Managing Knowledge Security

Managing Knowledge Security

Strategies for protecting
your company's intellectual assets

Kevin C Desouza

KOGAN PAGE

London and Philadelphia

Publisher's note

Every possible effort has been made to ensure that the information contained in this book is accurate at the time of going to press, and the publishers and authors cannot accept responsibility for any errors or omissions, however caused. No responsibility for loss or damage occasioned to any person acting, or refraining from action, as a result of the material in this publication can be accepted by the editor, the publisher or the author.

First published in Great Britain and the United States in 2007 by Kogan Page Limited

Apart from any fair dealing for the purposes of research or private study, or criticism or review, as permitted under the Copyright, Designs and Patents Act 1988, this publication may only be reproduced, stored or transmitted, in any form or by any means, with the prior permission in writing of the publishers, or in the case of reprographic reproduction in accordance with the terms and licences issued by the CLA. Enquiries concerning reproduction outside these terms should be sent to the publishers at the undermentioned addresses:

120 Pentonville Road	525 South 4th street #241
London N1 9JN	Philadelphia PA 19147
United Kingdom	USA
www.kogan-page.co.uk	

© Kevin Desouza, 2007

The right of Kevin Desouza to be identified as the author of this work has been asserted by him in accordance with the Copyright, Designs and Patents Act 1988.

ISBN-10   0 7494 4961 6
ISBN-13   978 0 7494 4961 2

British Library Cataloguing-in-Publication Data

A CIP record for this book is available from the British Library.

Library of Congress Cataloging-in-Publication Data

Desouza, Kevin C., 1979–
  Managing knowledge security : strategies for protecting your company's intellectual assets / Kevin Desouza.
       p. cm.
   Includes bibliographical references and index.
   ISBN-13: 978-0-7494-4961-2
   ISBN-10: 0-7494-4961-6
 1. Business enterprises–Security measures. 2. Knowledge management. 3. intellectual capital–Management. I. Title.
   HD61.5.D47 2007
   658.4'72--dc22
                                                                2007016440

Typeset by Saxon Graphics Ltd, Derby
Printed and bound in Great Britain by MPG Books Ltd, Bodmin, Cornwall

This book is dedicated to all my colleagues who have assisted me over the past six years. You know who you are, and this book would not have been possible if not for your words of wisdom, caring thoughts, and brave actions. I will forever be in your debt. Thank you.

Contents

Preface		*ix*
Acknowledgements		*xvii*
About the author		*xix*

1 The basics   1
Compromising your intellectual assets 3; Intellectual assets: the bedrock of organizations 6; Knowledge management 9; Competitive intelligence 15; Security management 20; Roadmap of the book 22

2 The human stain   27
Security breaches 30; Preventive measures 39; Closing thoughts 53

3 Technology hiccups   55
Security breaches 59; Preventive measures 67; Closing thoughts 74

4 When friends become liabilities   75
Types of alliance 79; Security breaches 88; Preventive measures 97; Closing thoughts 103

5 Guarding the fortress   105
Defining the fortress 108; Security breaches 109; Preventive measures 117; Closing thoughts 127

6	**From abnormalities to crises**	**129**

Understanding the beast 132; Preventive measures 154; Closing thoughts 171

7	**Securing your intellectual assets**	**173**

The seven strategic considerations 173; Closing thoughts 187

Notes	*189*
References	*191*
Index	*195*

Preface

This book is my story, a story that I wanted to write for a long time. In many ways, this book has taken over six years to write. Having been fortunate enough to run into the right sets of people on occasion and to stumble upon interesting opportunities, I became involved in the field commonly known as competitive intelligence in early 1999. My entry into this field was far from glorious or smooth, but it was stimulating, energetic and challenging. I began by examining how organizations gather information on their competitors from open sources (such as newswires, tradeshows, conferences and brochures), and use this information to plan tactical and strategic operations. This was mundane work which involved searching several hundred databases. While it was enjoyable at times, especially when I discovered latent connections within large sets of information, it was nothing to write home about. One of my biggest concerns was that as technology advanced, searching through open sources for information would become automated, and I would be out of assignments.[1] However, the more I learnt about the world of competitive intelligence, the more intrigued I became. My mentor kept reminding me to stay focused and energized, using a famous quote by Winston Churchill (1874–1965): 'The pessimist sees difficulty in every opportunity. The optimist sees the opportunity in every difficulty.'

Soon, around late 2000, I had my first look at an assignment that involved going beyond open sources for information. The assignment dealt with gathering information about a competitor by using human sources. Human sources are most often considered closed sources, as the information they possess is not easily accessible. Moreover, in competitive situations, one must access such information without the awareness of the source, so that the advantage derived from the information is maintained. Hence, accessing human sources normally involves some level of clandestine activity. Before your imagination runs wild, let me make one point clear: I am not talking about the type of operations you might see in *James Bond, Alias* or *24*. I wish I could charm all women like James Bond, or fight like Jennifer Garner, or even deal with nuclear threats in a matter of hours, as in *24*. I prefer a much blander role, one that involves playing behind the scenes and not causing too much ruckus or creating too much of a splash. Not drawing attention to oneself is a skill and a true asset in human penetration operations. Unfortunately, this characteristic of intelligence operations is lost on most people because of the fictions they encounter in the cinema or on television.

Since 2000, I have taken part in many competitive intelligence and security operations. (I do know the exact number, but let us keep that a secret!) Over 90 per cent of them have involved the use of clandestine techniques where organizations have been penetrated. While most of these operations were sanctioned by organizations who wanted to test their own security measures or investigate their own employees, some were commissioned by competitors of an organization. Some were even commissioned by consultants working for the competitors of a given organization. It is common practice for organizations to outsource their competitive intelligence assignments, especially when there is a need to go beyond open sources and to stay distanced from any links to the activity. Most of the time, these organizations asked me for a report or brief that documented the findings, and were never concerned with the actual measures and steps taken to ascertain the information. As I came out of each engagement, I always made notes on what I had learnt. These notes served me well as I stepped into new assignments, and also helped me build a viable security function for my own organization. This book provides me with an avenue to share some of my notes with you.

While I was executing competitive intelligence and security operations, I was also conducting work in the area of knowledge management, the discipline of leveraging intellectual know-how in and around an organization toward business objectives.[2] I continue to do research and consult in this area. I realized early on that the field of knowledge management lacked a thorough appreciation of the need for security and protection.[3]

After all, much of the practice, and even the literature, of knowledge management is premised on the notion that knowledge should be shared and made available to all, as it is a social good that grows when shared and combined with the experience of others. This thinking is appropriate so long as there is one caveat attached: sharing takes place only between authorized entities. After all, you do not want knowledge to be shared in an unauthorized manner with your competitor.

Most organizations lack significant programmes to protect their knowledge assets. The words of Henry Ford (1863–1947) come to mind: 'The only real security that a man can have in this world is a reserve of knowledge, experience and ability.' While organizations were spending a great deal of effort, time, and resources on creating their knowledge assets, they were not spending commensurate effort on protecting these assets. I remember commenting to one executive, 'It is easier for someone to tamper with your intellectual assets than it is for them to steal a computer monitor.' The executive laughed and dismissed my comment as a passing joke.

My comment was not meant to be a joke. Most organizations exert inordinate efforts to protect some of the most useless objects around. For example, in most organizations physical equipment such as tables, chairs, computer monitors and phones are tagged and inventoried. It takes a requisition order to get some of this equipment replaced (or even discarded), and in some cases, a security escort to move equipment from one location to another. Now contrast this with security policies in place for intellectual assets. Most organizations do not even know what their most valuable intellectual assets are. Furthermore, they lack an appreciation for the fact that these assets need to be secured and protected so as to preserve and extend competitive advantage. It is common to find organizations that think asking someone to sign a non-disclosure agreement (NDA) is enough to prevent knowledge leakage. Such thinking is not only naïve but can cost an organization its very existence. Here is an interesting statistic: according to the US Chamber of Commerce, corporate espionage penetrations cost US companies at least $25 billion a year in intellectual property losses. How much has your company lost as a result of corporate espionage activities?

In today's competitive environment, it is absolutely essential for organizations to leverage their knowledge assets. After all, intellectual assets are the only source of true sustained competitive advantage. Most other resources can be easily acquired and are common in the marketplace. An organization is differentiated by the knowledge it possesses, and how it employs that knowledge to further its business agenda. Lose this knowledge, or misuse it, and the organization may face disastrous consequences. Knowledge resides in the minds of employees, is embedded in work processes, and is captured in product and service offerings. Knowledge is not a product; knowledge is fluid, dynamic, and more mobile than any other physical product. Moreover, unlike other products, knowledge is in a continuous state of flux, making it difficult to pin down and capture.

Consider the simple case of a research and development (R&D) operation. Ideas are generated from informal meetings of scientists; these ideas are then tested, developed and nurtured through a series of trial-and-error experiments, during which some ideas are discarded, new ideas are developed, and some ideas go through a process of refinement. Given enough time and effort, a few ideas turn out to be valuable enough to inform future product development efforts. Needless to say, R&D efforts are costly and risky. What would happen if ideas being worked on by an R&D group were leaked to a competitor? What would happen if such ideas were featured prematurely in the business press? These are non-trivial issues which can harm current operations, and more importantly, the future viability of an organization. Hence, it is absolutely essential that intellectual assets be protected from unauthorized sabotage and accidental losses. Nowadays, just as information system security is not taken for granted by any organization, knowledge security should be given equal if not more attention. The importance of securing and fortifying knowledge resources is often disregarded: an oversight which presents organizations with a dire and immediate threat.

In addition to my interests in the areas of competitive intelligence and knowledge management, I became interested in the area of crisis management. Working with my colleague Tobin Hensgen, I began to examine how prepared organizations were for dealing with crises.[4] We started out by examining how organizations perceive signs – that is, warning signals – in their environments so that they can predict crises. We studied information failures surrounding the 9/11 attacks in the United States, among other disasters, and found that while all crises were preceded by warning signals, most organizations lacked adequate programmes to process these signs. As a result, many organizations fell prey to crises; some even witnessed similar crises time and time again (for example, the failures associated with the *Challenger* and *Columbia* disasters at NASA).

Through this work, I became interested in:

- how organizations can better develop their information systems to be more cognizant of warning signs in their environments;
- how information should be processed to help in preparing, managing, and recovering from crises;
- what measures organizations can put in place to exhibit resilience, agility and sustainability in volatile, complex and unpredictable environments.

One of the critical findings from this line of work is that most organizations do not know how to secure their assets, including intellectual assets, during times of crisis. As a result, many organizations lose their most valuable intellectual assets during their times of greatest vulnerability. This results in the inability of the organization to recover from crisis events. Consider the following: if an organization does not have people to help rebuild the organization after an event, no amount of financial reserves will help. Moreover, simply having the ability to hire new staff is not sufficient, as it is the knowledge in and around people that keeps an organization afloat. This is not easily replaced, especially during times of high stress. Securing knowledge before and during a crisis, and mobilizing knowledge during the recovery period, are important issues which cannot be left to wishful thinking.

The book

In this book, I share with you insights on how to ensure that intellectual assets are secured. I identify specific vulnerabilities present in today's corporate environments, including the risks of neglecting physical security, the susceptibility of business alliances, the potential hazards of outsourcing, the dangers of offsite meetings, the lack of adequate care in managing corporate travel, the perils of working without appropriate disaster scenarios, and finally, the dangers related to ignoring internal goals, neglecting to share and appreciate knowledge collectively, and overlooking organizational missions and core values. Each chapter presents actual cases from my personal experiences in competitive intelligence, knowledge management, crisis management and security operations, as a team member, manager and even as a procurer. The book presents a holistic view of securing knowledge from the perspectives of competitive intelligence, knowledge management and crisis management.

In addition to demonstrating how organizations are vulnerable to breaches, this book details how most breaches can take place without the use of sophisticated technology mechanisms. It illustrates the effects of breaches on the health and viability of organizations, and it provides organizations with preparation tools designed to avoid and thwart these breaches. I have changed all names to protect the identities of the organizations. I would strongly urge you not to jump to conclusions about their identities: believe me when I say that their identities have been disguised with great care to protect them.

Business books, such as this one, are supposed to contain a wealth of knowledge and insights that practitioners can readily consume to better their work practices and organizations. I hope this book achieves this purpose. However, one caveat needs to be addressed. This book contains case descriptions of how organizations were penetrated: please do not try this at home, and if you do, please do not tell me or call me! This book is not meant to be a learning tool for those who want to penetrate organizations; hence, I have not elaborated on all the details of the specific operations. Needless to say, a little knowledge can be a dangerous thing. The completion of penetration operations takes planning, diligence and execution of disciplined tradecraft; this book is not meant to be a reader on these issues. Hence, please use this book for its intended objective: to help you fortify your organization's security practices to protect your intellectual assets.

My goal in writing this book is simple, but salient: to help organizations realize that their core resources – intellectual assets – are under constant attack, and that protecting this resource is as important as any other strategic agenda. Organizations that take the necessary steps to protect their knowledge will thrive in today's competitive environment, often at the expense of their less-prepared foes. As noted by Confucius (551 BC–479 BC), 'The superior man, when resting in safety, does not forget that danger may come. When in a state of security he does not forget the possibility of ruin. When all is orderly, he does not forget that disorder may come. Thus his person is not endangered, and his States and all their clans are preserved.' Organizations that develop competencies in knowledge security capabilities will be able to seize opportunities that their peers can only dream of or shy away from. Securing the most critical assets of the organization – that is, its knowledge (or intellectual) assets – can be an opportunity to advance the agenda of the organization and be a true enabler of business value.

I welcome comments on the book (email: kev.desouza@gmail.com). Writing a book gives me the opportunity to reflect on past experiences and lessons learnt. I am always looking to learn of new ideas and practices, and to engage in constructive (and even heated) debates on the topic of securing intellectual assets. All comments, suggestions, criticisms and queries are welcome. I also encourage readers to visit my blog at the following URL: http://secureknow.blogspot.com. I shall do my best to keep this blog updated with content and discussions, which should make good complements for the book.

Acknowledgements

There are many people to whom I owe a depth of gratitude. However, not all of them can be mentioned here, at least not by their full names. First, and foremost, I would like to thank a mentor who showed me the ins and outs of the field of competitive intelligence, especially the human intelligence side. I normally describe this person as a combination of the knack of Kojak (as played by Telly Savalas), and the subtle, calm investigative personality of Peter Falk's Columbo. My mentor is bald, like Kojak, yet like Columbo, he retains the ability to hold a poker face, never disclosing his hand. I have thanked him numerous times over the years, and continue to rely on him for words of wisdom and guidance.

Second, I have had the opportunity to collaborate with numerous colleagues over the years on a number of projects; I will forever be in the debt of these individuals. There was never a project where I left with anything less than a renewed sense of passion for my work, and an expanded collection of insights and experiences. All of you know who you are, and I thank you.

Third, from the moment I decided to write this book, numerous associations, business networks and even private organizations have given me an opportunity to come in and present my ideas. All of you have my sincere thanks and appreciation for opening your doors and listening to me. I have tried my best to incorporate your comments into the text.

Fourth, I want to thank my colleagues with whom I continue to collaborate on projects outside the security realm, for example, in knowledge management and strategic information system deployments. I should like to thank especially Tobin Hensgen (my co-author for *Managing*

Information in Complex Organizations), Yukika Awazu (my co-author for *Engaged Knowledge Management*), Carlo Bonifazi and Mark Power (my co-authors for *The Outsourcing Handbook*), Roberto Evaristo (3M), Peter Baloh (University of Ljubljana), Ray Hackney (Manchester Metropolitan University), doctoral colleagues at the University of Illinois at Chicago (Sanjeev Jha, Sridhar Papagari and Chen Ye), and faculty at the University of Washington (Mike Eisenberg, Harry Bruce, Jeff Kim, Hala Annabi, Mike Crandall and Bob Mason). My graduate students, Caroline Dombrowski, Tyan Hynes, Jean Lee and Laura Horne, have read chapters of the book and provided me with insightful comments. This is my second book with Kogan Page. I thank my publisher, Jon Finch, for being supportive of the idea of the book and helping me to bring it to fruition.

Fifth, I am especially grateful to Dr George Kraft and Dr Margaret Kraft, who have been tremendous mentors to me over the past few years. During my graduate and doctoral studies, both of them took care of me as if I was their own son. I can honestly say that I would have gotten into a lot of trouble if not for the mentoring of Dr George Kraft. In addition, I would have never joined the ranks of academia if not for his guidance and mentorship.

Finally, my family (Mum, Dad, Ken, Karishma, Emily, and the eclectic group of cousins, uncles and aunts) and friends deserve a special note of gratitude. Often, my work took away opportunities for me to spend time with each of you. I thank each of you for your patience, kindness and words of encouragement. I promise to take a break from writing books until I have had a chance to come and visit each of you.

K C Desouza
Seattle, Washington
USA

About the author

Dr Kevin C Desouza is on the faculty of the Information School at the University of Washington. He is also an Adjunct Assistant Professor in Electrical Engineering at the College of Engineering. He serves as the Director of the Institute for National Security Education and Research, an inter-disciplinary university-wide initiative. He is Director and founding faculty member of the Institute for Innovation in Information Management (I3M) and is an affiliate faculty member of the Center for American Politics and Public Policy, both housed at the University of Washington. His immediate past position was as the Director of the Institute for Engaged Business Research, a think-tank of the Engaged Enterprise, a strategy consulting firm with expertise in the areas of knowledge management, crisis management, strategic deployment of information systems, and government and competitive intelligence assignments.

Dr Desouza has authored *Managing Knowledge with Artificial Intelligence* (Quorum Books, 2002), co-authored *The Outsourcing Handbook* (Kogan Page, 2006), *Managing Information in Complex Organizations* (M E Sharpe, 2005) and *Engaged Knowledge Management* (Palgrave Macmillan, 2005), and edited *New Frontiers of Knowledge Management* (Palgrave Macmillan, 2005) and *Agile Information Systems* (Butterworth Heinemann, 2006). His most recent book is *Managing Knowledge Security* (Kogan Page, 2007). In addition, he has published over 130 articles in prestigious practitioner and academic journals such as the *Communications of the ACM, Information & Management, Technology Forecasting and Social Change, Studies in Conflict and Terrorism, Disaster Recovery Journal, Journal of Engineering and*

Technology Management, Business Strategy Review, Across the Board, Journal of Contingencies and Crisis Management, Business Horizons, Communications of the AIS, European Journal of Information Systems, Government Information Quarterly, Journal of the American Society for Information Science and Technology, IEEE Software, IEE Engineering Management, Human Systems Management, Journal of Business Strategy, Information Systems Management, Journal of Knowledge Management, and the *International Journal of Technology Policy and Management*, among others.

His work has also been featured by a number of publications such as *Sloan Management Review, Washington Internet Daily, Computerworld, KM Review, Information Outlook* and *Human Resource Management International Digest*.

He has been invited to edit special issues of several prominent journals such as *Technology Forecasting and Social Change* (on Information Technology, Innovation and the War on Terrorism), *Information Systems Journal* (on Knowledge Transfer in Distributed Contexts), and the *Journal of Strategic Information Systems* (on eGovernment Strategies: ICT Innovation in International Public Sector Contexts), among others. In addition, he serves on a number of editorial boards such as the *Journal of Strategic Information Systems*, and has reviewed research for government agencies such as the *Research Council of Norway*.

Dr Desouza has advised, briefed and/or consulted major international corporations (eg Boeing, Microsoft, Accenture, the American Productivity Quality Center, etc) and government organizations (eg the Office of the Director of National Intelligence, the Department of State, the Department of Veterans Affairs etc) on strategic management issues ranging from management of information systems, knowledge management, competitive intelligence, government intelligence operations and crisis management.

He is frequently an invited speaker on a number of cutting-edge business and technology topics for national and international, industry and academic audiences. He was invited to give a plenary talk at the 2006 Command and Control Research and Technology Symposium, sponsored by the Office of the Assistant Secretary of Defense Networks and Information Integration (OASD-NII), and at the 5th Annual International Smart-Sourcing Conference (2006), Second International Conference on Knowledge Management (2005), among others. He has given over 40 invited talks in a wide assortment of avenues.

Dr Desouza has received over $575,000 of research funding from both private and government organizations. Dr Desouza is a fellow of the Royal Society of Arts.

1

The basics

Let me start with a story – a true story. There was once a boy named Kevin (yes, me), who was asked to penetrate an organization's physical perimeter. The goal was simple: use openly available information about the organization to get access to the executive offices. Kevin was hired by the CEO of the organization at the request of the Board of Advisors. The company was based in Chicago, Illinois, and operated in the financial sector. The organization had just implemented a new security system which combined the organization's physical security and information technology security apparatuses.

Soon after receiving his assignment, Kevin decided that he had to assemble a team to help him penetrate the organization. But before he could do that, he wanted to take a look at the building and gather some first-hand information. He decided to take a look at the building the next day on his way to the post office. Dressed in jeans, a T-shirt and a baseball cap, he walked past the building. He quickly noticed the number of exits, the number of back doors, the security guards at the nearby parking garage, the common reception desk shared by all tenants of the high-rise office building, and the café on the first floor, among other things.

As he walked by the common reception desk, purposely looking lost and perplexed, he was interrupted by the receptionist, who asked, 'Hello, can I help you find something?' Kevin still has a stutter at times, and before he could fully respond, the receptionist said, 'Oh, you're here to deliver the mail.' Kevin replied, 'Sure, I am, and since this is my first day on the job, I'm a bit confused and lost.' The receptionist assured him that he had nothing to worry about, and that she would help him find his way. Kevin then asked, 'Can you please tell me how I get to Alpha Consulting [the company that had hired him]?' The receptionist replied, 'They have offices on the 14th, 15th and 16th floors, and the mailroom is on the 14th floor. Please take the last bank of elevators up to 14 and you can deliver your mail.' Kevin was thrilled, as an opportunity to penetrate the organization had just presented itself. He replied, 'Thank you so much. Do I need to sign in?' The receptionist replied, 'No, it's fine. I know that you're just going for the mail. Don't give me any more work, as then I'll have to give you a badge and enter you into the system.' The receptionist smiled and gave him a visitor badge without logging any information about him. Kevin then headed up in the elevator to the 14th floor. Phase One was complete: he had gained access to the office floor.

Now came the more difficult part: locating the executive offices. He stopped by the mailroom and was greeted by a less than friendly receptionist. She said, 'Please sign in and bring the mail in.' The mailroom had a small window, and once a person signed in, he or she would then be buzzed in for entry to the receiving room where all packages were left and signed for. Kevin quickly replied, 'Good afternoon, I have some papers here for Mr John Smith [the organization's CEO]. I can't give them to you as they are highly confidential.' The mail receptionist was startled, but said, 'OK, hold on, let me locate his office for you.' She then looked up the corporate directory and told Kevin where the office was. Kevin replied, 'Thank you, I'll head up to the 16th floor. Sorry to have bothered you. Can you please tell me your name?' Kevin waited with his hand extended to shake hers. The receptionist hesitated then said, 'Sandy Lee.'

Kevin shook her hand and headed up to the 16th floor. Progress was being made on the penetration assignment; now all that was left was to pass through any interference on the 16th floor. Upon exiting the elevator on the 16th floor, he saw the receptionist, and then looked at his watch; it was about 4 pm. The receptionist was already getting ready to leave for the day. He approached her and said, 'I need to deliver this package to Mr John Smith.' The receptionist asked him to sign in and began to pick up the phone to make a call. Kevin quickly replied, 'Oh, I just came from speaking to Sandy in the mailroom. She called in ahead for me already and they are expecting me.' The receptionist said, 'OK, then just go in, walk down the hall and then make a right. Keep going till you can't any more, make a left and it's the fifth office.' 'Thank you,' Kevin replied.

Kevin then went in and knocked on the door of the CEO. His assistant had already left for the day and his door was open. The CEO, startled at what he saw, quickly closed his door and proceeded to have a three-hour meeting with Kevin about what he should do with his chief information officer (CIO) and the security director.

This is one case out of a collection that show how easy it is penetrate organizations. There are numerous safeguards that should have prevented Kevin from entering the CEO's office, but none of them worked. This book will detail how compromises around organizational security, and especially intellectual assets, can cost an organization competitive advantage. Most of the time, when organizational security is compromised, it is not a case of someone who wants to do some good and simply teach the organization a lesson. Organizational security is more likely to be compromised by a person who wants to do harm to an organization by sabotaging its intellectual assets. Someone like Kevin could very well have been hired by a competitor of Alpha Consulting, with a request to get hold of some product information or marketing plans. Once security is compromised, getting hold of assets of interest is, most of the time, quite easy.

Compromising your intellectual assets

This book will discuss how intellectual assets get lost or misplaced because of sloppy organizational practices and human carelessness. Most of the time, an organization is its own worst enemy! Organizations do not know how to care for their own intellectual assets, thus making those assets vulnerable to loss. In recent times, we have witnessed a slew of sloppy behaviours in protecting intellectual assets. Companies such as Bank of America Corp., Ameritrade Inc., Time Warner, ABN Amro Mortgage Group, Marriott Corp. and Ford Motor Company, among others, have all lost backup tapes containing sensitive information. Information on these tapes included data on individuals such as their social security numbers, account numbers and account balances. Most of the losses occurred as the backup tapes were being moved from one location to another. In some cases, tapes went unaccounted for as they were misplaced or lost on the premises.

Consider another type of intellectual asset breach: the misuse of assets. CartManager International sold personal information on one million customers to a third party for US$9,000 (Gray, 2005). This information included customer names, credit card information, phone numbers and dollar amounts of purchases. It is interesting to note that this data was not about direct customers of CartManager: the company provides shopping cart and checkout software for an online retailer, and it was the customers of the online retailer whose data was compromised. CartManager settled a lawsuit regarding this case in March 2005.

In 2005, ChoicePoint unknowingly sold 163,000 records of customer data to fraudsters who were posing as legitimate businesspeople (Greenemeier *et al*, 2006). The scam began in 2004, when the conmen posed as businessmen looking to join the ChoicePoint service. They allegedly opened about 50 fraudulent accounts. The incident did not result from the hacking of ChoicePoint's systems, but rather was caused by criminals posing as legitimate businesses seeking to gain access to personal information.

I could go on reporting more cases of intellectual asset security breaches, but I think the point is clear. Most organizations have faced such breaches in recent times. What is discomfiting is that many of these breaches occurred as a result of sloppiness (such as computer tapes being misplaced, lost during transit or not accounted for properly). It is worth noting about the above cases that none of them have the features of what one might consider a traditional information security hacker breach. The types of information security breaches that have fascinated techno-geeks are still common. Computer networks are routinely scoured for holes and entry points for attacks. Viruses, worms, Trojan horses and other evil creatures continue to cause havoc on the internet, not to mention the annoying case of spam. Dealing with sabotages to computer systems is an important issue, and it needs the attention of managers. However, I shall not focus on these kinds of breach in this book, as there are already several hundred books written on the topics of information security, network security and computer security. Moreover, there has been significant exposure on the issues of computer and network security, and organizations have taken these threats very seriously. However, the same cannot be said for non-computer or non-computer-network attacks.

Breaches and knowledge leaks may result from the behaviour of employees. Take the case of executives who, while waiting to board a flight, discuss sensitive business matters on their mobile phones. No one needs to go to the great lengths of penetrating an organization if its executives willingly disclose sensitive matters in public environments. Being a frequent traveller, I am continuously amazed at how sloppily sensitive organizational matters are handled.

Intellectual assets can be sabotaged by rogue employees as well. In May 2005, a group of former employees of Bank of America, Wachovia, Commerce Bancorp and PNC Financial Services Group was arrested for illegally obtaining and selling customer data (Marlin, 2005). In total, seven employees were arrested. Law enforcement officials seized 13 computers which contained data on 670,000 account holders. The scheme involved paying bank employees for account data and then reselling the information to law firms and debt-collection agencies. The publicity surrounding the case of the theft by bank employees is rare: these cases are not generally reported on, but are rather hushed up and never disclosed. Nonetheless, such incidents occur on a regular basis. I have personally been called in by organizations who have known that a breach has occurred and want to find a way to get rid of the perpetrator of the crime without drawing too much attention. After all, if an employee steals some money from the bank (let's make it a lot of money – $1 million), the cost to the bank is manageable, as long as the news doesn't get out. If the news does get out, the bank could lose more in terms of lost reputation, lost business and fines from regulatory agencies.

Today, with the increased interest in strategic alliances, security breaches can occur when organizations engage with business partners. In many of the occurrences mentioned above involving the loss of sensitive information, the loss took place during transit. Transit to and from destinations is normally provided by business partners, and hence the question of who is accountable and who should be responsible for these breaches also becomes important. Consider the following case. In August 2002, in New Delhi, India, Shekhar Verma, a former employee of Geometric Software Solutions Ltd. (GSSL), a Bombay-based outsourcer, was caught by the Central Bureau of Intelligence (CBI) when attempting to sell the company's source codes to an undercover FBI agent posing as a competitor (Fitzgerald, 2003). This is the first case involving intellectual property (IP) theft in outsourcing in India, and which criminal charges can be applied is still under debate. First, US non-disclosure laws, which include the Industrial Espionage Act of 1996, are not applicable to non-US citizens operating outside the United States in developing countries such as India. Second, India does not have a law that prohibits stealing trade secrets. Therefore, India may charge Verma under its laws relating to general theft for betraying the trust of his employer. However, this is also controversial, since the software codes he tried to sell are not owned by his direct employer, GSSL.

There are also cases in which an organization does not take adequate care to ensure that its intellectual assets are protected during times of crisis. Crises, whether small or large, internal or external, natural or human-made, cause stress on the organization. If an organization does not have adequate measures to protect its intellectual assets, chances are high that it will be severely impaired by a crisis, and it may not survive. To cite a recent example, the City of New Orleans had a contingency plan for disaster, but when Hurricane Katrina hit, buses that were intended for use in evacuation were left standing because there were no drivers, timetables or directions.

This book focuses on the concept of securing the intellectual assets of organizations. Before we get into the nitty-gritty of discussing the security of intellectual assets, it is important to take a step back and define what we mean by intellectual assets.

Intellectual assets: the bedrock of organizations

Organizations of all shapes and forms are in the business of asset management. Assets are any resource that can provide value when put to productive use. Traditional kinds of assets include buildings, which can be rented, and cash reserves, which can be invested. The fields of accounting and financial management are focused on helping managers with their financial assets better. Similarly, we have domains such as human resource management which focus on helping managers understand how to leverage their organizations' talent, its human assets. In this book, we shall focus on a particular kind of asset: intellectual assets. Intellectual assets can be defined as the knowledge housed in the minds of employees, encapsulated in products and services, or embedded in the internal and external networks of the organizations, which provides organizations with competitive advantage and differentiates them from competitors.

Intellectual assets are the bedrock of the organization. Consider the following: two organizations might have similar physical assets (such as technologies and facilities) and financial assets (such as cash), but if one organization has more experienced, knowledgeable and innovative employees it might be able to deliver better products and services to its customers and earn better rents on its investments. Without sound intellectual assets an organization will not be able to leverage its other assets. Intellectual assets are the creative juices behind the organization; they make the organization go or stop.

Intellectual assets, simply put, are the lifeblood of the business. If intellectual assets are compromised, a business will lose a significant portion of its competitive edge, and may even be subject to termination.

As a classic case of an intellectual asset, consider the Coca-Cola formula. This formula helps the Coca-Cola Company enjoy success in the marketplace by differentiating its products from those of its competitors. Similarly, for a pharmaceutical company, the formula of a drug pending review and approval from a government agency is a highly valuable intellectual asset. If the formula of the drug were compromised, the pharmaceutical company would be unable to enjoy profits from the drug's creation at the expected rate, as competitors might develop with cheaper alternatives, thereby reducing the value of the drug.

Intellectual assets help an organization differentiate itself from its competitors. For instance, the expertise housed in the minds of your employees is not found in your competitors' organizations, at least not in the purest sense. The reason is simply that you have your employees, and your competitor does not. Moreover, while you may be able to hire two people with just about the same skill sets at a given time, the chances of the two individuals having identical experiences is low.

A few years ago, technology assets were considered competitive differentiators. Today, this is no longer the case. Most organizations have access to the same technology offerings, and hence having access to certain technology does not necessarily lead to competitive advantage. As we shall see in the next chapter, the competition for talented employees can be fierce. Organizations that are not mindful of this challenge or do not know how to retain their most valuable employees will be at a constant disadvantage. Intellectual assets are the only assets that differentiate one organization from another.

Intellectual assets have other interesting properties: they encapsulate experiences and path dependencies. Intellectual assets take time, energy and resources to develop, and they are seldom purchased off the shelf. Why is this important? First, the time it takes for organizations to craft and develop intellectual assets means that losing these assets would leave a void that would not be easily filled. Consider the case of an experienced employee who leaves the organization. Not only do you lose the knowledge of the employee, you lose the knowledge embedded in the employee's social and professional networks. Most experienced employees know who to approach for answers and have rich networks they can tap into. Moreover, they have deep reservoirs of organizational knowledge that help them get their work done. Most organizations will not be able to hire a person from the outside, and in many cases may not even be able to mobilize a person from within the organization, to fill up this void. It will take time for the newcomer to get his or her feet wet, go through a learning curve, and accumulate the expertise and experiences to be capable of performing at a rate similar to the employee who exited. In a similar vein, if an organization does not have the necessary measures in place to protect its intellectual assets during times of crisis and disasters, the organization is flirting with disaster. After all, most other resources are easily replaceable and can be repurchased; however, the people required to put these resources to productive use cannot be purchased from the corner store.

Second, intellectual assets are built over time: that is, they have history. Take the case of pharmaceutical companies working on discovering the next drug. It takes years, not months or days, to come up with drug discoveries. The cost of these exercises is not cheap: they involve considerable money and effort (hours spent). Each successive experiment is viewed as a learning episode, and future experiments build on the lessons learnt. Now imagine if the results of some experiments were misplaced or leaked as a result of sloppy behaviour on the part of the employees. Not only would this breach diminish the value of these specific experiments, but with some level of creativity, it would be easy to extrapolate the other operations of the organizations. The practice of reverse engineering, where one works backward from a finished product to identify how the product was constructed, is commonplace. Not only can one work to identify the past steps, it also becomes possible to extrapolate future steps.

Exposure of path dependencies is a critical problem, as this may negate most of the effort that went into charting these courses, and will call for the organization to reconsider its plans, which it is not easy to do. Consider the case of leaks of classified information in the context of government intelligence operations. Leaking classified information can jeopardize current operations, but it also exposes the plans, personnel and activities of the organization, producing cascading negative impacts, with the end result being the inability to achieve strategic, tactical and operational objectives.

In sum, intellectual assets are vital aspects of the organization and need to be managed with care. Now consider the following: did you take a class in graduate school that was titled 'Management of intellectual assets', or have you ever heard of a field called 'intellectual asset management'? Probably not! Why? For a long time, organizations were focused on management of physical and financial assets. This approach was ideal when these resources were scarce in the marketplace and were sources of competitive differentiation. As we have already discussed, this is no longer the case today. In response to this, the field commonly known as knowledge management has come to the fore.

Knowledge management

Knowledge management as a field is concerned with how to create, mobilize, store, retrieve and apply organizational know-how towards the attainment of business objectives (see Davenport, 2005; Nonaka and Takeuchi, 1995; Desouza and Awazu, 2005a). The practice and literature around knowledge management continues to grow at an astounding pace. Today there are dozens of books and several hundred articles that address the intricacies of knowledge management. However, as noted in the preface, there is a dearth of advice on how to protect and secure knowledge.[1] The aim of this book is to address this gap in practice and the literature.

An organization's knowledge resources must be proprietary to the organization. In order to keep them proprietary, we must secure them from unauthorized use, tampering, acts of vandalism and sabotage. Competitive intelligence activities are on the rise and will continue to rise exponentially. Competitors are spending a great deal of resources trying to understand an organization's next moves and to make its proprietary technology common knowledge in the marketplace. If they are successful, they may be able to extinguish the profits earned by the organization.

Moreover, with the current rise in alliances between organizations, the need for security of knowledge takes on increased prominence. Organizations have accepted the fact that they must home in on their core competencies and forge alliances for securing their non-core needs. Alliances call for sharing and relying on a business partner's knowledge. An organization must not only make sure that its internal controls and security protocols are apt, but must also ensure that business partners have security measures in place. As the old adage goes, you are only as good as your weakest link. An organization must establish agreements about how its knowledge will be used by its business partner, where it will be stored, and who will have access to it. Regardless of where a knowledge leak occurs, within the organization or at the business partner's location, the ramifications could be disastrous. Recently, we have seen an increased number of IT outsourcing agreements, many of them with partners in different countries. Technology sourcing agreements call for organizations to provide business partners with access to their critical resources: knowledge of the business, data and information on constituents, and process methodologies. These are prime opportunities for an organization to suffer serious knowledge breaches unless it is sincere and holistic in its security protocols and their implementation.

The sophistication, ubiquity and pervasive nature of technology can compromise the knowledge security of an organization. Most of us use multiple devices for knowledge communications and sharing. These can range from the office phone and e-mail to personal digital assistants, laptop computers, personal computers and so on. This is complicated by the fact that we work and communicate in multiple environments, and hence we use these devices in multiple settings. For instance, I could use my laptop computer at my office, taking advantage of the office communication network; then over lunch I could go to the neighbourhood café and use an open wireless connection; and then at home I could have a personal communication network that taps into a local internet service provider. The use of heterogeneous devices over heterogeneous environments makes the act of securing knowledge exponentially difficult, because an organization has a larger number of devices, gadgets, environments and systems to monitor and protect. With increases in hacking, spamming, spyware, worms, viruses and other nuisances that intercept, harm, sabotage and destroy electronic networks, knowledge communications over electronic networks are increasingly at risk. However, it is not only communication over electronic networks that is at risk. Even if we are capable of securing communication mediums, we must still be concerned about the devices on which the data and information reside. If an executive loses a laptop on which an organization's strategic documents are stored, these could be easily used by unscrupulous individuals to their advantage.

Given all these reasons, and many more, it troubles me that many organizations that have knowledge management programmes ignore the aspect of protection. Throughout my consulting efforts, I have seen organizations spend inordinate amounts of resources to build systems to help in knowledge transfer and set up incentive schemes to promote the capture and codification of knowledge. However, commensurate attention to knowledge security is absent. There are several reasons for this. First, most organizations are still grappling with the ABCs of knowledge management. For example, getting employees to share knowledge is still a big problem. Hence, these organizations take the stance that they will address issues around knowledge protection at a later date. This thinking is flawed. Good knowledge management habits need to be built in from day one, because changing behaviour at a later date is not easy. After all, this is one reason that knowledge management is hard. For ages, people have not been accustomed to sharing their most valuable resource. Just imagine: if we all started sharing things from the day we were born, chances are high that we would continue this behaviour with ease.

Second, among those organizations that have mastered the ABCs of knowledge management and have viable programmes in place, there is a feeling that putting in security measures might derail the spirit of knowledge sharing and openness. After all, security measures can be restrictive in nature and may be seen as an additional headache. This kind of thinking leads to confusion, as we shall see in the next chapter. Employees may not understand the sensitive nature of knowledge and hence may make costly mistakes. Moreover, while a knowledge management programme is designed to encourage the sharing of knowledge, sharing must occur only between authorized entities.

Third, organizations have a difficult time identifying what knowledge to protect. After all, it is common today to consider organizations as knowledge-based: most organizations run on knowledge. So does this mean that all knowledge has to be protected? What is knowledge? Is a method for fixing the broken copier knowledge? How about the presentation from the last sales meeting? Moreover, should the knowledge about how to fix the copier be treated with the same amount of care as the presentation from the last sales meeting? For someone in the photocopier maintenance business, a note on how to fix the copier does represent knowledge. Similarly, for a consulting firm the PowerPoint presentation qualifies as a knowledge resource. These artefacts represent knowledge in the domain of interest to particular organizations.

Now, consider the following: will the note about how to fix the broken copier represent organizational knowledge for the consulting organization? The answer is not a simple yes or no; it is a maybe. If the copier has been problematic to the organization, and the note summarizes a method to quickly address the problem, there is value in the note. The note helps those who want to make a copy. However, does this knowledge directly help the organization win business deals or attend to the needs of its consumers? Probably not! Hence, the answer is that the note represents organizational knowledge of an operational nature, but not of a strategic nature.

The challenge most organizations face may be considered analogous to the consulting organization trying to manage both the sales presentation and the note to fix the copier with the same amount of care and attention.

To avoid this inefficiency and ineffectiveness, the first step is to segment and clearly define what kinds of organizational knowledge merits being considered as an intellectual asset. Failure to clearly define what knowledge needs to be secured can lead to failed security programmes, and can also make the security of knowledge a daunting task.

Identifying intellectual assets[2]

Knowledge is a fuzzy term. Defining what constitutes knowledge and how we measure and capture knowledge has puzzled philosophers since the dawn of time. The good news is that we do not need to engage in this thought-provoking discussion. From an organizational perspective, we need to be quite specific in determining which organizational knowledge truly represents intellectual assets. Remember, intellectual assets are nuggets of knowledge that can be put to productive use. Not all knowledge that an employee has can be put to productive use. (For example, in my current job, my knowledge of Italian and Spanish red wines has limited, if any use. It is probably counterproductive, as it may distract me from work!) Moreover, not all knowledge resources have equal importance. Some kinds of knowledge may be more valuable than others.

Any asset needs to contribute value. Value emerges when we put an asset to use. In order to use an asset, one must have the necessary capabilities and intent. In our context, *necessary capabilities* come down to having the organizational processes required to take advantage of the asset. *Intent* is the strategic direction and focus of the organization. Put another way, to a software organization, methods on how to improve project management can be considered an asset, because the asset can be mobilized (that is, used in the improvement of project management protocols) and there is an intent on the part of the organization to continuously improve how projects are managed. Consequently, other knowledge resources (such as notes on travel destinations for vacations) do not contribute value for the organization. Resources that do not contribute value should not be managed; this rule applies to both traditional resources and knowledge resources.

Once we determine that a resource does in fact contribute value, the next question to ask is, what kind of value does the resource provide? At the basic level, a knowledge resource should contribute to the operational effectiveness and efficiency of the organization. Going back to our previous illustration, the note on how to fix the copier is an example of a knowledge resource that contributes to operational improvements in the consulting organization. Knowledge resources at the next level up can contribute to the tactical processes in the organization. Tactical processes represent the nature of how work is done: for example, project management methods and accounts receivable functions. Both the sales presentation and the methods for improving project management can be thought of as knowledge resources at the tactical level. At the final level, a knowledge resource can be of interest for its contribution to the strategic level. New business ideas and business development proposals are examples of knowledge resources at the strategic level. Knowledge resources across the three levels – operational, tactical, and strategic – need to be cared for differently. For instance, knowledge resources at the operational level might be plentiful in number, while those at the strategic level might be limited. Moreover, it is rarely desirable to give all members of the organization access to knowledge resources of a strategic nature. It would, however, be beneficial to provide operational and tactical knowledge to most members of the organization.

Another question to ask here is, what is the future value of the asset? Is the asset increasing in value, or is it decreasing? To take the case of accounting firms, are the skills for preparing personal income tax returns increasing in value? With the arrival of computerized tax preparation software this skill has become less important and less valuable. The value proposition trend is important here. Unless an asset has future potential, the cost one will incur in securing it will not be justified.

Once we have ascertained that a given resource contributes value to the organization, the next question we ask is, how rare is the resource? A resource that is not rare can be easily replaced. Hence, while we may want to spend a lot of time to store, manage and even protect a resource, these costs may not be justified. The lack of rarity is commonplace when we consider knowledge resources that contribute at the operational level. Knowledge resources at the tactical and strategic levels are more likely to exhibit the characteristic of rareness.

The next question to ask is, is the knowledge resource non-imitable and non-substitutable? Non-imitable means that the knowledge resources cannot be duplicated, at least not at a reasonable cost and/or effort. For example, knowledge housed in the minds of skilled engineers is very often non-imitable. The knowledge in the minds of engineers cannot be easily duplicated, and copies cannot be made. Non-substitutable means that a knowledge resource cannot be replaced by a variant knowledge resource. Most people substitute Pepsi and

Coke products without difficulty. However, knowledge resources are not easily substitutable. As an example, an engineer looking to fix a product defect cannot substitute the solutions for one product (such as a video camera) with those for another product (such as an automobile).

Knowledge resources that are non-imitable and non-substitutable, in addition to being valuable and rare, need to be given the utmost care. These knowledge artefacts are the highest-valued intellectual assets of the organization. Most knowledge resources will meet the condition of being valuable; however, only certain knowledge resources will be able to meet the condition of rarity. At the bare minimum, for a knowledge resource to qualify as an intellectual asset, it should be of value to the organization.

Just as we can segment explicit knowledge resources, we can also segment knowledge workers and the capabilities and expertise they possess. Not all knowledgeable workers are alike, and treating them as such will result in a failed management approach. Some employees work in a highly autonomous way and are highly skilled; they often know their work in great detail. Others are highly skilled, yet their work is more dependent on an external party such as a boss or supervisor. A hospital nurse for example, is certainly a knowledge worker, yet a nurse's schedule and work practices are likely to be dictated by a doctor and/or the hospital. By comparison, an artist knows best how to create a masterpiece and will work independently to meet the need of a client.

Other types of knowledge workers are not highly skilled, yet know how to follow knowledge-based procedures and perform tasks. The most common example for this class of worker is call centre personnel. Incoming calls are handled based on a predefined routine which dictates the opening greeting, method of problem resolution, problem reporting and other intricacies. The role of the worker is to follow these knowledge-based routines and complete the call in an effective and efficient manner.

Each type of knowledge worker needs to be managed differently, and offers different value propositions to the organization. For example, if an organization has an apt knowledge base on which to draw and a mature call-handling procedure, the knowledge worker who takes the call can be substituted easily. Any individual with basic speaking skills and simple etiquette should be able to follow the procedures outlined in the call manual. If the organization does not have a mature and valuable call manual (a knowledge asset), the skills of the call takers become paramount. Without a call manual, the organization is at the mercy of the experienced call takers, since these individuals will need to have the expertise necessary to complete a call optimally. It would be a shame for an organization to lose a knowledge worker whose capabilities are rare, valuable, non-imitable and non-substitutable in the organization. Losing such an employee to faulty management practices leads to gaps in an organization's knowledge structure, and will have a negative impact on business outcomes.

To summarize, while there is an abundance of knowledge in organizations, not all knowledge resources or capabilities possessed by knowledge workers merit consideration as intellectual assets. An organization must have a clear and coherent picture about what knowledge constitutes intellectual assets so that it can focus on protecting these (see the box). The security of intellectual assets has become a critical issue because of the rise in competitive intelligence activities and poor security management practices in organizations.

Identifying intellectual assets

1. Is the resource or capability valuable?
2. Is the resource or capability rare?
3. Is the resource or capability non-substitutable?
4. Is the resource or capability non-imitable?

If the answer is yes to all questions, the resource or capability is an intellectual asset of the highest value. If the answer to question 1 is no, the resource or capability is not an intellectual asset. If the answers to questions 3 and 4 are no, the resource and capability might be an intellectual asset depending on organizational context, or they could be assets of a lower value.

Competitive intelligence

What is competitive intelligence? Just like government intelligence operations that acquire information on future threats and opportunities for a nation, competitive intelligence (CI) involves gathering information on competitors that can advance the objectives of the organization. CI as a field has been around for several decades. Much like the field of knowledge management, the reasons for the growth of CI have been simple yet salient. We must be able to gather, analyse, interpret and predict competitive moves so that we can better inform strategic, tactical and operational endeavours. Failure to have a viable CI programme will leave an organization vulnerable to surprise moves by competitors, which could be detrimental to the health and well-being of the organization.

The field of CI has blossomed recently as the nature of competition has intensified, in both volume and variety. Today, organizations have many more competitors than they did before. Moreover, because of advancements in information and communication technologies, competitors can come from every corner of the globe. Furthermore, technology has also removed some of the traditional barriers to entry. Take the case of large marketing and advertising agencies: in the past, it was not uncommon for these agencies to compete with peers of equal size and reach. Today, these organizations must also compete with the lone individual who has a computer, video and imaging software, and artistic talent. The world of blogs and the internet has revolutionized the field of advertising, changing whose voices get heard and how attention is captured. Today, if a large advertising and marketing agency does not have a viable CI function that can understand the changing nature of competition in its environment, it will soon be out of business.

Most practitioners in the field of CI rely on the use of open sources (that is, publicly available information) to make assessments about competitors. CI as a field has long been dominated by the analysis of open sources of information, which include news releases, websites, trade exhibitions and scholarly research papers. Access to open sources does not require clandestine measures. These sources have several advantages. Many of them are easily accessible. With the advent of sophisticated search technologies and the internet, retrieving information from open sources has become easier. In addition, it is now easier to triangulate information from these sources; we can verify the reliability and quality of information by seeking convergence and resolving conflicts in information from multiple sources. Moreover, the methods used to gather, analyse, visualize and interpret information from open sources are fairly well understood. Any research methods class in graduate school or a tutorial on data analysis methods will be sufficient to provide the basic knowledge required to engage in analysis of open sources. Given all these advantages, it is easy to think of open sources as a panacea. However, the advantages an organization can obtain from them are limited: open sources are available to all and hence are seldom differentiable. Moreover, since all organizations engage in analysis of open sources, seldom is there anything out there that someone does not already know or is not already looking at.

There are some people who go beyond what is available publicly; I have been known to be one of these individuals. After all, public information has limited value: if it is out there for free, then why should a company pay someone like me a lot of money to get it? A fairly well-educated individual, maybe with a library science or information science background, should be able to gather, integrate and present the information. Getting information that cannot be accessed from open sources is of greater value to most organizations. The reason for this is quite simple: information that is inside the company is of greater value than information that is out in public.

For example, a financial analyst may want to know information about a company's financial performance one or more days before the public announcement, information that the analyst can then use to make gains in trading. A competitor may want to know details of a new product offering being released by an organization. A potential investor of one organization may want to know what is being developed in the R&D department of the organization's competitor. A marketing manager may want to know which other organizations a potential client is in discussion with for signing a new deal. The list can go on and on.

Information of this kind is not available out in the open: it is normally held within the confines of the organization. For example, as we shall see in later chapters, one way to access such information is to simply follow some of the executives and eavesdrop on their phone conversations. Most executives lack cognizance of their surroundings when using their mobile phones. Many feel quite comfortable talking about sensitive business matters on the train ride to work, as they wait in line to pick up their coffee, or even as they take a ride in a taxi. What is even more interesting is that they do not mind raising their voices as the noise in their surroundings gets louder, making the job of people like me very (very, very) easy. Another way such information can be compromised is through sloppiness in how organizations host offsite meetings (we shall explore this issue later in greater detail). Failing to safeguard against eavesdropping on offsite meetings, or lack of diligence in how employees use offsite facilities such as business centres in hotels, among other oversights, can lead to information leaks. Yet another way for information leaks to occur is when laptops – or those handy portable USB disk drives – get stolen (or, more commonly, misplaced). I shall stop disclosing ways that such information is compromised for now, but I explore these issues in greater length in the remainder of the book.

You might think when reading this book that what I do could be illegal. Perhaps surprisingly, the answer is that it is not. Keeping your ears and eyes open as people speak in a public space is not a crime. Moreover, using a fake name and identity when introducing yourself is not a crime; young adults do this all the time, giving out fake names in clubs or bars to weed out people they are not interested in. Furthermore, I have been asked many times by organizations to test their reflexes to a physical security breach, as was the case in the story that opened this chapter; my actions in such a case would not be illegal. Under no circumstances have I or anyone I know ever used measures that would be considered illegal to get access to information within a company. After all, we wouldn't want to get caught and be subject to arrest and other avoidable unpleasantness.

The question then becomes, is it ethical? You might argue that what I do is unethical and morally irresponsible. To that I say, 'You could be right.' However, there is one caveat: before you judge such actions to be unethical, you should have some understanding of the values that are in place in our current competitive environment. First, I can tell you that even the most respectable companies, even those that you would want to work for and those that aspire to do good for society, engage in competitive intelligence activities. They also engage in activities to procure information that is not publicly available. Second, if an organization were to claim that it does not engage in these activities – which I find hard to believe – it will become the unknowing victim of such activities, as its competitors are sure to be engaging in them. Third, many companies do not want to be directly involved in such activities. Thus, they outsource the activities to third parties. Outsourcing the activities makes them legally not responsible for the acts, but does not absolve them from the ethical considerations. Finally, in order to consider the ethical implications of such activities one must be a realist. Businesses compete, and they do so in a fierce manner. Information gives companies the edge they need to outperform competitors in the marketplace. Hence, any valuable information that can further corporate objectives is fair game. Moreover, if an organization is sloppy in handling its own information, that is one of its weaknesses; and just like any other weakness, that sloppiness is fair game for exploitation by competitors.

In conclusion, while the activities I have engaged in may be unethical, they are not illegal. Rest assured that if I did not partake in those engagements there would be plenty of other people waiting to pick up the assignments. I performed these assignments knowing that what I was doing was sometimes questionable, and I do not claim to know whether I did the right or wrong thing. I guess time will tell.

Consider the case of Hewlett Packard.[3] At the annual Hewlett Packard Board of Directors meetings in 2006 and 2005, one board member released detailed business plans to CNET news.com. This reduced HP's competitive advantage, as it made public what was once private company information. The leak persisted for over a year. Finding the source of the leak was a priority for former CEO Carly Fiorina as well as former Chair of the Board Patricia Dunn. During their respective terms as CEOs, Fiorina and Dunn authorized private investigators (PIs) to find out who had caused the leak. During the course of that investigation, the PIs followed several common practices:

- **physical surveillance**: the PIs followed HP board members surreptitiously.;
- **e-mail surveillance**: the PIs embedded tracing mechanisms in e-mails to see whether board members forwarded sensitive information;
- **pretexting**: the PIs pretended to be other people in order to get access to phone records.

None of these practices is strictly illegal. In particular, pretexting has received much attention because it is unethical and borderline illegal, but PIs across the country use it frequently in other contexts (such as obtaining the phone records of a cheating spouse for divorce proceedings). Pretending to be someone else is not always illegal. For instance, the founder of REI often enters stores dressed like a scruffy backpacker to assess how employees treat customers.

In response to the public outcry, Dunn stepped down from her job as a result of her role in the PIs' actions. Another board member whose records were obtained through pretexting (Tom Perkins) resigned from the board. A third director who was revealed to be the source of the leak left the board voluntarily. A congressional inquiry is under way in the United States. The California state attorney-general indicted Patricia Dunn on four charges and she could face up to 12 years in prison as a result of the investigation. On 4 October 2006, HP's stock hit a 52-week high.

In this book I discuss how intellectual assets of an organization can be compromised by CI operations by competitors, and what can be done to prevent these occurrences. In order to prevent these operations from materializing we need to pay attention to security management.

Security management[4]

The one area of an organization that is supposed to act as a defence against competitive espionage types of activity is its security apparatus. Unfortunately, in most organizations the security programmes are beyond weak; they are in a piteous state. Organizations have had guards to keep an eye on corporate premises since the early days, yet the nature of how physical security is handled has not changed much.

A large percentage of the personnel who are thrown into a 'security' role do not have the necessary knowledge, experience or skills. I spoke to over 60 different private security personnel who were charged with protecting office buildings in downtown Chicago. Over 85 per cent of them had never attended a university or had any training in aspects of crisis management, security or law enforcement. Of the 15 per cent that had attended universities, most were college dropouts and had minimal training in security management. Moreover, most of the job descriptions for security personnel were vague about the minimal requirements for hiring. As one of our respondents put it, 'In the interview ... the most important question was if I knew how to use a walkie-talkie.' If organizations do not hire the right calibre of personnel, organizations should not expect much in terms of protection. To be effective, security personnel must have requisite knowledge in the areas of security, crisis management and law enforcement. Without these skills, we might as well leave our doors open to intruders, as our security guards will not know how to effectively detect and deal with intruders.

Most organizations view their physical security measures as an expense, not an asset. As such, the first line of thinking is often, How I can reduce this expense. In the current era of shrinking budgets and difficult growth periods for organizations, any means of reducing expenses is looked upon favourably by management. Most organizations outsource their security management functions, many times to the lowest bidder, without executing due diligence in evaluating the capabilities of security vendors. In the Chicago downtown area, most security guards barely earn $8–12 an hour in wages, with minimal fringe benefits. With such salaries, organizations cannot expect to attract the best and brightest to take up security positions. What is more critical is that with such low pay, security personnel may be easily subject to manipulation by unscrupulous individuals. For example, if in the process of attempting to access an office space, I encountered a security guard who was having a hard time making ends meet on his salary, chances are high that I could get access to the space after a bit of convincing and upon offering some extra income. Organizations put themselves at risk by creating such environments where employees' allegiance to the organization can be tested. Would you pay your best software programmer or salesperson minimal wages? Of course not! If you did that, the employee would probably leave for another organization; or if he or she did stay in the organization, would perform below his or her true potential. Organizations need to start thinking in a similar fashion when it comes to security personnel.

Security personnel are like puppets in uniforms. In the majority of organizations they lack significant authority or accountability. Consider the following case. In one organization a security guard was fired after not allowing a person without an ID card to enter the office building. The security guard did his job: he had been hired to prevent unauthorized individuals from entering the building. However, the person he stopped was a senior member of the organization's management team. Because he questioned the senior official of the organization and delayed him for a few moments, the vigilant and innocent-minded guard was relieved from his post. Why? Because he inconvenienced a senior manager. After this incident, do you think any security guard at this organization would stop a person who looked like a senior manager?

Security guards also have a hard time enforcing 'security rules'. For example, most organizations have a rule stating that ID must be displayed at all times. Try this for an exercise: walk around your office premises for a day without your ID and see whether you are questioned by a security guard. Unless organizations give security personnel the requisite authority they will not be successful in protecting intellectual assets. Just as the police have authority to ensure that all citizens abide by the law, security personnel must have the authority to enforce security policies.

Most security personnel do not have any vested interest in the organizations they protect. If you are not convinced by this, walk by your office premises during off hours. Your security guards will be quite busy: watching television, using the phone to call their friends, leaving back doors open while they go for a smoke, and even sleeping on the job.

Now obviously, I do not want to claim that every security guard behaves in such a manner. But in my experience a lot of them do not have any motivation to protect their organizations. They are not going to risk their lives or the ease of their jobs to protect organizations that do not care about them.

Except in a few organizations, physical security is viewed as a secondary concern compared with information system security. Most organizations have executives who are in charge of information security programmes. These individuals have the luxury of hiring some of the brightest minds and securing needed resources. This is all well and good; however, what troubles me is the fact that the same attention is not given to physical security, especially in the context of protecting intellectual assets. Yes, technology systems are increasingly at risk of attack by unscrupulous individuals. I don't wish to debate this point; however, I feel that businesses have become so caught up in technology security that they have forgotten the more basic, yet very salient, notion of physical security. Physical security has lost its glamour in recent times and has taken a back seat to issues of technology security. However, an organization can be brought to the ground in seconds if the right perpetrator is able to breach physical security and gain access to sensitive areas in an office building.

Given the apathy towards physical security, it should not be surprising to find that only a handful of organizations have safeguards in place to protect their intellectual assets. Security programmes around intellectual assets are in a primitive stage of development, although there are some exceptions to this rule. For example, defence and national security agencies take great care in ensuring that sensitive material is not jeopardized or leaked. Similarly, some R&D labs and pharmaceutical labs have sophisticated security measures in place to ensure that secrecy is maintained around projects. However, these exceptions are few and far between. In this book, I provide guidelines for building security programmes around intellectual assets.

Roadmap of the book

We are ready to get started on our journey. Here is the roadmap to help navigate the terrain we will cover.

Chapter 2 will discuss issues that surround securing knowledge from the perspective of employees. Employees are hired because they have knowledge and skills of interest to the organization. Unless an organization is able to use its employees' skills to accomplish goals and objectives, it will not be able to recoup returns on its investments. Today, the competition for talent is fierce, and trends indicate that competition will intensify in the future. Skilled employees and those with expertise and knowledge in certain domains are scarce. Competitors are trying to lure away your employees, and unless you understand how to address this issue, your organization will be at a loss. Your organization might spend the time, resources and energy to train and equip employees only to have the employees eventually leave your organization for others.

In this chapter, I also discuss issues of knowledge leaks (communicating knowledge to unauthorized sources, like the press), knowledge sloppiness (accidentally using knowledge incorrectly, resulting in unintended consequences), and knowledge misuse (such as wilful misuse of organizational knowledge to further personal agendas).

In Chapter 3, we shall look at knowledge losses that occur as a result of information and communication technologies (ICTs). ICTs have made it possible for organizations to work in distributed and virtual environments. Employees can now work from home, as they can easily connect to the organization using ICTs. Similarly, employees use mobile technologies to communicate about business matters and USB disk drives to take their work home. While the advancements in ICT have made it easy for employees to be more agile and mobile in how they work, they also pose considerable security challenges. Consider the case of an employee who takes sensitive work materials home. What happens if the home is burgled and the material is compromised? This is a non-trivial issue, and in recent times, these types of security incidents have continued to rise in number. ICTs also pose other challenges. For example, very few organizations have guidelines in place outlining the kinds of conversations that may occur in public environments (that is, outside office premises), and the kinds of communication channel that may be used.

Chapter 4 examines issues of knowledge security in the context of strategic alliances. All organizations must forge alliances with external entities in order to accomplish their business objectives. When an organization chooses to collaborate with an external entity, it opens up some aspect of its business; in doing so, it must pay attention to issues of security. Consider the case of licensing agreements. When engaged in a licensing agreement – let's say for software – an organization must ensure that the software does not have malicious content. Similarly, in more complex forms of alliances, such as joint ventures or production and development agreements, it is important for an organization to ensure that its business partners have adequate security measures in place and do not act with guile. As the adage goes, you are only as strong as your weakest link. If there are vulnerabilities in the security practices of your business partners, there is a chance that you may feel the impact of a security breach.

The less glamorous part of security management today is physical security: securing the physical locations of organizations, including office buildings, offsite conference facilities and so on. But as the introductory story noted, an organization's inability to secure these premises can cost it dearly. In Chapter 5, we examine issues of physical security. Physical security is a major challenge today. Today, organizations have many more offices than they used to, and these offices are spread across all corners of the globe. We discuss how to secure sensitive knowledge work within these premises. In addition, we shall discuss issues of securing knowledge in the extended organization. For example, how do you ensure that facilities used for offsite meetings are secure, and how do you ensure that employees and executives who travel or are in transit from one location to another are protected?

Chapter 6 looks at knowledge security issues in the context of crises and disasters. Organizations can be affected by crises both natural (such as hurricanes and floods) and human (such as terrorism and wars). How an organization secures its knowledge during these periods can be quite critical. If an organization does not secure its knowledge, which involves not only preventing knowledge losses but also planning for resumption of operations, the consequences can be deadly. During times of crisis, organizations are under undue stress and hence are abnormally reactive. They seldom think through all implications before executing actions during these periods. It is hence important to think through, plan, rehearse and be ready for these situations before they materialize.

In the concluding chapter, Chapter 7, we shall assimilate and integrate lessons learnt from the previous chapters. I discuss how organizations should implement strategic processes and practices to address knowledge security issues. Here, we address issues of getting employee buy-in for security programmes, changing management practices, crafting incentive schemes, and engaging in cost–benefit and risk analysis, among others. Issues of how to measure the effectiveness of security programmes and how to continuously improve them are also addressed.

Taking these subjects together, it is my hope that this book will help you to examine intellectual asset security issues through a critical lens. For those of you that were not aware of the wide array of intellectual asset security issues that must be contended with, I hope this book opens your eyes. For those who already knew that securing intellectual assets is a challenge that needs to be addressed, I hope this book will provide you with some thinking points. For those who are engaged in crafting intellectual asset security programmes, I hope you can relate to some of the experiences here and get a few new nuggets to try out.

Now, let us get started on our journey. The first stop is securing knowledge in and around employees.

2

The human stain

Organizations run on their employees. Employees take organizations to great heights (think of Bill Gates and his work with Microsoft, Jack Welch and his tenure with General Electric, Steve Jobs and his work as the CEO of Apple). Employees can also bring an organization to a screeching halt and destroy the vitality of the business (as with Ken Lay and Jeffrey Skilling of Enron, and the eclectic groups of senior executives who ran Global Crossing, Tyco International and WorldCom). Managing employees is central to the ability to sustain an organization.

Consider the following: individuals such as Ken Lay and Jeffrey Skilling were hired because of the skills and capabilities they possessed. I am quite sure that they did not disclose their skill in executing large-scale corporate financial fraud on their CVs. So chances are high that they were hired for some other skill they possessed, and from the salaries paid to these individuals, we can deduce that these skills were seen as highly valuable. How were they then able to orchestrate the crimes they were convicted of? What went wrong? Why weren't these scoundrels caught before it was too late? Why did thousands of individuals have to lose their jobs and suffer economic hardship as a result of their actions? The answer to this is surprisingly simple: oversight of their activities was minimal at best. These individuals misused their knowledge and skills to further their personal gains at the cost of the organization. Now, think for a second: are you sure that your employees are using their knowledge and skills for productive purposes? Failure to ensure that employees use their most valuable resource, their intellect, towards productive ends in the sense of both creating ideas and using skills, can lead to all sorts of very costly headaches.

Employees represent the core intellectual assets of any organization. They are hired for their ideas and skills, and they are remunerated for the ability to use their knowledge towards the objectives of the organization. In addition, they receive training and other knowledge development opportunities. These may include covering the cost of courses in areas related to the work of the company, or even classes towards the attainment of professional qualifications. The organization provides these opportunities, not only for the betterment of the individual employee's knowledge and well-being, but also for the betterment of the organization through the realization of organizational goals. Therefore, it is vital that companies do their best to secure the know-how and skills these employees possess.

One vital concern for organizations in this arena is retaining valuable employees. Employees are storehouses of knowledge, which makes them of interest to competing organizations that operate within the same industry. After all, it is the knowledge of a company's employees, operationalized into products and services, that is purchased by consumers. Employees often have contextual knowledge both about the operations of their employer and about its business partners, clients and industry dealings. Most employees navigate multiple jobs within a given company or within a given professional field (such as accounting); those employees tend to possess more experience and knowledge, and are of greater interest than those who do not. Furthermore, such employees do not have such a steep learning curve to manoeuvre when joining a new organization since they already have knowledge about the given industry and are comfortable with its operations. How do you keep such valuable employees from leaving your company?

Another vital concern for organizations is ensuring that employees do not disclose sensitive information, either intentionally or unintentionally. There can be good employees who accidentally use unsecured channels for communication, thereby possibly disclosing sensitive communication to outsiders. Competitors may also gain critical knowledge assets through deliberate and accidental leaks of information. As noted in the preceding chapter, one area that has become infamous for such behaviour is in the various intelligence agencies of the United States. Contrary to these agencies' mission of keeping secrets and protecting the national security agenda, there have been many cases of leaks of classified information to the press. It never ceases to amaze me how many leaks result from careless behaviour, putting actions and plans in jeopardy.

In a similar manner – though most often of a less serious nature – employees of an organization will at times leak information to external sources for personal gain. This commonly occurs when an employee leaks information about his or her current work activities during a job interview at a competing firm. Does your organization have a policy stating how to handle sensitive information? Are you aware of what your employees are saying during interviews with rival organizations?

There may also be cases of employees falling prey to external pressures. For instance, an employee in severe financial distress might be easily motivated to engage in competitive intelligence activity for a competing organization. In government agencies, especially in the intelligence world, counter-intelligence can become critical to prevent the possibility of employees behaving in such a manner. Are you aware whether any of your employees, and the knowledge they represent, are at risk? Do you know how to protect your employees from external pressures to reveal secrets?

The concept of conscious and malicious intent is also critical here. There can be employees who become rogue, engaging in the deliberate mishandling of intellectual assets or misusing them for their own advantage. How are you minimizing this risk in your own company? Are there company practices that marginalize or trivialize employees and create dissatisfaction? How do you assess the trustworthiness of your employees?

Were you unsure about the answers to many of the above questions? Not knowing the answers to those questions can lead to disastrous consequences. The costs to an organization in terms of knowledge security when dealing with employees can be quite severe and comprehensive. These include the costs of compensation (such as salaries and benefits) and development (such as training and educational programme assistance); opportunity costs (such as the cost of not having a more capable and dependable employee); and damage (the cost of the damage an employee may inflict). In this chapter I explore the security issues of protecting intellectual assets at the level of employees (see below).

Causes of security breaches

- Employee sloppiness.
- Employee obsolescence.
- Competition for talent.
- Entrapment of employees.
- Malicious intent on the part of employees.

Preventive measures

- Background checks.
- Regular check-ups.
- Counter-intelligence.
- Aligning with organizational goals.
- Incentive schemes.
- Educating employees.

Security breaches

Security breaches can occur in a multitude of scenarios. These breaches can occur both knowingly and unknowingly, but the results are devastating either way. Understanding the reasons behind security breaches and the mechanisms by which they occur allows an organization to put proper preventive measures in place. We begin by discussing the ways in which intellectual assets can be compromised unknowingly, then move on to the cases where an employee wilfully decides to sabotage intellectual assets.

The case of sloppiness

Intellectual assets can be compromised by sheer sloppiness. In these cases, intellectual asset loss occurs when employees reuse assets without appropriate care for the context in which they were created. Consider the following case. Claire was responsible for product development in a high-tech company. She had access to the company's knowledge assets in the form of presentations, past sales documents, marketing plans and so on. In her job she was responsible for securing new business by engaging with customers, both current and potential. However, Claire was not an expert in all aspects of the company's products, such as product capabilities and engineering details. She was more of a salesperson: she specialized in managing client relations. One day, in an attempt to quickly prepare a presentation, she decided to reuse an existing presentation on the company's intranet site. She copied and pasted the name of the clients she was presenting and quoting to into the original presentation. In her haste she forgot to check the presentation, and e-mailed it right away to the client. She did not realize that the person who originally created the presentation had inserted extensive notes and details about the original client for whom the presentation had been created. Now all of this material was compromised. Not only did Claire lose the business deal, her organization ended up being sued for breach of confidential information.

Security breaches may also occur as a result of accidental leaks. Some employees may not be aware when they cause intellectual asset losses simply because they aren't aware of what constitutes an intellectual asset. The most common case is when an employee discusses confidential matters of the corporation with external entities. This can take place when an employee makes a statement to a journalist or discusses sensitive work among a set of external peers or at a social setting. For instance, an employee may need to attend trade shows or educational conferences. During these events, people inevitably run into members of competing firms. What gets discussed in these settings can be quite critical to the viability of an organization's ongoing efforts.

Consider the following case. Mona worked for a company that specialized in making accounting software. At a trade conference she struck up a conversation with the employee of a competitor. Mona was so forthcoming with information that she disclosed the current enhancements to a product being developed by her organization. The new version with the enhancements was scheduled for release in about four months. To the dismay of Mona's organization, it found its competitor announcing similar enhancements to its own product a few days after this conference. Not surprisingly, the competitor had a significant edge over Mona's organization. First, the competitor did not have to spend the marketing dollars to understand the needs of customers for product enhancement. The competitor also reduced any losses it might have suffered if the enhancements had given Mona's organization a competitive edge in the marketplace. Situations like this are not rare occurrences or anomalies.

In both of the above cases, the employees did not act with the intention to compromise the intellectual assets of the organization. However, regardless of their innocence, their actions led to the compromise of intellectual assets. I have heard hundreds of these stories over the past few years, and each of them has resulted in devastating blows to organizations. In the case of a sloppy employee who unknowingly discloses sensitive organizational matters, does the fact that he or she did not intend to do so make a difference to the outcome? Probably not.

Consider another case, albeit one in which the employee has a wilful intent to compromise intellectual assets; ask yourself whether the outcome would have been any different if the employee were simply acting carelessly. An employee was frustrated with his current job because he felt he had not received sufficient recognition. The employee was one of the newest members of the organization's R&D team, and was a very diligent and honourable worker; however, he never received any credit for his work. The culture of the labs was very hierarchical, and hence the most senior personnel always got most of the credit. (For example, in research papers that were the outcomes of research projects, a lower-level employee was never listed as the primary author even when he or she did most of the work.) This employee decided to make a move to a competing organization. During his interview, he not only decided to share knowledge of his skills, but purposely disclosed information about half a dozen major research projects that were under way. The employee's primary intent was not only to show that his work was the basis for these efforts, but also to jeopardize the projects' potential by disclosing them to a competing organization. This put the primary organization in jeopardy: although the interviewing organization decided that the employee lacked basic credibility and trustworthiness and did not hire him, it likely used the knowledge about the ongoing research projects to its advantage. This issue is quite serious if you have not talked to employees about what they can and cannot say during interviews, especially about sensitive matters. Most organizations do not train employees about these details or provide any information about this. They do not address this topic, as they fear that they will somehow motivate employees to leave the organization. This thinking is quite futile. Rather, you should deal with this issue head on rather than avoid it, as turnover in personnel is a normal cost of doing business and you want to prevent incidents such as the one above.

The case of obsolescence

Intellectual asset loss also happens when skills that an employee possesses no longer meet the requirements of the current work environment. This normally occurs when an organization does not adequately train its employees to keep their skills updated. Take the case of an organization that has to downsize its workforce as a result of the movement of work to offshore locations. The challenge here for the organization is quite salient: it must find a way to retool or reskill its current employees, or else fire them. The losses that can occur here can severely disrupt an organization. For example, employees may not possess the skills that are needed, but they often have important contextual knowledge about an organization's operations. If the organization loses or fires these employees it cannot easily replace them with new hires, since new hires will not have the requisite contextual knowledge about where to deploy their skills. Intellectual assets can lose value as a result of technology advancements as well. As we discussed in Chapter 1, before the arrival of computerized tax preparation software, tax accountants were in high demand. Today, however, technology has made their skill sets less valuable, especially in the case of routine and simple tax preparations for individuals. Similarly, online travel websites have made traditional travel agencies all but obsolete.

In today's fast-paced and competitive landscape, organizations need to pay adequate attention to intellectual asset obsolescence. Just as we would not neglect to take our cars in for routine maintenance and repairs, organizations should not try to run their intellectual assets without appropriate maintenance and care. One aspect of caring for intellectual assets is ensuring that their value keeps increasing. Here is where most organizations have a difficult time. Most organizations have a tendency to continuously use their intellectual assets to get near-term or short-term rewards. Consider the case of an experienced programmer or a veteran consultant. Chances are high that these individuals have no downtime; soon after one project is complete they move on to the next effort. The reason for this is that their skills are in demand, and the customers of the organization are ready to pay a high premium for these assets. This is good for the organization in the short term. However, if the organization does not pull these individuals out of daily operations and give them time to update their skills, acquire new skills, or even just reflect and document their experiences, in the long run the viability of their skills and knowledge will be sacrificed.

The case of competition

Competition can be a source of intellectual asset loss when an organization's competitor hires away talent. Consider the case of two software giants, Microsoft and Google. Both organizations have been known to engage in battles over talent. After all, both companies would like to hire the best and brightest individuals so as to retain their competitive position in the marketplace. Who is the ideal candidate for a job at Microsoft or Google? In many cases it is an employee who currently works at the other organization, or someone the competing organization is about to hire. The reason is simple: employees of interest have skills and knowledge that are in demand. Hence, both Google and Microsoft have been quite fierce in their attempts to lure talent away from each other. This battle for talent can happen even between organizations that do not operate in the same industry, as long as the competing organizations need employees with similar skills and knowledge. As another example, the banking and sales industries regularly work hard to 'steal' employees from their competitors. Many banks, especially in the commercial arena, lure seasoned bankers away from their competitors, not just because of their knowledge, but because of the client relationships they will bring. By hiring a given banker, the bank may extend its client base and consequently its market share. Similar dynamics occur within the sales industry, where headhunters constantly call successful sales personnel to entice them to work for competitors.

Academia is another well-known example of this phenomenon: top-tier professors continuously field job opportunities from rival institutions. The challenge of the recruiting school is to show professors that some of their current needs (such as research assistance or funding) are not being met in their current environments. Seldom is it just about the increase in pay. The exception is when a good professor is being underpaid, which is a rare occurrence. Universities that are able to recruit the best professors, and more importantly keep them, will be able to sustain their competitive advantage. The opposite is quite dangerous: a university that recruits the best but fails to keep them will be doing itself a major disservice. It will be expending a lot of energy to recruit the best, and will not be able to recoup these costs when the employee leaves. Moreover, as the academic community witnesses this constant turmoil and turnover, the university's reputation will spiral downward, eventually leading to its inability to even recruit the best.

Fierce competition for talent is taking place continuously in the corporate world. Most of us seem to be oblivious to this reality. Consider, however, that some organizations have one or more 'recruiting researchers' or 'recruiting and personnel intelligence analysts' on their payrolls. These individuals have several tasks: understanding how competitors lure away their employees; understanding the kinds of incentive schemes and offers their competitors provide and how they can match or beat those; and how to identify potential talent in the competing firms that they would like to recruit. If your organization does not have such a person, be wary of your HR department: it is neglecting an important part of its function. Recruiting and luring employees away from a competing organization is a skill that only a handful of organizations have mastered.

It is important to note that when your employees leave to join competing organizations, these losses can be devastating (see the box). The best-case scenario when an employee leaves is loss of the employee's skills and capabilities, but this best-case scenario is seldom realized. It is more likely that the worst-case scenario will be realized: the employee leaves, and in addition to taking knowledge and skills, he or she also takes professional networks, disrupts information and communication patterns in the organization, and even shakes up the morale of the unit left behind.

The pub

Consider the case of a local pub that I used to frequent. Jaime, the bartender, was the most charismatic, charming and friendly bartender I had ever met. She had been working at the pub for over 10 years since dropping out of her university studies. During that time, she not only got to know everyone who frequented the bar, she was also well known in the local neighbourhood. When the bar hit tough times during 2002, the owner sold it to his friend. The new owner decided that Jaime was being paid at a premium, and decided to lower her pay to help balance the books. Jaime, naturally upset, decided to leave and work for a competing pub a few blocks away. She lured away all her regular customers to the new pub. The new owner tried his best to convince Jaime to reconsider and come back to the original pub, and even offered to double her earnings, but it was too late. The first pub closed down within two months.

The case of entrapment

Compromised employees put themselves in vulnerable positions, making their allegiance to the organization suspect. In addition to external pressures, such as competition, there are cases in which an employee might become compromised for internal reasons, such as financial trouble. If an employee is nearing bankruptcy and is scrambling to make ends meet, he or she might succumb to pressures to act with guile. Whether the compromise happens because of internal or external reasons, the presence of a compromised employee can pose a serious threat to an organization.

It is important to note that in many cases, simply a perception of being compromised may be as dangerous as any act that actually leads to a compromised situation. For example, the very suspicion that a professor is flirting with students can lead to serious outcomes, regardless of whether inappropriate activities have actually occurred. Similarly, if an employee is perceived as unethical or acting in an unauthorized manner it can lead to serious consequences, both for the individual and for the organization. Employees need to understand that even a small action can be taken quite seriously, as a small action has the potential to compromise a good employee.

To cite an example, an executive who was travelling through foreign countries was befriended by a woman who was able to exploit him by threatening to disclose this relationship to his spouse. Moreover, the executive was known to spend corporate money on questionable entertainment choices, such as patronizing strip clubs. Such behaviour made him vulnerable to external pressures.

In one R&D organization, a researcher was compromised after attempting to falsify the results of an experiment. A fellow colleague discovered the errors and threatened to report the researcher if he did not share his future results and help the discoverer advance up the corporate ladder.

How might one go about coercing an employee? Let us imagine that an agent, Joshua, wants to extort information from an executive. Joshua might meet the executive at a business function such as a conference. During this event Joshua might befriend the executive and then invite him out for cocktails. During the meeting for cocktails, Joshua might engage the executive in conversation about his work. With every passing moment, Joshua might begin to probe a bit deeper into work activities. Soon, the executive might feel more comfortable and at ease. Then, at a future meeting, again over cocktails (or coffee), Joshua might ask the executive to share details about his work engagements, and even get him to bring a copy of his CV. Joshua might, for example, tell the executive that using email to send his CV might be detectable by his IT department, and hence it would be best if he brought it in person.

During this meeting, Joshua might have an envelope with a few dollar bills in it. Joshua would give it to the executive as a sign of good faith and to see whether he accepted it. Joshua could come up with a hundred reasons for this offer of money. For example, Joshua might say that if he found the executive a new job, the executive's new employer would more than willingly pay Joshua for his expenses – something like a finding or referral fee. What the executive does not know is that Joshua has a friend taking pictures of the exchange of materials. Then, at a later date, Joshua might ask for more sensitive materials. The executive might refuse, upon which Joshua could share the pictures that his friend took. Reminding the executive that he has already exchanged sensitive material for money, Joshua will insist that he now either follow through or risk exposure. Chances are high that the executive will follow through, as keeping up mortgage payments while trying to explain the situation to his superiors is not a feasible strategy.

This is an example of a baiting strategy. The agent sets the bait and sees whether his victim will bite. If the victim bites, he is hooked, and then can be reeled into deeper and more significant operations.

The case of malicious intent

Not all security leaks result from mistakes made by innocent employees. Often, rogue employees are the culprits. This is normally a disgruntled employee with a score to settle. In most cases the employee feels undervalued in the organization, or in some cases is just an employee who has a criminal bent. Most employees would like to be recognized when they make contributions to an organization above and beyond normal expectations. After all, employees work for an organization not only for monetary rewards and remuneration, but also for non-monetary and social rewards. What may be more troubling to an employee is when his or her peers are recognized for contributions that the employee thinks are inferior. A disgruntled employee, upset because he or she did not receive a promotion, may get angry to the point of being motivated to jeopardize the organizational agenda. The employee may engage in any number of disruptive behaviours, from simply not meeting deadlines and not sharing knowledge that is of interest to peers, to more covert manoeuvres, such as disrupting information systems or fishing for information in restricted spaces so that he or she can gain personal advantage.

The most common cases of rogue employees damaging an organization's work have been in the information technology (IT) field. As a result of downsizing, layoffs and outsourcing initiatives, IT departments have seen their numbers of employees decrease and their job security disappear (see the box). Employees who are about to lose their jobs may want revenge against the company, and they can get it by compromising information systems (ISs) they have been paid to maintain. This commonly takes the form of planting back doors and viruses into ISs, distributing sensitive materials, sabotaging information by corrupting it, and sometimes even delivering faulty software. In the last case the employee often not only sabotages the intellectual assets of the organization, but also takes steps to ensure that the organization realizes who compromised the assets and why.

Early on we highlighted the issue of intellectual asset obsolescence. When their employees' intellectual assets became obsolete, few organizations, especially those in the IT sector, were prepared to retrain their employees and move them to new positions within the organization. As a result, during the early part of 2000, when many in the IT sector lost their jobs, it was common for organizations to witness malicious attacks on their information systems, many coming from inside the organization.

The disgruntled employee

Cliff, an employee for a large information technology firm, discovered he was about to be laid off. Angry over the loss of his job, he decided to plant a critical bug in the corporate information system. Upon discovery of the bug, the executives in the organization quickly realized that Cliff was the perpetrator. The organization knew that it could not go public with the story or call local law enforcement, since word of the incident would cause severe damage to its reputation and well-being. The organization instead decided to pay Cliff a premium to fix the bug. In addition the organization guaranteed that Cliff would receive a salary for the next five years as long as no other bugs were discovered in the IS. Needless to say, if other employees knew about this deal they too might be enticed to conduct similar activities and cause similar damage to the organization.

There are also cases in which an employee is, by nature, prone to criminal activities. In some cases, employees' criminal activity may lead indirectly to security breaches (see the box). In other cases, employees with a criminal bent may be able to access sensitive corporate materials and jeopardize the well-being of the organization. For example, at a biotechnology firm, the janitorial and maintenance staff were involved in stealing sensitive materials from the company on behalf of a competing organization. The janitorial staff took pictures of whiteboards, copied printouts, and at times even recorded passwords that employees taped on their monitors. It is important to realize that an organization needs to take great care in selecting employees, especially those who have access to sensitive materials.

The criminal element

A large manufacturing firm in the Midwest of the United States outsourced the physical security of its corporate buildings to a security management organization. It was up to this security organization to hire the necessary personnel to monitor the premises. The manufacturing firm did not know that the security-outsourcing vendor never ran thorough background checks on its hires. Upon investigation it was found that two of the guards, George and Alan, working in night shifts at the manufacturing firm, were stealing high-end office supplies such as printer toner and reams of paper. It was even discovered that George and Alan were using unprotected computers (computers that were not locked) to surf pornographic websites during their night shifts. The investigation commenced only after a routine IT audit discovered that two computers had traffic to the pornographic websites. Besides the minor expenses involved in replacing stolen office supplies, these actions might have had a more severe cost, such as viruses or spyware being inadvertently downloaded onto office computers.

Preventive measures

Preventing damage caused by loss or misuse of intellectual assets is vital to the ongoing success of any organization. Although the previous examples in this chapter paint a grim picture, there are several important steps organizations can take to prevent these errors. By making a few simple changes in policies and procedures an organization can ensure that its most valuable knowledge assets, its employees, remain with the organization and use their knowledge in an appropriate manner.

Background checks

Doing background checks on potential employees is very important. Without conducting adequate checks we can only hope that prospective employees have good intentions. This holds true for most new employees, but a few bad apples is all it takes to corrupt the bunch. Organizations often fail in their efforts to properly screen out employees harbouring criminal intent. Most organizations only conduct very basic background checks on their employees, and usually only for what some might consider white-collar work. Companies avoid doing more because background checks can be costly, especially when detailed information is required. It is possible to conduct a very basic background check of criminal, financial and work history via the internet for under US$50. However, ascertaining detailed information, such as the employee's associates and social habits, pressure points and degree of trustworthiness, requires a more detailed background investigation.

When conducting background checks it is important to be upfront about the detailed search you will conduct. Moreover, ask prospective employees to be honest with the information they share with you. For example, for most positions, use of recreational drugs in the past is not, in and of itself, an issue for the potential employer. However, if an employee who has used recreational drugs in the past answers a question about past drug use dishonestly, this would constitute a good reason not to hire him or her. After all, if the employee cannot be trusted to share accurate information initially, then there is no reason to trust the employee with the intellectual assets of the organization.

Beware of the use of previous background checks as a method for vetting your potential employee. Consider the case of the US government. Today, if you have security clearance, you can sell the government nearly anything and they will pay you a premium for it! The reason for this is that for certain activities (that is, work projects) individuals are hired not for their expertise but because of the clearances they hold. So, any John Doe (or Jane Smith) who spent several years in some government function and was lucky enough to get security clearance can move to the private sector and charge the government a premium for his or her knowledge. Time and time again I have seen unqualified people get paid for knowledge they supposedly possessed, when in fact they were just being used to fill numbers in a budget sheet. Beware of individuals who flaunt their security clearance; this might be their only asset. Yikes! I am always amazed by how easily an organization will give highly classified and important work to people with security clearance but no knowledge or expertise in the area. Rather, companies should make the efforts to identify skilled people who have the requisite knowledge, then have an efficient and effective process to provide them with security clearance.

A similar dynamic occurs in organizations. Most often employees' levels of access are not a function of the expertise they possess or their work-related needs. They are more likely a function of how long they have been there and who they know. Moreover, once an employee is given access to the organization there are very few mechanisms, besides minor security protocols on the computer system, to prevent the employee from traversing the entire organizational knowledge space.

I would estimate that almost 70 per cent of the organizations that I have consulted for either do not have good processes in place for conducting background checks, or overdo background checks to a point that they become an impediment to business. It is important to create an efficient process for background checks. Overly detailed checks can waste valuable time and money, resources that are better spent on training new employees. Always strike a balance between a thorough, effective background check and an efficient one. Companies who have robust background check processes know how to conduct various types of checks depending on the kind of employee who is being screened. For example, the checks that would be required on a manager or senior executive are considerably more extensive than those that are required on other personnel who have less access to the intellectual assets of the organization. In addition, the organizations that have mastered the art of background checks do not give all-purpose clearance upon the completion of these checks; instead, background checks are used to vet employees for very specific tasks, projects and roles. If the job of an employee should change, as a result of either lateral or vertical movements, a new check may be required to upgrade the employee's access levels.

Finally, the issues involved in handling information that comes up during a background check need to be considered. The first issue is inconsistent information. It is possible to get different pictures of an individual depending on the sources consulted. For example, in assessing the creditworthiness of an individual, an examination of bank records might find that she is fairly well-off; however, other records might indicate that she is regularly late with her mortgage payments. Does this mean that she is simply sloppy and does not get round to making the payments on time, or is this an indication of a deeper issue? In cases such as these, when there is conflicting information, the best piece of advice is to gather more information and wait for some level of convergence. Do not jump to conclusions or make arbitrary decisions. In this case, the inconsistent information could be a result of the credit reporting agency obtaining bad data from a particular financial institution, and the individual not having rectified the mistake.

There are also cases of missing and incomplete information. If missing information arises during a background check, it is wise to make a decision upfront on the value of the information. If this information is not of significant interest, it is best to move on and examine other information that is available. You do not want to burden the person whose background is being checked with every small request, as the situation is stressful enough. Moreover, you do not want tip people off to the kind of searches you are conducting, as this may lead them to take actions to counter the information.

The last issue to manage is when you get information indicating that the employee may have lied, hidden information or provided false information. In these cases, it is very important to handle such information with care. First, never accuse the person of any wrongdoing. Accusing a person means that you are sure about the information (300 per cent sure!). This is never possible during a background check. Hence, do not accuse someone, as he or she can retaliate and sue you! Instead, call the employee in to discuss the information that has been uncovered, give him or her a chance to explain and clarify the information, and then make an informed decision. If the information cannot be explained or if it is discovered that the employee did lie or hide information, you have an easy explanation for why employment is not an option.

Regular check-ups

The use of background checks should only be the first step. Even if an employee passes the background check, don't just leave the treasure chest of organizational intellectual assets open for him or her to access and use. Once employees join the organization, the next step is to begin a serious evaluation to gauge performance and also to assess their trustworthiness. During the annual, biannual or quarterly review, managers should rate employees on measures of trust. Do employees display integrity in their work? Has an employee engaged in questionable behaviours that might compromise organizational security? Has the employee contributed insights to help increase the potency of organizational assets? Only after the employee has been vetted, displayed integrity, and demonstrated that he or she follows security procedures should unsupervised access be given to sensitive intellectual assets of the firm. It is important to note that employees do not gain access to all the intellectual assets of the organization; they only gain access to the knowledge they actually need.

In addition, regularly perform basic checks on employees, especially those who work in sensitive areas. Routinely scan details such as the well-being of employees, their financial health and so on, so that any signs of potential problems can be identified upfront. Most organizations only do such checks when an employee joins the organization, then later leave such details to chance. These organizations are then very surprised when a disaster does take place. Employees who engage in rogue behaviour or those who act under coercive pressures may come into the organization with clean slates. However, conditions may develop after hiring that sway them in different directions.

It is vital to be upfront with your employees so they know these checks will occur on a regular basis; otherwise they might interpret these backgrounds checks as a sign of distrust or displeasure on the part of the company. The organization needs to explain that the background checks will be exhaustive, and that they are being conducted to protect the organization. Moreover, employees should have the right to decline the check, but this should be grounds enough for barring them from continuing with the organization. One organization that I know of has used the analogy of a doctor and patient relationship to frame routine background inspections. Employees are screened before they join the organization, and this is used to establish a baseline and weed out employees who have malicious intent. Once employees join the organization, they are then asked to subscribe to yearly and/or as-needed background checks. The yearly background checks are analogous to going in for a yearly medical check-up, while the as-needed checks are analogous to being screened when a symptom appears. The use of these check-ups ensures that the organizational climate is preserved, integrity is maintained, and that everyone can work in a safe and secure environment.

Organizations need metrics to gauge employee trustworthiness and continued integrity. Things can change at any time, and it is important for organizations to recognize and identify changes in employee behaviour upfront (see the box). Changes in employee behaviour may be indicators that the person's integrity or trustworthiness is suspect. In order to build metrics, an organization must be able to collect data on its employees and analyse them in a centralized manner. To this end, it is important for an organization to have clear reporting mechanisms. For example, if a manager in one division finds an employee engaging in questionable behaviour, he/she should not simply handle the matter locally. There should be a report filed to a centralized reporting agency, like the security department. Failure to report incidents will make the process of regular checks-ups difficult, cumbersome, and even incomplete.

Suspicious behaviour

A boutique strategy consulting company based in downtown New York had about 30 employees and just under a dozen clients. The firm received an offer to participate in a project involving a firm based in Shanghai. No one in the firm had any serious experience in the Chinese market, and hence it decided to hire a new employee: a recent graduate of a prestigious law school who was interested in international law with a special focus on Asia. The graduate passed the initial background check with flying colours and began her assignment.

During the course of the assignment, suspicious behaviour started to emerge, including loss of documents and extended phone calls with Chinese counterparts. The organization decided to commission a new check on the employee. During the investigations, which included information on the exchanges with the colleagues in China, it was discovered that the employee was in serious financial trouble and had ailing parents who needed her immediate financial assistance. As a result, she had become involved in illegal activities, which included the sale of sensitive information and spying on the organization's clients for the benefit of the Chinese business counterparts.

Counter-intelligence

One necessary aspect of an organization's security apparatus is the counter-intelligence function. Organizations need to have in place programmes that monitor how competitors are interacting with the organization's employees. Interaction can be as simple as headhunters calling employees to lure them away with job offers. One of my colleagues got a call from a headhunter asking him to switch jobs three weeks after he started at his new job. He accepted the call and spoke with the headhunter. What he did not know was that neither the headhunter nor the job offer really existed: it was the organization's counter-intelligence function that had made the phone call to see how quickly my colleague would switch jobs.

Counter-intelligence functions are very important in today's competitive marketplace. Your employees, especially your most valuable ones, are attractive candidates for your competitors. As noted earlier, only a handful of organizations have counter-intelligence programmes in place to address this issue. Counter-intelligence functions must be able to clearly identify the sources of threats to an organization's intellectual assets. In addition, they should uncover the methods used by external entities to compromise the intellectual assets. Once the sources and methods are deduced, counter-strategies can be developed to address them.

In building a counter-intelligence function several points need to be considered. First, it should be clear what the charter, goals and objectives of this function are. Employees do not like to be monitored or investigated. Hence the counter-intelligence function should be clearly defined, to help avoid confusion about the purpose of the unit. Second, it is very important that these groups stay within legal bounds. Engaging in illegal activities to get at information and sources of leaks is not advisable. Think about the HP case we discussed early on. The fact that HP's counter-intelligence programme will now be discussed within a courtroom is not good. Third, the counter-intelligence function should not be viewed as only a reactive mechanism. For instance, in most organizations this function is called into action only after a breach occurs. Ideally, the function needs to prevent breaches by having a good understanding of the environment in which the organization operates and the environments the employees traverse.

The outcomes of counter-intelligence activities do not always have to be negative from the point of view of employees. In one organization that I know of, upon completion of a successful counter-intelligence project, the organization identified the top 100 employees at risk of being lured away by their competitors. Once these employees were identified the counter-intelligence function worked in conjunction with the human resource team to devise ways of changing these employees' compensation, reward and benefits packages to make the decision to move to a competitor a difficult one. The moves on the part of the HR department were viewed favourably by these individuals, and they came to respect the organization for taking proactive steps to value their contributions and expertise.

Aligning with organizational goals

Intellectual asset breaches, such as the compromising of assets by employees acting either wilfully or under coercive pressures, often stem from a lack of appreciation for employees in most organizations. Today's organizations place very little emphasis on allegiance, taking very little care to ensure that their employees become part of the fabric of the organization. Put in another way, very little effort is made to bond an employee to the organization. In the past it was common for people to spend their entire careers in one organization. Employees came to respect and bond with their organizations. Their co-workers were often their closest friends. The organization became more than a place to earn a paycheque: it was a place that helped define who they were.

Now contrast this with the current generation of employees. During a ten-year span a person may work for a dozen different organizations, often as a temporary employee on a short-term contract. As a result, allegiances do not lie with any of those organizations but rather with the individual. The reason for this is simple: at any point in time an organization may, and often does, terminate employment. So why should employees work for the best interests of an organization? This is a classic problem in the principal-agent relationship. What is good for the principal (the organization) may not always be what is good for the agent (the employee). An agent may therefore sometimes engage in activities that are not in the best interests of the organization. In the case of rogue employees, the propensity of such agents to pursue their own agendas and goals at the cost of the organization is high.

Employees must find their goals to be in congruence with the goals of the organization. They must understand the criticality of their work, the fact that the organization treasures them, and that they are more than a number or a record in a database. The employees must feel it is important and good to protect intellectual assets and use knowledge for the betterment of the organization. Such congruence in employee and organizational goals comes with recognizing the value each employee adds to the organization.

Consider the case of small businesses that have a familial environment. Here, employees help each other, as it is in their best interests to make sure that the overall organization does well, which in turn means that each of them will be better off. Employees who work for such organizations have great allegiance to the organization. They will go out of their way to make sure that the customers of the organization never see any disruption to services. For example, they might cover shifts for each other or work extra hours. The point is that they have an allegiance to the organization and understand that the competitive ability of the organization is directly tied to their ability to give the organization their best work and outperform their competitors.

For a larger organization, this point may not be as apparent or clear. There are now teams, departments and units in place, which may be the primary points of allegiance for employees. For example, at universities, most faculty will identify themselves first as members of their college or department, and then as members of the larger university setting. This is quite natural, as the local context (the department or college) is where faculty members have most of their dealings. This way of thinking, however, is problematic as it may lead to such problems as lack of appropriate coordination and integration of activities across the various units. Units might be at odds with others for resources and attention, which will result in problems for resource allocations and incentives.

To build allegiance to the organization, it is essential that employees know that their work directly contributes to the viability of the organization.[1] The links between each employee's job and the organization's bottom line need to be made visible and clear. In addition, the relationships between all employees' jobs and those of their peers must also be made clear. In most organizations the first link – tying employees' work to the bottom line – is made explicit only for personnel in senior management positions. For senior management, the linkage is achieved through compensation that is directly tied to the organization's bottom line (such as stock options), but for the rest of the organization this connection, if made, is only weakly established.

The connection is most commonly made by providing incentives. For example, a portion of the employees' compensation may be tied to how well the organization is doing. This is fine, but not enough; employees need to be given more clear indicators. For example, at 3M employees are given the opportunity to transform their ideas into businesses. An employee who develops an innovative idea or product can run a business within 3M to commercialize and leverage the idea. 3M provides the employee with the environment for this to happen, and also shares a portion of the profits with the employee. Thus, entrepreneurial employees do not need to leave 3M but can use their energies creatively within the organization. In addition, this protocol builds allegiance to the organization, as each employee is given a greater stake in the well-being of the organization.

Incentive schemes

Another way of building allegiance to the organization is to have clear protocols about what it takes to gain promotion or advance in the organization. Organizations also need to create incentive schemes that give employees the right motivators to promote behaviour that takes account of security needs. For instance, violating security procedures to get a job done more quickly should not be tolerated. One employee might find it justifiable to violate security protocols in order to meet individual and local goals, but this may cost the organization dearly at the global level.

Organizations fail to appropriately align incentives to ensure that ideal behaviour by employees is rewarded. Most organizations give out rewards to their top performers. Very few give out incentives to employees who develop and protect intellectual assets. For example, most project managers are rewarded based on project completion dates, the amount of money saved, the amount of business secured and so on. Similarly, most executives are rewarded with stock options. These incentives do not always promote the most ideal behaviour. Thus, during the course of a project employees may have to cut corners, go around organizational protocols and even subvert organizational practices in order to meet their objectives.

In order to quickly wrap up tasks it is common for members of a programming team to share passwords or avoid writing detailed documentation. In the short term these practices might be beneficial to the organization, but in the long term they could cost it dearly. Similarly, executive compensation packages may encourage executives to engage in questionable behaviours in order to show relentless performance. Upon hiring, it should be made clear to employees that their promotion and career development paths are directly tied to how well they perform according to the mission and values of the organization. They should not just be rewarded on the financial contributions they provide to the organization. Instead, they should be evaluated on how well they exemplify the values of the organization. For example, have they helped other team members? Have they gone beyond what is required to make sure that the organization is successful on a particular effort? Rewarding these types of behaviour promotes greater allegiance to the organization.

Good incentive schemes will reward those employees who are working in the best interests of the organization, and more importantly displaying the kind of behaviour that the organization respects. Simply 'making the numbers' should not be viewed in isolation; rather, it is making the numbers while not cutting corners that is of importance. Developing the right work ethic is quite critical.

A handful of executives that I have talked to understand the real nature of incentives. They do not give out incentives as easily as their peers, but the incentives they do give out have the necessary impact. For example, these executives do not give out bonuses or prizes for employees who engage in knowledge sharing or work to be innovative. The reason for this is twofold. First, they pay their employees a premium over their peers; hence, they do not need to engage in a constant salary negotiation game. Second, and probably more importantly, sharing knowledge with your peers is expected and should not be considered an exemplary activity that needs to be rewarded. On the contrary, employees who do not share knowledge or engage in the production of innovation might lose their jobs very quickly. These executives understand the true nature of incentives in that they focus on recognizing employees who are exemplars of the tenets of the organization. In these organizations, employees are promoted for their contributions to organizational missions and values. Employees are given promotion, which by default mean greater pay, but more importantly signify to the rest of the organization what kinds of behaviour are valued.

Finally incentive schemes should also address the issue of intellectual asset obsolescence. Incentive schemes should allow for employees to update their skills and knowledge. Employees who are known to use their skills and capabilities for the betterment of the organization should be rewarded by getting opportunities to develop new know-how and skills. In addition, as conditions in the environment change – for example, with the development of technological solutions – the organization should take proactive steps to think about the implications of these changes for their employees. They should work proactively to preserve employee jobs by having them learn new skills and enabling them to take on new functions. These kinds of actions do more to build allegiance than any number of dollars or speeches can. Employees will come to respect the organization, and will do their best to contribute to it.

One organization that I know of stated its commitment to its employees unambiguously: 'If you do your best to increase productivity and lower the cost of products, we will do our best to ensure that you do not lose your job. Even if the job moves to another location, we guarantee each of you the opportunity to take part in a new effort and will train you for it. You are our most important asset and we want you to do your best.'

Educating employees

The most important preventive mechanism an organization can implement is to educate employees about the issues that surround the protection of intellectual assets. An educated employee cannot claim ignorance of the issues, and hence the possibility of negligence or accidental loss of intellectual asset can be minimized. There are a number of different topics about which employees should be educated.

First and foremost, employees need to be educated about the risks faced by the organization and the risks to the organization's intellectual assets. As part of this training effort, it should be made clear to employees what constitutes the intellectual assets of the organization and why every employee must use these assets with the utmost care, and prevent unauthorized access and sabotage to them. Employees should leave this training with an understanding of how their work assignments affect the intellectual assets of the organization, and the steps they can and need to take in order to handle such assets with care.

Second, employees need to be trained on how to recognize risky and dangerous situations. For example, employees who handle major client accounts, especially in the sales and business development areas of the organization, need to be trained on how to recognize danger signs. When is a deal *too* good? When should they say no? Learning about cultural issues is also important. Knowledge of what is considered friendly behaviour and what is not is vital. In addition, organizations need to have reporting mechanisms whereby employees can share information about situations they thought were risky and dangerous in order to prevent colleagues from repeating these mistakes. In the next chapter, we discuss issues associated with employee travel. The need to train employees to recognize risky and dangerous situations in foreign lands is especially relevant.

Third, it is especially important to train employees on how to communicate about sensitive matters. Two kinds of training about this issue are important. First, organizations need to train employees about the topics that can and cannot be talked about outside the organization, or even within the organization when guests or visitors are present. Second, employees should be trained about how to handle external inquiries that might arise in relation to their knowledge. For example, researchers in an R&D department may wish to publish their knowledge. The firm should have a protocol in place for clearing material for publication so that the researchers are satisfied and organizational knowledge is protected.

Training employees about appropriate conduct during an interview for another job is also important. Most organizations do not address this issue head on, and in my assessment, this is one of the most common ways for knowledge leaks to occur. Organizations need to have clear protocols about what knowledge employees can share about their jobs, work assignments and so on. These are issues that are better addressed in an open manner, rather than leaving employees to guess about what is allowable.

One strategy that I have seen succeed is clarifying the type of assets that are sensitive and confidential. Start out with *sources*. Sources might be clients, customers, repositories from which an organization retrieves information, employees of the organization, advisers to the organization and so on. An organization should clarify what information about sources used in an employee's day-to-day work cannot be disclosed. Next, the *organizational processes* that are in place at the organization, such as information systems and manufacturing processes, should be addressed. While employees may wish to discuss the systems they worked on, they should not be allowed to disclose the complete workings of these systems, especially if these systems are proprietary and not commercially available. The next items that need to be addressed are *projects* and *strategic efforts*.

Most employees do not have clear guidelines on how to address these matters to the external world. Projects under way at the organization may be sensitive and need to be protected. In addition, information about strategic efforts – for example, discussions with a competitor about a possible merger and/or acquisition – needs to be held in confidence. For projects, it is advisable to be clear from the onset – that is, when the project is commissioned – about the people who will and will not know about the effort, and the reasons for this. Similarly, for strategic efforts, the simple rule is to restrict such information to those who need to know, and to limit the number of people who need to know. The larger the number of people who know, the greater the chance of a leak.

Fourth, risky situations can also occur when intellectual assets are used improperly. To avoid the misuse of intellectual assets through sloppiness, organizations need to take time and effort to preserve the context around knowledge artefacts. Three guidelines are important here. First, make a clear distinction between what represents an intellectual asset and what does not. As noted previously, an organization needs to clearly identify the intellectual assets in its midst and then carefully manage and control them. Second, train employees about how to use these assets. In one consulting firm, all employees who needed to access or interact with the core knowledge assets of the organization had to attend a training session first. During this session employees learnt how to use the intellectual asset in context. In addition, changes or modifications to the asset were carefully controlled so as not to compromise its integrity. Third, provide context along with the intellectual asset. Think of warning labels on drugs: these warning labels help both the patient and the physician know the context in which the medicine should and should not be used. Similarly, no intellectual asset can be used without any regard to context. It is important to deploy knowledge artefacts within the right context. Having warning labels on intellectual assets is one way to ensure that the consumers or users of the assets know when and where to use them.

Fifth and finally, organizations too often discover intellectual asset losses or misuse too late because the employees who were involved or their peers do not have safe ways to report mistakes. It is important for organizations to create these mechanisms. Two types of mechanisms are needed. The first allows employees to clearly report errors and mistakes that might have happened as they conducted their work. Companies have a greater chance of preventing or minimizing damage from errors if they are reported right away. The second mechanism allows peers who witness knowledge misuse by other employees to report the misuse without any fear of repercussions. This is very important, as ideally the organization wants to be the first to know of a mistake, rather than hearing about it from the press. One excellent method is having a contact, external to the organization, to whom employees can talk without fear. This external person then interfaces with the senior executives of the organization and works to resolve the matter.

A reporting mechanism works only if it is used to improve the security programmes in place. Hence, reports of errors and mistakes should be investigated to *learn* what went wrong and how to improve the programmes. They should not be used to assign blame and reprimand employees. Employees will not share such information if they feel they will be penalized for it. Consider the case of commercial aviation. Mistakes or near misses in commercial aviation occur on a regular basis. Not all of these result in calamities. In the past, airline pilots were penalized for these mistakes when they were discovered. As a result, such errors were seldom reported. The consequence was a lot more errors and mistakes. Only recently did this process change, such that pilots today are encouraged to report mistakes so that a learning process can occur and the findings from investigations can be used to build better travel protocols. Pilots are not blamed for such errors and are not subject to penalties or fines. The philosophy behind this process is to help improve the overall safety of air travel.

Closing thoughts

As discussed in this chapter, employees face many kinds of risk. The smart organization will build security programmes that monitor these risks and try to address them in their formative stages. For instance, we can use the age of the employee to assess the risk that the employee will retire shortly. We could also use travel logs to see how frequently an employee travels, and more importantly, to which locations. In other cases we can see the nature of sensitive material to which the employee has access, and based on this we can assess the risk of compromise. This kind of thinking is pervasive in the national security arena, where security details and other protective measures are put in place to ensure that individuals who interact with highly sensitive material are protected and stay free of external pressures. We can also estimate the reputation risk posed by an employee. If a high-profile employee engages in sloppy use of corporate knowledge, what kind of exposure will the organization get?

To sum up, securing intellectual assets in and around employees is important for organizational success. Failure to secure its intellectual assets can cost an organization dearly. Moreover, employees are the foundational intellectual assets of the organization: without them, no other assets can be leveraged or mobilized. Hence, it is even more important to secure these assets and preserve their integrity and value.

3

Technology hiccups

How many technology gadgets (phones, pagers, mobile devices, personal digital assistants and so on) do you have? Are your house, car and office wired or wireless-enabled? What about your data: how many data stores (hard disks, USB drives and so on) does it reside on? We live in a world where technology gadgets are pervasive. Technology helps us get our work done in a highly effective and efficient manner. For example, through the use of information and communication technologies (ICTs) such as the internet, web browsers and mobile phones we are able to converse and communicate with individuals who reside in multiple places across the globe. This helps us coordinate and manage projects that may involve people in multiple continents and across multiple time zones. In the absence of such technologies we would not be able to work in such a highly effective manner, thus limiting our ability to leverage resources that may be present in distant lands.

Technology has also helped us automate some types of routine work, thus saving us time and effort, not to mention increasing the effectiveness of such tasks. For example, before the use of barcode scanners, grocery store checkout procedures were quite cumbersome and even error-prone. Technology has also helped us cross global boundaries. One of the most brilliant forms of technology is the aeroplane. Today, commercial airline travel contributes significantly to the growth of companies, economies and countries. The reliability, flexibility and efficacy of commercial airline travel have improved in recent times. This has made air travel more affordable to the masses. Consider the following. Using the internet, many of us can plan an entire trip from origin to destination. The ease with which we can now make travel plans has lowered many of the costs of flying. In the past, we would have to go to a travel agent and go through a somewhat cumbersome and time-intensive process to get tickets.

To sum up, technology has revolutionized all aspects of business, and even of society. Several factors have contributed to this. First is the increasing sophistication of these gadgets. Consider the following simple case. A few years back it was common for your calls to be cut off when using your mobile phone; today, such occurrences are not as common. Moreover, today you can not only use your phone to share voice messages, but you can also take photos, shoot videos, exchange short text messages, and even send e-mails. Wow! What's next? Phones that will automatically call the person you think of? We are actually quite close to this being a reality: there are phones that can dial a number if you speak a person's name.

Second, the cost of technology gadgets continues to decrease at an astounding rate. The capabilities one can get from gadgets today is amazing in comparison with the cost. What we paid for a basic telephone a few years back is higher than the cost of some of the fanciest and sophisticated mobile phones today (considering that many firms give out these phones for free or for nominal fees when customers subscribe to a usage plan).

Third, the size of gadgets continues to decrease. What once filled a room or a desk can now fit in the palm of your hand; think about the data you can fit onto a tiny USB drive today, compared with a hard disk drive of a few years back. The miniaturization of technology devices has made them more pervasive, and their use more casual. Today, most of us do not give the same attention to things like disks drives (especially the smaller and more portable ones) as we did a few years ago. For instance, several years ago, in one of the first organizations that I interned with, to get a floppy disk you had to walk to a storeroom cabinet and then retrieve one. Over the last four months, I have received over a dozen free USB disk drives.

Fourth, technology gadgets have moved from being a luxury to a necessity. Can you imagine running your business without having your people connected via mobile phones, pagers or laptops? Probably not! However, a few years back, only if you were in the senior echelon of a firm did you get such devices, and many times only as a perk! Now, there is a craze to continuously keep up to date with the latest technological trends. Technology-enabled processes have made manual processes outdated, and have in many cases replaced them. Thus on one hand we have made processes more efficient and effective; on the other hand, we have also become heavily dependent on technology. In many cases there are no ways to conduct processes other than by technological mechanisms.

To summarize, technology gadgets are omnipresent in modern society, especially in work environments and commercial settings. These gadgets can be used for productive purposes and can enable the optimal achievement of business objectives. However, these technologies can also be the source of tremendous liability, especially if they are not cared for properly and deployed in a secure manner.

As noted in Chapter 1, there have been several cases of data disks containing intellectual assets going missing or getting lost. Almost all large organizations have had data breaches in some form or another. Some have even had cases in which employees took sensitive information home, only to lose the information or – as in the case of an employee of the US Veterans Administration – have their houses burgled and the assets compromised. Consider the case of the Los Alamos National Laboratory, a US Department of Energy Laboratory, which is known to conduct classified research on sensitive matters such as nuclear technology. In June 2000, it was made public that two computer disks containing sensitive material (allegedly nuclear weapons secrets, including information on how to disarm Russian and American nuclear devices) had gone missing. These disks had apparently gone missing from the most secure vaults of the labs. Workers realized they were unaccounted for when wildfires raging in the area prompted them to enter the secure storage area to move some of the disks to an even safer location. The hard drives were missing for 11 days and were found behind a photocopier. Do you think Los Alamos learnt to be careful and to avoid such pitfalls in the future? That may very well be wishful thinking.

There were at least three more incidents like this at Los Alamos between 2000 and 2004. During a December 2003 routine inventory of classified electronic storage media, nine classified computer floppy disks and a large-capacity storage disk were found to be missing. In July 2004, two more disks were found to be missing. Once again, these two removable computer disks contained classified nuclear weapons data. In 2005, upon completion of the investigation into the missing disks, it was determined that the two disks had never been created. Barcodes to identify the disks had been created, but the disks had never been produced, hence leading to an incorrect record of disks. Now do you think that Los Alamos has learnt its lesson? I don't like to be the bearer of bad news, but the answer is no. The lab has had several other security incidents since these discoveries.

In this chapter, I explore how technologies can become the Achilles heel of an organization by compromising the security of intellectual assets (see the boxes). One point should be noted: there are hundreds of books that cover the technical aspects of information security. These books cover details such as encryption of information, protection of computer networks and password protocols, among others. I do not attempt to cover these issues in this chapter, and especially not from a technical stance. I think the books that are already available in the market are very good: they provide readers with a lot of the ins and outs of information security and assurance. Hence, I urge readers who do not have backgrounds in these areas to consult these external sources.

This chapter will focus on the human aspects of technical security breaches. I discuss points that need to be considered in conjunction with the technical issues. For instance, while there are many technical solutions to encrypt e-mails that work well, I discuss how to build protocols for determining what material should and should not be communicated via e-mail. In this way, should material be communicated via e-mail, at least we know that the decision to send this information over a technical medium was deliberate, and we can apply the appropriate technical encryption method. The human aspects of technical security breaches are foundational issues that need to be considered before technical solutions can be applied.

Possible causes of security breaches

- Travellers compromised.
- Technology-enabled mobilization.
- Technology-enabled storage and duplication.
- Technology-enabled application.

> **Preventive measures**
>
> - Securing travellers.
> - Securing electronic channels.
> - Securing duplication and storage.
> - Securing application.

Security breaches

Understanding the role played by technology in the management of intellectual assets is a critical first step if we are to prevent security breaches. As described earlier, intellectual assets are represented either in the minds of individuals or in explicit artefacts such as documents and processes. For instance, intellectual assets may include knowledge housed in the minds of researchers in our labs; similarly, insights into future marketing opportunities housed in the minds of our marketing and sales professionals also represent intellectual assets. Some intellectual assets may be physical in nature – for example, the printed-out copy of a business plan or a PowerPoint presentation detailing engineering designs. Technology plays distinct roles in the management of intellectual assets that come from a variety of sources.

For intellectual assets that are housed in the minds of employees, technology helps us bring the minds together. For instance, video or web-based conferencing technologies allow us to host meetings where we bring together people to discuss and debate important issues. Aeroplanes allow us to fly people around the globe to provide opportunities for face-to-face meetings. The point of bringing minds together is to create new intellectual assets and to engage in work that might call for the use of intellectual assets. In this chapter, I discuss the security implications of employee travel. In Chapter 5, I discuss protecting the physical space of the organization, one aspect of which is protecting offsite meeting facilities. I have chosen to cover offsite meeting facilities later: while they are enabled by technology (for example, people flying to a common location to meet up with each other), they occur in a physical space. An ideal security programme will account for the risks of using technology to bring intellectual minds together.

For intellectual assets that are in explicit form, technology helps us make them accessible to a wider audience. For instance, we can make copies of documents (duplication), use e-mail to get documents from source to destination, or telephones to share ideas and thoughts (mobilization), and store documents on common directories to increase their accessibility (storage). In addition, technologies allow us to automate the application of intellectual assets. For example, financial institutions now allow individuals to apply for loans and mortgages on the internet. Using intelligent decision support systems and rule-based inference techniques, a financial institution can automatically pre-approve a user for a loan and determine the loan amount and monthly payments. Technology has provided financial organizations with a new avenue for deploying their intellectual assets. They can now use online systems to handle routine applications while the time and energy of their analysts can be spent addressing more complex situations in which automated rules do not apply or are difficult to apply. People designing security programmes should take the above issues into account when considering the ramifications of technology-enabled mobilization, duplication, storage and application of intellectual assets.

Travellers compromised

Depending on the organization, employees may be asked to travel to distant lands that are not completely secure. In most cases, these employees are senior executives travelling to secure business deals. The kind of protection given to these employees is of interest and can play an important role in the protection of knowledge. Does your organization have a policy in place to protect travelling employees? Do your employees know how to recognize and avoid dangerous situations when travelling? How can you protect the knowledge assets these employees physically carry?

Most employees shuttle among multiple locations during the course of a given day. At the most common level, employees leave their residences, arrive at their work sites, and then depart for their homes. Today, the distinction between the workplace and the home is blurred. Employees routinely take work home; they also engage in what one would consider home activities (such as making dinner reservations, talking to the kids and e-mailing friends) at work. It is important to note the movement of work between office premises and other locations.

Consider the data losses at the Veterans Administration (VA) (Greenemeier, 2006; Messmer, 2006). A VA analyst decided to meet deadlines by taking home sensitive data to work on. As far as we know (I suspect we do not know everything yet) the data contained the social security numbers, dates of births and even the health records of 26.5 million people. The data included information on veterans and currently active military personnel. Information for as many as 1.1 million active-duty service members, 430,000 National Guardsmen, and 645,000 members of the Reserves may have been included in the data theft. The data was stolen when a burglary occurred at the analyst's house on 3 May 2006. The burglars took a government-owned laptop and disks from the analyst's home in suburban Maryland.

Security practices at the VA leave a lot to be desired, but the sad news is that the VA is neither an exception nor an outlier. A large percentage of organizations lack basic protocols, mechanisms and practices to ensure that their intellectual assets (such as sensitive data, information and knowledge) are protected and maintained in a secure manner. In the VA case, the analyst was given permission to access the data because of his involvement in a project; no authorization was given to take the data out of the office. Moreover, the investigation uncovered that the analyst had been taking data home since 2003. In addition, the data was not encrypted, and senior executives were not made aware of the breach until two weeks after the incident. Here is the icing on the cake: the analyst, whose annual salary was between US$90,000 and $120,000, got to take an early retirement for his actions. Nice!

Some of the most common spaces for intellectual asset breaches to occur are those spaces around airline travel. Using aeroplanes to move personnel from one location to another is quite common today, and many of us could not imagine what organizations would look like in the absence of commercial aviation. Given this reality, I am continually surprised how sloppily employees behave on aircraft. Many times I have seen employees read sensitive corporate material while people are situated only a few centimetres away from them. It has been hilarious to see people in some cases read material that has a big stamp on it saying 'Confidential' or 'Sensitive'.

In a case that my firm handled several years ago, we were asked to provide consultative services to the senior executives of an emerging biotechnology organization. During the course of our work we determined that the organization's senior executives travelled to parts of the world that were not the most secure. These executives often carried highly sensitive corporate material with them while travelling. We advised the executives of a simple strategy: do not carry sensitive material during travel. We devised a process whereby travelling executives would meet with a local computing vendor in the country of interest, purchase a laptop, and download the requested material from their home office using a secure telecommunications channel. Then they would conduct their business. Before leaving the country, they would upload any material that they needed over a secure connection. Soon afterwards, they would destroy the hard drive of the laptop and return the rest of the laptop to the computer vendor.

This strategy was not easy or cheap. The organization had to forge alliances with local computing vendors in three frequently visited but insecure locations. The organization was required to pay fees for use of the laptops and reimbursements for the hard drives. Moreover, the executives had to spend time and effort to upload and download material. However, in our opinion this strategy was worth the costs: it minimized the loss of intellectual assets during transit, and moreover reduced the threats faced by the executives. After all, in the countries the executives visited, it was not uncommon for business executives to be taken hostage and held to ransom.

In addition to giving this piece of advice, we briefed the organization on other useful practices. For example, we provided guidance to the executives on how they should behave at airports and on flights, how to catch a cab, how not to draw attention to themselves, how to change their patterns of daily travel so as not be predictable, and even how to identify whether they were being followed or watched. Given all of the advice we provided, we were fairly sure that the executives had what it took to protect themselves and their knowledge assets. However, this was not to be the case.

One December, while relaxing during my annual vacation, I received a call from the organization informing me that an executive had been taken hostage. Needless to say, my Christmas and New Year celebrations came to a screeching halt. Upon investigation, we discovered that the executive had ignored most of our advice. The executive had decided that he needed to wear a three-piece suit while travelling, not to mention flaunt his Rolex. He flew first class, which in and of itself is not too bad; but the minute the flight landed he started talking on his phone, boasting about the business deal he was going to make. He also spoke about his plans for the week.

Then, when he decided to take a taxi from the airport, he ignored our advice to avoid the lowest-cost provider. It was during his taxi ride from the airport that he made his most crucial mistake. He engaged the taxi driver in a conversation about the most popular tourist spots and places to go for dinner and drinks. The taxi driver offered to be a personal chauffer to the executive in return for a small fee. The miserly executive took up the offer, which sealed his fate.

What was most interesting to me was that the organization's primary concern was not the fate of its executive, but the sensitive material the executive had in his possession. As my contact at the organization said, 'Our first priority is to ensure that the material in the possession of the executive is not compromised.' When I probed deeper about what this material constituted, I was not surprised to learn it was the executive's laptop. During our initial briefing of the organization, we had emphasized that in the areas where the executives travelled, there was an abundance of software engineering talent that could be recruited for unscrupulous purposes. Many of these persons were engaged in hacking, stealing identities and so on. Our suggestion to not bring a laptop while travelling was meant to help the executives avoid this risk. Even more troubling – yet understandable – was the fact that the organization did not want to engage local law enforcement authorities. The chances of an information leak leading to a public relations disaster were high, and this would have exponentially compounded the potential damage.

Luckily (and I do mean luckily), we were able to resolve this crisis, but it cost the organization an arm and a leg. Moreover, this was an endeavour where, regardless of how much we had prepared, it was luck at the end of the day that helped us resolve the matter. The biggest mistake you can make is to leave the care of your intellectual assets up to luck.

Technology-enabled mobilization

Employees use mobile phones, personal digital assistants and other devices to communicate about work matters while they are outside the organization. This, in and of itself, is not a bad thing. However, lack of care on the part of employees in ensuring that their surroundings are secure does pose a risk to the organization. I cannot tell you how often, when I travel or visit a café, I encounter executives who are careless in the way they communicate. I remember one executive who was waiting in line for his latte at a nice café in Chicago. He was talking on his mobile phone and was so careless that he started to scream every time the noise of the espresso machine got too loud. Within five minutes, I was able to deduce not only what company he worked for, but also his division, the business deal he was in the midst of closing, and how he was going to con his client into closing the deal. If I had been sent on behalf of his client, I would have been able to provide the client with favourable information that would have given it the leverage to renegotiate the deal.

Similarly, the use of e-mail to send material from source to destination is common. This is where things get very interesting. In one organization where I worked with the IT department to check the content of e-mails for sensitive material, we found that over 40 per cent of the e-mails contained material that was considered sensitive and proprietary. Moreover, when we shared these e-mails with the senior executives, 99 per cent of them contained information that was considered too sensitive to be shared in e-mails. Think about this: have you ever forwarded someone a message by accident? What happens if you add the wrong person to an electronic distribution list? These are common ways sensitive materials leak from an organization. I know of an employee who added the e-mail address of an external discussion list to which he used to subscribe to the mailing list of a sensitive corporate memo. The memo was consequently made available to over 10,000 people across the globe!

Technology-enabled storage and duplication

Advancements in technologies for storing and sharing intellectual assets constitute both a curse and blessing. Think about the concept of the printer and the ingredient of paper. The printer has made it possible for us to make copies of and share material, facilitate discussions, and also improve the documentation of intellectual assets. However, it has also increased the challenge of ensuring that we do not allow papers containing sensitive material to get into the wrong hands. Similarly, hard disk drives of all shapes and sizes, from the mini-disks that go into mobile phones and digital cameras to their larger counterparts that are part of desktops and servers, have greatly facilitated the storage and exchange of intellectual assets. However, they have also increased the need to be vigilant about how these artefacts are handled, especially during the decommissioning stage. Most organizations lack adequate procedures to ensure that intellectual assets are destroyed appropriately.

Think about how paper documents are handled today. In 1975, some thought that advancements in computing would result in the paperless office (*Business Week*, 1975). Needless to say, like most claims about computing that came out of that era, this prediction has not come true. Offices are filled with paper. I have entered some offices where occupants are buried under paper, or where there is so much of it that it would take a few weeks of effort just to sort through all the paper. Organizations cannot afford to have a free and open policy or a careless attitude to the handling of paper. Sensitive material printed on paper might make its way into the wrong hands. In one organization, a well-intentioned employee interested in reducing paper waste took to reusing paper, so that both sides of paper were consumed (the printer on the employee's desk printed only on one side). There was only one problem: during a meeting, the employee provided hand-outs printed on paper that was previously used to generate the monthly payroll, with names of employees and their bimonthly pay noted on the other side! Do you know when it is appropriate to burn a piece of paper and when to use a shredder?

Now think about how obsolete computer equipment is handled within your organization. Is it just thrown away in a skip? Or is your organization in the habit of giving obsolete computer equipment to charity? What measures do you have in place to ensure that sensitive material is removed from these devices before they are decommissioned? This is a non-trivial issue, and if an organization does not have a policy addressing the destruction or decommissioning of intellectual assets, chances are high that it will open itself to all kinds of trouble. Let me share one case. A major public university in the Midwest lacked adequate measures for destroying intellectual assets stored on computer equipment. One day, the newspaper ran a feature article containing photographs of university computer equipment (monitors, keyboards, processors and so on) that had been thrown into a skip. Since the university was a state school, it was funded by taxes paid by state residents. As a result, the newspaper article expressed anger that the university was wasting and mishandling state resources. In particular, the article questioned why the equipment was not given to high schools or local charities, where it could still be put to good use. Later in the week, the press ran another story: sensitive material had been found on the hard disks of the discarded computers. Even though the computers had been wiped clean (that is, material had been deleted from the disk drives), this data was recovered with minimal sophistication. Needless to say, the university got hammered on both counts.

A classic case that demonstrates the issues involved with the security of systems and channels is John M Deutch's mishandling of classified information. John M Deutch was director of Central Intelligence (DCI) in the United States from May 1995 to December 1996. Upon his departure from the position, it was discovered that his personal computer at home contained classified material. Even though the computer was government-owned, it was designated for use with unclassified material only. CIA personnel services retrieved sensitive material such as Top Secret communications intelligence, information on covert actions, and information on the National Reconnaissance Program Budget from Deutch's unclassified computer, which was connected to the internet via a modem and hence a prime target for hacker attacks. Moreover, Deutch had used his government e-mail addresses and aliases for unclassified communications over the internet and for posting on websites. Out of all personnel one might expect to engage in such sloppy work, the last person would be the DCI.

Technology-enabled application

Technologies can help in the application of intellectual assets. However, breaches do occur during such cases. Consider some of the common ways for breaches to occur. Today, one of the most commonly used pieces of software is PowerPoint. PowerPoint has become part and parcel of every meeting, briefing, presentation and talk that most of us participate in. Have you ever had material in your slides that you should not have? What about having material that is considered sensitive? In one organization, as an employee was creating a presentation for a talk, he accidentally copied and pasted certain formulae and commentary onto the slides. The employee then proceeded to make these slides available to the audience, and as part of the talk, it was agreed that the slides would be placed on a website. Three days after the slides were posted, the employee received a call from a colleague informing him about the sloppy error. In this case, sensitive material was leaked to the general public.

In another case, an employee lost his laptop, which contained sensitive proprietary programs and data. The employee's company was in the information technology industry, and the employee lost the laptop at a trade convention. It is suspected that one of the organization's competing firms got hold of the lost equipment and has used it for advantage. Once again in this case, while technology was used to apply intellectual assets to productive use, it also caused loss of value to intellectual assets.

Technology application of intellectual assets is governed by the development of software programs and applications. These applications are the electronic realization of physical processes. For instance, the applications that we use to manage our financial transactions online are the electronic counterparts to physically going to the branch and conducting these activities. It is important to be sure how we secure the development process around these intellectual assets. There are two aspects to this, the people and the technical aspects.

The people aspects of this include ensuring that the right personnel work on these projects. The right personnel are those that have the necessary capabilities, and more importantly, the required integrity. In the previous chapter, we discussed the need for background checks, and this applies here. Failure to assure that individuals working on projects have integrity will lead to trouble. In one organization, a group of software engineers compromised critical applications by adding malicious code. In one case, the malicious code involved the manipulation of interest rate payments on a financial application. On the technical side, we need to ensure that the applications we build are sound, robust and secure. In the computer gaming industry, a common occurrence takes place. When a game is released, there is a high probability that a gaming enthusiast will develop ways to add code to the game, generate cheat codes, manipulate the application and so on. In some cases, these alterations can change the nature of the game, and impact the user experience. Organizations cannot afford to release technically compromised applications. Just imagine, if you could add new add-ins to a financial application.

Preventive measures

The previous pages have alerted you to the means by which the sloppy usage and management of technologies can sabotage your intellectual assets. I shall now discuss several preventive mechanisms you can consider. To reiterate, these preventive mechanisms, especially those dealing with security of explicit intellectual assets, should be supplemented with the vast set of practices found in the field of information system security and assurance.

Securing travellers

In building a security programme for travellers, we must start with the basics: training travellers about how to conduct themselves during travel. Most organizations do a hopeless job of this, and this is the root cause for a lot of headaches. Here are some best practices to consider.

First, pay close attention to the intellectual assets being transported by the traveller. As far as possible, you should minimize the carrying of intellectual assets, in either print or electronic form. Today, with the advancements in technology and logistical support, assets can be moved from one location to another independently of the traveller. For instance, if an executive were giving a talk in Cairo or Cape Town, you could send the presentation material via a registered courier (such as FedEx or DHL) to meet the executive at a hotel location. Similarly, you could provide the executive with the means for securely connecting to the organization's information network and accessing the material. The executive could then send the material back to the home office or destroy it (see my later point about this) before travelling home. Reducing the carrying of intellectual assets will lower the risks to the executive's personal well-being, as well as the risks that the material will get lost or sabotaged.

Second, organizations need to provide training so that employees can recognize risky and dangerous situations (see Pelton, 2003). It is not necessary for all employees to go through such efforts, though it is highly advisable and desirable. But at the bare minimum employees who travel need to have some training in how to recognize dangerous situations and how to read environmental cues. For instance, employees who are travelling to foreign lands need, at the minimum, to have some basic language skills, to understand the cultural nuances of the place, to learn how not to draw attention to themselves, to know how to identify whether they are being followed, to learn how to change their patterns during the day so as not to be predictable, and so on.

Third, organizations should advise employees on how to conduct themselves while in transit. For example, designating what an executive can and cannot read on a flight is important; similarly, while travelling on a train, it is important to be aware of your surroundings. Let me be clear: I am not talking about having all of your employees become paranoid that they are going to be attacked. But employees need to be alert to their surroundings, rather than oblivious, which could put them in dangerous situations. Remember that employees travelling for personal reasons should not be of concern to you; however, it is when employees are travelling for business purposes and/or are travelling with intellectual assets that you need to be concerned.

Fourth and finally, organizations also need clear policies in place regarding travel. This is vital because such policies can, for example, ensure that senior executives do not all board the same flight, lest the aircraft crashes or meets with another unexpected tragedy. Solutions can include using a centralized travel scheduling agent that handles all the bookings, policies to make sure that only the required number of senior executives is travelling at any given time, controls and checks to account for diversity in where people are travelling, and travel arrangements that adhere to a succession plan. As part of its travel policy, an organization should ensure that it has alliances with reputable hotel chains, that the locations of the hotels are not in compromising environments, that there are local contacts that employees can seek out should they need information, and that local travel to and from locations is provided through reputable organizations.

It is also important for organizations to learn from the travel experiences of their staff. When employees come back from travel, especially if they are returning from an area they have just visited for the first time, there should be a debriefing process whereby the learning and experiences acquired during the trip can be captured. In one organization, any employee can use the company's intranet to see the places that other employees in the organization have travelled to, the dates and duration of their stays, the accommodation they have stayed at, and so on. Once an employee books tickets for travel, the travel office lets the employee know who he or she should talk to before leaving to gain knowledge about a location.

Securing electronic channels

In order to secure electronic communication channels, we must ensure that the right messages are being passed via these channels. An organization needs clear-cut guidelines on what material can be passed through a given communication channel. Some organizations have protocols which employees must follow when writing the subject of an e-mail. The subject line might contain the level of sensitivity of the e-mail (such as classified or secret). Some other organizations take the additional measure of creating two networks. An internal network is used to send material within the organization, while the external network gets the message to those outside the organization. Messages sent on the external network are monitored more closely, and typically need to be cleared before they are transmitted. The use of automated technologies to parse the language of e-mails and identify sensitive material is also becoming more common. Once e-mails with potentially sensitive content are identified, they are sent to the security department for clearance. Should the security department need more information, it can get in touch with the sender. Having clear-cut protocols on the kinds of messages that can be communicated, how messages should be structured, and the process for evaluating messages over electronic channels is very important.

It is important to have means for encrypting messages of a sensitive nature before they are sent through communication channels. Any book on information security or network security will cover the intricacies of encryption methods, so I shall not cover them here, but I do want to point out two things. Encryption of messages costs resources, which includes the time and effort needed to identify messages that need to be encrypted, the application of the encryption algorithm, and the application of a decryption method by the recipient. Hence, you need to choose wisely which messages get encrypted and which do not, as encryption is not a costless consideration. The other point to remember is that no matter how many advancements we make in encryption methods, there will always be those who will find ways to break them. Hence, the best line of defence is to minimize, if not avoid, the passage of sensitive material through electronic channels. A strategy might be for an organization to limit who can send sensitive or confidential e-mails to external entities. An organization might want to designate a point-of-contact (POC) whom external entities can send documents to and receive them from.

Securing duplication and storage

Practices from government intelligence organizations might provide useful solutions in securing the paper in an organization. First, the easiest thing to do is to limit the opportunities available to people to create paper-based outputs. Sensitive documents should not be printable. An organization can limit output of sensitive documents to on-screen display. In the rare case that sensitive documents need to be printed, special permission should be obtained from the security department.

Second, limit the number of printers. The good news is that this will not only reduce the amount of paper, but will also save you some maintenance costs. Employees most often print simply because they can, and not because they have to. Hence, taking personal printers away from employees is one sure way to get them to think twice before printing. You can also limit the number of pages an employee can print during a given time period.

Third, material printed should be traceable. The easiest way to do this, especially for documents that are printed for internal consumption, is to include an employee identifier and a time stamp on the printed document. Including this information will help us ensure that you know who is printing what, and whose papers are not handled with care.

Technology hiccups ▌ 71

Fourth, ensure that employees know how to dispose of paper. While some paper can be dropped off in a recycling bin, other paper might need to be shredded, and yet other paper might need to be disposed of in a more thorough manner (such as by burning). At the very least, it is earth-friendly to have paper make its way to the recycling bin. Employees should be advised and counselled about why hoarding paper is not a desirable practice.

Paper should be disposed of right after it has been repurposed or consumed. No paper should be kept idle for more than three days. Employees should be advised that they may print documents only if they are going to read or act on them within three days. Papers that have sensitive information, such as customer information or employee payroll, should be shredded immediately upon completion of the tasks for which they were printed. It is important that employees know it is not an option to keep these papers lying around. Depending on the kind of organization, it may also be advisable to have these and other kinds of papers burnt.

In government intelligence organizations, employees are given brown bags in which they can place material to be burnt. For example, documents that detail ongoing plans of a company and sensitive operations (such as R&D programmes) should be burnt so that there is never a possibility of these being recreated. (With a lot of patience and careful ingenuity, shredded documents can be recreated!) Of course, not all paper should be burnt, as this would be too costly and would result in a lot of waste.

Finally, it may be beneficial to conduct random inspections of garbage to see whether there is any sensitive material that is not being handled with care. I once conducted such a task for an organization, and found an entire internal report of a sensitive nature in the recycling bin. The employee who had discarded the report was immediately reprimanded. The consequences of not adhering to these policies should be made clear.

The solution for disposing of computer equipment is also fairly straightforward. First, you need to identify the best way to utilize an old computer or system. For example, sometimes only certain parts of a computer are reusable; other times, the entire system can be reused. Because of the decreasing costs of technology, most organizations are not too concerned about reusing old systems and are more likely to just destroy them. It might be wiser and more socially responsible to ensure that we do not waste equipment. To build goodwill, an organization could help disadvantaged global economies by providing them with old equipment. There might be costs associated with doing this, but these costs are not very high.

Second, you need to be concerned about intellectual asset security. Wiping data is the most effective solution (Berinato, 2005). However, you need to be aware of the costs associated with wiping. The more complete the data wiping, the higher the cost. For example, degaussing guarantees that nobody gets the data, but it also damages the hard drive, which usually is the most valuable recyclable part. The level of data destruction used will depend on the kind of information that was stored and processed on the equipment. If sensitive information was never stored on a disk drive, then it may be worthwhile not to completely destroy the drive, but to use a less intensive data destruction process. However, if sensitive information was accessed on the drive, then the drive must be made unusable.

Third, you need to make a decision about the type of disposal, such as reselling, recycling, scrapping or redeploying the equipment. Reselling is not a common option in most organizations, as the costs are high and the returns marginal. It is more common to recycle the equipment. Recycling equipment has an advantage in that it is easy to do. Moreover, an organization can give the equipment to less fortunate organizations who might gain from receiving it. Scrapping equipment is another option, but it is not a wise one unless the equipment is damaged and cannot be salvaged. A lot of waste may result from disposing of equipment that could have been salvaged. Finally, redeploying might be an option. Redeploying involves using the equipment for other purposes within the organization. For example, if the computer used by a researcher to process large data sets became obsolete, chances are high that this computer could be used quite effectively by an administrative assistant. The administrative assistant will not require a machine that is as high-end as the researcher requires. If an organization chooses to redeploy equipment, it should have a sound process for ensuring that sensitive data is removed from machines before they are moved around the organization.

Securing application

In order to secure the application of intellectual assets via technological devices, the organization needs to take certain critical steps. First, the organization must have a plan in place to ensure that it can track and manage its technology devices. To this end, it is important for an organization to inventory all of its technology assets. For each asset, the purpose, owner, current state (active, obsolete and so on) and other details need to be recorded. Technology assets should be given to users under strict agreements. For example, when a mobile phone is given to an employee, the employee should be informed about the kinds of intellectual assets (in the form of data and information) that can be stored on and communicated via the device. The devices should be used for specific purposes; this will help the organization devise appropriate device security profiles. A device that will be used only to make basic phone calls will require minimal security: if it is lost, it can be replaced by another device. However, a device that will be used to read e-mails, download and work on material, or store a list of contacts needs to be given a higher priority and more attention in terms of security.

Second, the organization must have an approval process that ensures intellectual assets are being applied appropriately. For example, before an employee sends a presentation to an outside entity, the presentation should be checked for the presence of sensitive information. This can be done by the person's immediate boss or some kind of review board. Checking for and removing sensitive material from explicit artefacts is absolutely essential. This is because once the presentation leaves the confines of the organization, it can be made available to just about anyone. Having a clear approval process will limit the number of leaks resulting from the application of knowledge.

Third, as part of the review and approval process, any intellectual asset that is applied via technology should be given boundary conditions. For example, if a presentation has been built for a given client, then permission should be given only to share the presentation with the client and provide the client with physical (paper) copies. Providing only paper copies makes distribution a bit more costly, though not by much, as we now have scanners. The more important point is to control the environments in which assets are applied via technology and the people who are doing the applying. For example, a trainee and an expert giving the same presentation may have two different outcomes. Hence, if the material being presented is highly sensitive, you may want only a specific group of individuals to be able to access it and talk about it.

Fourth, as noted earlier, when we develop intellectual assets in electronic form, we need to secure the people and technical aspects. For the people aspects, I strongly urge you to consider the points we discussed in the previous chapter. In addition, as we shall discuss in the next chapter, there are security issues that need to be considered when we work with business partners via production and development agreements. On the technical side, it is important that the organization has a reliable quality assurance process to inspect its software applications. I shall not explore this issue here in any detail, as there are several books on the topic that can be consulted (such as Galin, 2003).

Closing thoughts

This chapter has discussed a few of the technology-centred issues one needs to consider when protecting intellectual assets. The most common reasons that the above measures are not attended to in organizations are carelessness and lack of attention. Failure to implement adequate policies for securely using technology equipment and artefacts that interact with intellectual assets can come back to haunt an organization.

Here is a case in point. An executive was given a new computer as part of a routine IT maintenance effort. The executive asked the person installing his new computer if he could take his old computer home and use it as another workstation. The IT staff member wanted to please the executive and gave him the green light; he even told the executive to remove the corporate tags from the equipment and to not mention it. In this company, the process of tagging assets, especially those that were deemed obsolete or those that were replaced, was poor. The executive took the computer home. A few months later several sensitive files were found on the internet. The breach was traced back to the executive's home computer: the executive had allowed the computer to be used by his kids, one of whom was a frequent visitor to chat rooms and was the subject of a malicious electronic attack.

When friends become liabilities

When friends become liabilities things can get very bad. Here are a few examples. Think about the current global war on terror. Is Pakistan a friend or a liability for the United States? Most of my close friends in the government tell me that Pakistan has become a liability. Pakistan has not only become an impediment to dealing with terrorists on the border between Pakistan and Afghanistan, but the very fact that the United States bet on Pakistan instead of India early on when picking allies has now come to be a major thorn.

India is significantly more modern than Pakistan and has a stable democracy, which could help the United States. However, India has reservations about cooperating with the United States given the United States' relationship with its unfriendly neighbour Pakistan. After the bombing of the *USS Cole*, when the United States received intelligence on the location of Osama Bin Laden, it wanted to act decisively; however, it first had to communicate its intention to attack to Pakistan. The reason is that the United States did not want Pakistan to think that the missiles being launched were coming from India, which could have resulted in a heated confrontation between the two nuclear neighbours. The passing of information to Pakistan resulted in the leak of this information to the Taliban, resulting in the movement of Bin Laden, which meant that the United States ultimately was unable to achieve its goal of capturing him.

Think of a more corporate example: to Arthur Andersen, was Enron a friend or a liability? As Arthur Andersen learnt in the most severe way, doing business with friends who do not act with integrity can cost one dearly. Arthur Andersen had several hundred accounts, one of which was the Enron account. However, involvement with the Enron scandal immediately brought the company and its entire workforce to a screeching halt. Arthur Andersen lost its credibility, and this impacted on the quality of its intellectual asset – the practice of auditing – resulting in the demise of the organization.

All organizations have to engage with external entities in order to conduct business. Alliances between organizations are on the rise. These alliances come in many shapes and sizes. At the simplest level, businesses engage in licensing agreements with each other. These agreements deal with the purchase of products and services, and the capacity to use them within a structured and limited manner. For example, when an organization decides to purchase software from a vendor (such as Microsoft) it receives the rights to use this software within the context of a licensing agreement. The organization must trust that Microsoft is producing software that is of superior quality, that the software is credible and does not have malicious content, and that entering into the agreement will not jeopardize the strategic posture of the organization. The organization might be in big trouble if there is malicious content (such as keystroke loggers) in software it purchases, or if the software provider should go out of business and fail to provide ongoing support for the products. Similarly, there might be risks in more complex forms of alliances. For example, as I shall discuss later, in a joint production and development agreement, there are risks that intellectual assets might leak outside the context of the specific agreement, thereby making an organization's competitive advantages vulnerable.

The nature of alliances has undergone fundamental changes in recent times. First, there has been a shift from dependence on business partners for simple capacity or auxiliary resources, to the case today, where organizations depend on outsiders for critical resources and ingredients: knowledge and innovations. In the past, organizations would structure relationships to help them meet their auxiliary and capacity needs. For instance, it was common for organizations to form alliances with office supplies organizations to provide them with office stationery, printer toners and so on. Today, in addition to these alliances, there are organizations in which not only is the entire office supplies function outsourced, but so is the design and management of the corporate brand and icons that make their way onto the stationery.

Similarly, in the past, organizations would enter into alliances for warehouse space and even production capacity. Today, in addition to these alliances, organizations receive specialized knowledge in the form of logistical and distribution planning solutions, which make their way into supply-chain processes. Each member of the supply chain is supposed to be an expert in a given area, and produce and deliver products and services of a specialized nature. The point is that alliances have evolved from being vehicles that are conducive to meeting operational efforts, to integral parts of strategic efforts. The products and services exchanged in alliances have also shifted, from simple mechanistic goods to more complex goods and services, including intangible ones such as the movement of knowledge and expertise. Alliances now also contribute to the development of intellectual assets, while ensuring that an organization has a broader reach in how it might deploy intellectual assets.

To appreciate how alliances have evolved, consider the case of outsourcing, a form of alliance that has become quite popular recently. While the outsourcing of manufacturing has been around for ages, the new variants of outsourcing are more sensitive. Outsourcing of manufacturing was viewed as a good business and societal initiative, especially in the developed world. Structured and routine work – which most often required limited knowledge and was the least cognitively engaging – was seldom a high-priority job in the developed portions of the world. This work was gladly sent to developing and under-developed nations, which contained a cheap labour pool which could be exploited. The developed world focused its energies on innovation and the knowledge-driven activities of crafting the designs, requirements and specifications of products. The actual physical manufacturing of the products was carried out in offshore locations.

While there has been no decline in the manufacturing form of outsourcing, two newer forms of outsourcing have also taken hold.

The first form is the sourcing of knowledge work, in which work that was traditionally considered a mainstream job in the developed world is moved offshore. Moreover, these work assignments have been the mainstay of middle-class professionals in the developed world. The prime example of this is the offshoring of software development work. Today, most organizations employ offshore outsourcing vendors in a wide assortment of information system development projects. Another example is the management of help desks and call centres. Here again, most organizations have call centres located in offshore locations, most notably India, Ireland and the Philippines, among others.

The offshoring of knowledge work is more complex than the offshoring of basic manufacturing work. Knowledge work requires that the agent (or organization) conducting the work has some domain knowledge in the area. For example, the execution of software programming assignments requires knowledgeable workers who have basic skills in computer programming.

The most recent form of outsourcing is the sourcing of innovation. This is probably the most difficult form of outsourcing engagement to manage, and these alliances have the most at stake. The very process of making an organization's products and services is outsourced in these alliances. As an example, pharmaceutical companies have begun to outsource portions of the drug discovery process. Needless to say, these types of alliance require an organization to be highly diligent in how intellectual assets are managed and secured.

The success of a business partner can have direct impacts, both positive and negative, on an organization. Today, this becomes ever more evident when we consider the global war against terrorism. The alliance between the United States and the United Kingdom is an exemplar in this respect. The national security of both nations is ever more intertwined. The security (or insecurity) at one location has impacts on the perceived and real security (or insecurity) in another location. Moreover, if a competing organization (for instance, a group of terrorists) wants to disrupt the goals and ideals of either nation, it has three critical options: attack the primary organization (either the United States or the United Kingdom); attack the partnering organization (also, either the United States or the United Kingdom); or, as in the most recent case of a plot to blow up commercial airlines travelling from the United Kingdom to the United States, attack the flow of material between the two countries. In an analogous way, an organization is very closely tied to its business partners.

In this chapter, I discuss security issues with regard to intellectual assets posed by engaging with external entities (see the boxes). In order to truly appreciate the nature of intellectual asset security when engaging with external entities, we shall begin the chapter by outlining the various types of alliances that an organization can engage in. While describing the various alliances I point out how the issues of managing intellectual assets play out across two vital dimensions, control and coordination.

Causes of security breaches

- Sub-par performance.
- Acting with guile.
- Leaks from the business partner.
- Movement of intellectual assets.
- Hijacking and incapacitation of the alliance.

Preventive measures

- Building alliances based on trust.
- Monitoring behaviour and performance.
- Incentives.
- Balancing risks.

Types of alliance

Alliances among business entities come in many shapes and forms. Figure 4.1 depicts the various types of alliances. I have mapped out alliances among business partners on two axes, control and coordination, which represent critical dimensions.[1] *Coordination* is the extent of synchronization that is expected between a business partner and an organization in the alliance. *Control* is the extent of influence an organization has over the behaviour and actions of its business partners. For example, on the one hand, licensing agreements call for the lowest degree of coordination among business partners and involve the least amount of control that one business partner can exert over another. On the other hand, in a merger and acquisition, the level of coordination and control is the highest. Understanding the nature of control and coordination in the various types of alliances will help us appreciate the issues of intellectual asset security from both a risk and preventive perspective.

I have also mapped out the differences between the types of links that are called business relationships and those that are called strategic alliances. A *business relationship* is defined as a transactional link between two entities. This normally involves the purchase of products or services

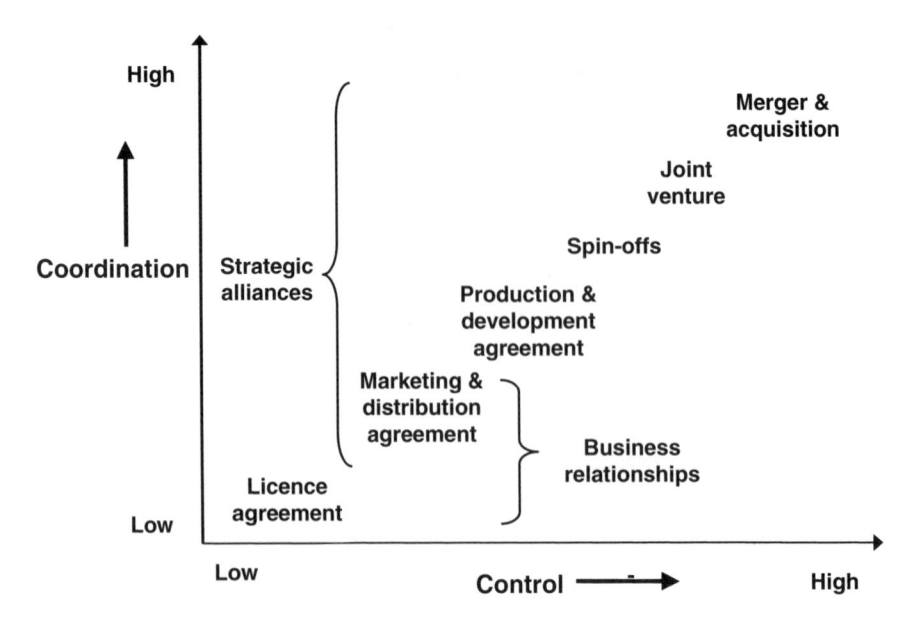

Figure 4.1 Types of alliance

between the entities. Business relationships are most often governed by the logic of lowest cost, and there is relative ease of switching between partners involved in a business relationship. Business relationships are normally renewed (or terminated) on a periodic basis and are viewed in a more operational light. *Strategic alliances*, as the name implies, are not operational linkages. These normally involve the exchange of intellectual assets between partners. Strategic alliances are not based solely on cost and are seldom short-term in nature. Moreover, these alliances have high switching costs, and there is a high cost to be paid should these alliances fail.

Consider the example of a logistics company such as UPS or FedEx. To the local grocer or even the local bar, the linkage with FedEx is for operational purposes and hence is viewed as a business relationship. At any given day, the grocer can change with ease the provider that is used to ship a product. Now, consider Amazon. Amazon's relationships with its logistics providers are more than simple operational linkages: they are strategic linkages. Amazon would not be able to survive if not for the various logistics providers it engages with. Amazon's success in reaching its customers relies on its logistics providers. The point is that we cannot view any linkage in an absolute sense, but must analyse it in the context of its environment. Understanding which alliances are business relationships and which are strategic alliances will also help in allocating resources for the protection of intellectual assets.

Licensing agreements

The most basic form of alliance that an organization can enter is a licensing agreement. Licensing agreements are most common in the technology industry. Most organizations and individuals enter into licensing agreements when they purchase a given piece of software. The licensing agreement tells them what they can and cannot do with a piece of software: the terms or conditions that govern the use of the product. In addition, the licensing agreement dictates the kind of intellectual asset that is being exchanged in the alliance. For example, when you purchase a piece of software, you do not get access to all of the software producer's knowledge or intellectual assets. Rather, it is the knowledge that is encapsulated in the product that is made available to the purchaser. To be more concrete, when you purchase a copy of Microsoft Office you do not have access to all of the knowledge of the software engineers and researchers employed by Microsoft; you only get to access knowledge that is encapsulated in the CDs that contain your software. Now why is this important?

First, because of the restrictions on the access to the producer's knowledge, some forms of products or services should not be accessed using licensing agreements. Licensing agreements should not be used, for example, when you are purchasing mission-critical software, where lack of an adequate connection to the intellectual assets behind the product could be detrimental to the health of the organization. On the contrary, you should enter into licensing agreements for products or services that are of an auxiliary or supporting nature.

Second, you should enter into licensing agreements for products and services that are well-defined and mature. You do not want to enter into licensing agreements for products that are at an immature stage of development, for the risk is just too high. The reason is that if things do go wrong with the product or service, you are limited in the amount of control you have over the producer of the knowledge artefact.

Finally, you should enter into licensing agreements when you want your relationship with the producing organization to be loose: that is, you do not wish to control the intellectual assets of the other organization, and you do not want to expend a lot of energy to coordinate your work with the work of others. Licensing agreements are ideal for products and services that need to be used in a basic plug'n'play manner: you get it, you use it, and there is little overhead in terms of implementation.

To summarize, licensing agreements involve the least amount of coordination and provide an organization with the least amount of control over a business partner. Hence, most licensing agreements are viewed as business relationships.

Marketing and distribution agreements

Marketing and distribution agreements are links that involve one organization mobilizing its products and services via the infrastructure of another organization. In today's environment it is common for organizations to engage in these sorts of alliances due to the emergence of specialized marketing organizations (such as Leo Burnett) and distribution organizations (such as FedEx, UPS and DHL). The cost to an organization to maintain these functions has become too expensive. Moreover, the specialized knowledge (intellectual assets) that is available at organizations that specialize in marketing and distribution cannot easily be duplicated. For example, today, the logistics planning services offered by organizations such as FedEx and UPS are world-class. If a firm had to build these capabilities in-house, it would use up resources, both financial and intellectual, that it could otherwise put into its core business processes, products and services. In comparison to licensing agreements, marketing and distribution agreements require greater effort in terms of coordination and control between two organizations.

In coordination, marketing and distribution agreements require the partnering organizations to have some level of synchronization so that the products and services involved can be mobilized effectively and efficiently. This may be as simple as agreements about shipping and delivery times, or include more detailed plans for packaging, handling of returns and so on. On the control dimension, unlike licensing agreements that involve use of a producer's knowledge in a plug'n'play manner, marketing and distribution agreements require service providers to have some understanding of an organization's products and services so that tailoring and fitting of knowledge can occur. For example, it is rare for an advertising firm to use the same campaign materials for two different clients. Each client is different, and campaigns need to be tailored to the needs of individual clients, especially to meet the needs of their communication goals and their products and services. Hence, the control that is exerted here over the nature and movement of intellectual assets between firms is higher than the control exerted in a licensing agreement.

There is another aspect of control and coordination that becomes relevant in marketing and distribution agreements. Let us say a firm entered into a distribution agreement with a major logistics company such as UPS, and the products that were ordered by a customer arrived late. Who would the customer blame or hold responsible? The average customer would hold both organizations at fault, with the primary product producer more responsible for choosing the logistics company that delayed the shipment. Now, let us consider another case: imagine that a logistics company entered into an agreement with a company that produced defective goods: that is, the primary producing organization purposely put damaged goods into packages for transportation by the logistics organization. Now who would the customer hold responsible, and whose reputation would be in jeopardy? The logistics company, innocent in this case, could start to lose its business and reputation through no fault of its own. The point is that when entering into a marketing and distribution agreement, the firms become bound together. These ties are strong, but not as strong as the ties in production and development agreements.

Production and development agreements

In production and development agreements, organizations are jointly involved in the development of new intellectual assets in the form of products and services. These agreements are more complex than marketing and distribution agreements, as they involve the infusion of knowledge among, and joint development of intellectual assets by, business partners. For instance, Boeing actively solicited business partners in the innovation process for its new 787 jetliner, the Dreamliner (Kotha and Nolan, 2005). Boeing's new factory model for this plane integrated assemblies from global partners. In a vast departure from tradition, Boeing created a team of 15 companies from more than 10 states in the United States and seven countries just to make the structural sections of the plane. To innovate a complex product (such as a jetliner), innovation processes themselves must be rethought, reorganized and creatively reconstructed. For example, Japan's Mitsubishi Heavy Industries is responsible for the wing box. Vougut and Alexia, from Italy, are building the Dreamliner's horizontal stabilizer and the centre and aft fuselage. Another novelty in the innovation process is that Boeing has asked its business partners to fund their own R&D costs for the parts of the Dreamliner they are assigned to build. Boeing believes that this will help align business partners' interests with the creation of the new plane, as the partners will have stakes in not only minimizing the costs of R&D but also eventually marketing the plane. Suppliers thus become invested in the success of the new jetliner. This is a significant departure from the past method of aircraft design, in which Boeing centralized not only R&D but also the costs, risks and benefits of making a new aircraft a success.

Organizations involved in these alliances do not simply exchange intellectual assets, but create new intellectual assets together. This means that the organizations have to be more tightly bound in terms of both coordination and control. In terms of control, an organization needs not only to control its own knowledge flows but also to have some control over the knowledge of its business partners. For example, the organization needs to ensure that its business partner protects the intellectual assets being developed and does not share them with other partners. In terms of coordination, both organizations have to be considerate of each other and capable of working jointly so that they can achieve a mutually beneficial objective.

Because of the degree of coordination and control required to sustain these engagements, they take a lot longer to get off the ground and, if fruitful, are normally engaged in for longer periods of time. It is not as easy to switch business partners in production and development agreements as it is to switch partners in licensing agreements. The cost of switching is considerably higher, as partners that are part of these links are chosen for their unique skills and intellectual assets.

Production and development agreements are seldom viewed as simple business relationships. Instead, it is more common to consider these as strategic alliances. Whenever an organization engages with another entity to develop intellectual assets, these need to be considered as strategic efforts. Considering these as simple business relationships will lead to inadequate attention being paid to these relationships, which almost certainly will lead to disastrous outcomes.

Spin-offs[2]

Situations can emerge where an organization has either more knowledge than it knows what to do with, or needs a new approach to realizing valuable internal knowledge. Both of these situations may result in knowledge leaving the organization in the form of spin-offs. Spin-offs are a special form of alliance. Spin-offs are new organizations that emerge around knowledge in the parent organization and then separate from the parent organization.

An organization might spin off a new entity for several reasons. First, the organization might need to develop new ideas, intellectual assets, products and services that do not fit the current organizational environments. Second, the organization might feel that the new organization needs an independent space to try out new ideas and not be bogged down with the legacy infrastructure and the organizational history of the parent organization. Third, organizations might want to mitigate risks. Spinning off a new entity allows the organization to preserve its traditional business and allow risks to be borne by the new entity without direct impacts to the parent organization.

In terms of control and coordination, a spin-off poses interesting challenges. The critical dilemma is to strike a balance between the independence of the new entity and retaining some control and coordination with the parent (sponsor) organization. While the new entity needs to be given independence to pursue new ideas and think outside the traditional confines of the parent organization, the parent organization does exert control over the resources of the spin-off. Simply put, the parent organization gives the spin-off its budget, personnel, and the other necessary administrative and infrastructure resources to get its work done.

In terms of coordination, ideally there will be loose coordination. Loose coordination will take the form of exchanging ideas and intellectual assets. In order to be successful, it is recommended that the spin-offs have the capabilities to leverage the parent organization's knowledge about market opportunities and general administrative issues. The parent will normally have deep pockets of market knowledge that can be of vital importance to the spin-off in positioning its new products and services. Spin-offs normally operate in the same industry spaces as the parent and hence do not need to reinvent knowledge about the market. Moreover, the parent will have knowledge on general administrative details, such as how to handle payroll and taxation issues. Rather than trying to reinvent the wheel here, the spin-off should tap into such knowledge and leverage the parent's know-how. It should, however, think very carefully before importing the parent's governance mechanisms. It is better to invent mechanisms to meet the needs of the new entity rather than attempt to superimpose previous structures, since the spin-off is different from the parent and may need different management protocols in order to be successful.

Needless to say, spin-offs are strategic partners of the parent organization and need to be viewed in this light. Spin-offs emerge from intellectual assets constructed in the parent organization in the form of ideas, processes, practices and market insights. It is therefore important that these assets, the very reason for the spin-off's creation, are appropriately secured in the new entity.

Joint ventures

In joint ventures, two or more businesses go into partnership to create a new organization; this new organization is jointly controlled by the primary organizations, but is run as an independent unit. Organizations enter into joint ventures when they want to share resources and risks and want the new entity to be a stand-alone business.

Several situations warrant the creation of joint ventures. The first is when a business does not want to disrupt its ongoing operations but feels a need to explore the development of new products and services with a partner that has complementary resources and similar interests. The creation of the new organization means that both organizations can continue their current operations as is, and then use the new organization to test out the new development. The creation of the new organization also reduces the impact of any losses or other damages that might occur: the new organization would absorb these, and the impact would stop there, rather than affecting the operations of the primary organizations. Second, joint ventures are common when a firm is trying to enter geographic markets it has not penetrated before. A firm can enter a new market by collaborating with a local subsidiary that has knowledge about local markets and has the necessary connections and complementary assets.

Firms enter into joint ventures for strategic advantages. The entity that results from the collaboration between two or more organizations is jointly owned by the organizations; hence, the parents can exert control over the new organization. However, the new organization must also be able to create its own identity. Thus, the control cannot be absolute, as in the case of mergers and acquisitions, which we shall discuss next. The control of the new entity will rest in a management team that is generally appointed through the collaborative work of the parent organizations. Moreover, control issues are also critical in one other important respect. For instance, the knowledge that goes into the new entity from the parent organizations must benefit the new entity, and should benefit the parents equally. Hence, the coordination of intellectual asset issues also becomes important. There must be coordination among the parents and the joint venture to ensure that knowledge flows effectively and efficiently among the entities.

Mergers and acquisitions

The final and probably most complex form of linkages is mergers and acquisitions. Mergers and acquisitions occur when two companies decide to merge their forces and become one organization. This can occur in one of two ways. In one way, two organizations join up their assets, liabilities, infrastructures and so on, and create a brand new company that has the combined resources of both the original companies. In the second way, one organization acquires another one and subsumes the acquired organization's operations within its operations. In this case, the acquiring organization retains its original external façade, while the acquired organization loses it.

Mergers and acquisitions occur for several reasons. First, two organizations might merge their resources to create a more powerful entity that can compete with existing players in the industry. This normally occurs in the financial sector, where banks combine resources to be able to compete in a fierce environment. A company might acquire a smaller organization that it sees as having strategic capabilities and resources of interest. These kinds of acquisitions are common in the technology and pharmaceutical sectors, where established large organizations acquire smaller organizations that are working in emerging areas of interest to the larger organization.

During mergers and acquisitions the issues of control and coordination play out quite intensively. There needs to be absolute coordination of efforts between the parties so that the merger or acquisition takes places smoothly and there is not much disruption felt by the customers of either organization. If there is disruption, the customers may not be tolerant and might decide to take their business elsewhere. In terms of control, the acquiring firm will have absolute control over the acquired organization's resources. Needless to say, the issues of intellectual asset security are most prominent in these kinds of relationships. After all, these alliances can be considered as akin to getting married. For good or bad, the two organizations are joined at the hip, and any weaknesses, liabilities or other intellectual asset security ailments afflicting one organization will have an impact on the other organization.

Security breaches

Given the above understanding of business relationships (which mainly constitute licensing agreements, and for some firms, marketing and distribution agreements) and strategic alliances (all other forms of partnerships), I shall now discuss the various security breaches that might arise when engaging with external entities. The important thing to remember is that the intensity of a security breach will vary depending on whether it occurs in a business relationship or a strategic alliance.

Sub-par performance

Business partners that an organization engages with might under-deliver on their promises, and in some cases fail to deliver anything at all. This normally occurs when a critical mistake has been made in the choice of business partner. Consider the following example. A government agency wanted to engage in a production and development agreement with civilian vendors. To this end, the agency issued a tender and screened the responses to its request for proposals. The government agency ended up choosing a firm that on paper had the lowest cost offerings, the best collection of resources, strong references, and that met all the criteria (such as the ability to conduct classified work). Three months into the engagement, the business partner failed to meet the first milestone. About a year later, the business partner had missed two other milestones and also was over-budget. Instead of pulling the plug, the government agency decided to provide a supplementary budget and continue with the engagement. Three years later, the project was $5 million over budget, and still none of the deliverables had been met.

Examples such as these are not rare, although I wish they were. Here is another example: a consumer goods producer forged a relationship with a transportation company to ship its products to international markets. The transportation company, once again, had a good track record on paper. In addition, the owner of the transportation company was a relative of one of the senior executives of the consumer goods organization (this relationship doubtless helped the transportation company get the work assignment). Over the period of one year, the transportation company not only managed to misplace 5 per cent of all items shipped, but had late deliveries on over 20 per cent of all orders. Needless to say, this had a negative impact on the reputation and the well-being of the consumer goods organization. Quite surprisingly, the transportation company was able to pick up over 10 major new clients after signing the deal with the consumer goods organization. It had used the fact that it had obtained the deal with the consumer goods organization to boast about its capabilities and market reputation!

Sub-par performance on the part of the business partner is a security breach and needs to be addressed head on. When a business partner does not keep its end of the bargain, it undermines your intellectual assets and more importantly undermines the credibility of your organization. In the above example, the reputation of the consumer goods organization was damaged, and its clients lost respect and trust in the organization's ability to deliver quality products and services in a timely manner. As noted earlier, in these kinds of marketing and distribution agreements, the average consumer will hold the organization responsible for failures on the part of the business partner.

If we were to analyse sub-par performances in business engagements, we would find that they commonly stem from lack of care in how business partners were chosen in the first place. Organizations commonly get suckered by lucrative attractors such as lowest-cost providers. Lowest-cost providers are not always the most reputable or trustworthy. Moreover, organizations sometimes do not conduct due diligence in checking the backgrounds of their providers, and hence may engage with a questionable entity. Another reason for sub-par performance is a lack of checks and balances in a contract or agreement that helps align the incentives of a business partner to ensure that it acts appropriately. For our purposes, from a security perspective it is important to be concerned when sub-par performance is the result of intentional actions by business partners. Here is how sub-par performance may play out in the various types of alliances:

- **Licensing agreements**: sub-par performance occurs when the products and services licensed do not live up to their billing. This commonly occurs when software has numerous bugs and works erratically. In other forms of renting agreements, for example in hiring temporary staff, the capabilities of the staff may not be up to par with what was advertised or promised.
- **Marketing and distribution agreements**: as noted in the examples above, this occurs when vendors do not deliver on their promises to market and distribute the products and services of organizations.
- **Production and development agreements**: as in the case of the government agency, sub-par performance in these agreements affect

the intellectual assets being developed. The business partner will lack the necessary capabilities and/or the effort to use its intellectual assets to further the joint effort of creating new intellectual assets.
- **Spin-offs**: sub-par performance on the part of a spin-off rarely happens purposely. If it does occur, it is because of the immaturity of the idea or products that are being spun off, or the management team that is leading the new organization. These are issues that are manageable and do not represent a cause for concern from the vantage point of security.
- **Joint ventures**: because of the tight coupling of the two organizations and the sense of joint ownership of the new entity, the chances of sub-par performance occurring in the joint venture as a result of purposeful action are rare.
- **Mergers and acquisitions**: Similar to joint ventures, the chances of sub-par performance occurring in a merger or acquisition through intentional actions are rare. Mergers and acquisitions do routinely fail, but these are seldom because of deliberate efforts by a business partner to act less than its best.

Acting with guile

There are numerous cases that document business partners acting with guile. Consider the case of outsourcing relationships, a form of production and development agreement. There have been several cases where an outsourcing vendor has tried to use the business relationship to further its objectives at the expense of its partner. In one case, upon completion of a software development assignment, an outsourcing vendor attempted to sell the software built for one organization to competing organizations.

Consider another case: counterfeit operations (Datz, 2006). There are three types of counterfeit operations in China. The first type of counterfeit operation is conducted in a legalized factory. This kind of factory has two faces, a legal face and an illegal face. It produces goods and products legally, and in different shifts it may produce illegal goods and products. Factory workers may not know whether the products they produce are illegal or legal. The second type is operated by a joint partnership between a multinational company and a Chinese company. In this case, the Chinese company produces goods in excess of the contract's stipulations and sells the surplus illegally to make profits. The third type is operated in underground facilities. Those facilities are hard to find since they are hidden. They may be located in basements, for example.

Sometimes these facilities are built around important machines and equipment. Also, some counterfeiters do not have fixed locations, but are movable. In this way, they can avoid tracking by the authorities. China is not the only country where counterfeit operations exist, but it is one of the most significant.

In another case involving business partners acting with guile, a firm that entered into an agreement to bring in a contingent staff of 100 workers to help address a temporary surge in workload discovered that 10 of the contingent employees were stealing customer information. These employees had been asked by a competing organization, which also hired contingent workers from the staffing organization, to get access to customer contact information.

As in the case of sub-par performance, intellectual asset loss that results from business partners acting with guile can be traced to poor choices in how business partners are screened and chosen. In addition, organizations that suffer these fates almost always lack good ways to monitor the performance and behaviour of business partners. As we shall discuss in the next section, having preventive mechanisms, such as conducting announced and unannounced inspections, is critical to ensuring that all is well with a business relationship.

Here is how guile may play out in the various types of alliances:

- **Licensing agreements**: the products and services being licensed or rented may contain hidden nuisances. For example, software products might contain viruses or keystroke loggers. Contingent workers might be asked to engage in corporate espionage activities.
- **Marketing and distribution agreements**: acting with guile here includes activities that destroy products and services being marketed or distributed. Within marketing agreements, acting with guile is rare. Acting with guile is also rare in distribution agreements today, given the advancements in the tracking and shipment of products. However, it can still occur.
- **Production and development agreements**: following the examples noted above, acting with guile is quite common in these efforts, as there are opportunities for one party to take advantage of the intellectual assets of its counterpart.
- **Spin-offs**: acting with guile is almost never a concern here.
- **Joint ventures**: acting with guile is seldom a concern here as both parties have a vested interest in seeing the joint venture materialize and become profitable.

- **Mergers and acquisitions:** acting with guile is almost never a concern here.

Leaks from the business partner

The two previous types of security breaches result from purposeful actions; there may also be breaches that occur accidentally. A common form of this is when intellectual assets are leaked from the premises of the business partner. As noted in the introductory chapter, we have recently witnessed several cases in which computer tapes and disks were lost. Most of these losses occurred as data was being moved by a third-party logistics company to an offsite storage facility, which is normally managed by yet another company.

Consider another type of case. Khalil Abdulla-Raheem, a Unisys Corp employee, was charged with stealing a desktop computer with information on as many as 38,000 US Department of Veterans Affairs medical patients (McMillan, 2006). Unisys Corporation was a contractor to the Department of Veterans Affairs. In this case, Unisys failed to secure the assets of its business partner through lack of control over how its employees engaged with the partner's intellectual assets. What is even more troubling is the fact that Unisys had not encrypted the data, thus making the intellectual assets less safe and more easily susceptible to theft.

A business partner might lack adequate measures to protect intellectual assets, both its own and those of its partners. Most organizations fail to conduct due diligence on their business partners' security programmes. This is quite unfortunate. A large manufacturing plant suffered a terrible fate when its business partner, a marketing agency working on the brand and logo designs for the product launch, suffered an information breach. A designer working at the marketing agency left his bag on the train, which led to the breach. Within a matter of hours, the story of the new product being designed broke out in several internet chat-rooms.

Security teams are seldom made part of the negotiation and dealing leading to the formation of an alliance. As a result, the security protocols of a business partner are seldom scrutinized and evaluated. Here is how leaks may occur in the various types of alliances:

- **Licensing agreements**: because intellectual assets are not transferred from the organization to the business partner, leaks do not occur under this arrangement.

- **Marketing and distribution agreements**: leaks occur through communications between the business partners about intellectual assets, and also as intellectual assets are moved from one location to another.
- **Production and development agreements**: leaks occur as intellectual assets are being developed by the parties, and also when work in progress is tampered with at business partners' locations.
- **Spin-offs**: leaks that occur here result from lack of care in developing the new organization's security programmes. The parent organization bears the responsibility of ensuring that adequate protective mechanisms are in place to protect the intellectual assets of the new organization.
- **Joint ventures**: leaks that occur here are similar to those that take place in spin-offs, and are the result of a lack of adequate security programmes in the new organization.
- **Mergers and acquisitions**: leaks that occur here are caused by a lack of appropriate attention as the organizations merge or as one organization is being acquired.

Movement of intellectual assets

Most mergers and acquisitions fail. The percentage of failure of mergers and acquisitions is in the range of 70 per cent. While there are many reasons for the failure of these alliances, one issue is critical: lack of cultural fit between the two organizations. Lack of cultural fit essentially means that two merging organizations, or an acquiring organization and the organization being acquired, are so different that it is inconceivable that the two have any chance of comprising a functioning whole. One potential outcome of a lack of cultural fit is that weeks, months, or in some cases a year or two before the merger or acquisition is finalized, critical intellectual assets leave the organization.

In one case, two medium-sized technology organizations were planning to combine their operations in order to avoid duplication of efforts and to engage in joint development of core competencies. About a month after news of the potential merger got out, 10 of the core software developers of one organization left their posts to join competing firms. They were unsure about their futures in the new organization. As a result, the new organization that resulted from the merger failed to reach its objective of developing a distinctive offering to clients based on the combined expertise of the two original companies. (After all, a large percentage of the expertise did leave!)

In another case, consider the issue of spin-offs. When a company spins off a business it walks a fine line between giving the new business the attention it deserves and the necessary resources to operate while also preserving its traditional business and operations. One company that I know of learnt a hard lesson about balancing between the new, spin-off organization and the old organization (Thomas *et al*, 2005). The organization created a spin-off to help it take advantage of the dot-com movement. The new organization was given new facilities and new locations, and its critical staff included some of the best minds from the parent organization. However, frustration grew. The new organization was allowed to take critical resources – the most important resources being seasoned project managers and software engineers – to the new firm. These employees were offered attractive packages to leave the parent organization and join the spin-off. As one manager at the parent organization commented:

> We XYZ [the parent organization] were treated like a third-party vendor. We were invited for a meeting in ABC's [the spin-off organization's] First Avenue location and we were made to wait in the lobby. They had us check in, made us sit in the lobby until they were all assembled, and then we could go in the conference room and meet. Why were we not allowed to talk to our friends who were in ABC [the spin-off] from XYZ [parent organization]?

As the above comment shows, there was little care in ensuring equity in how intellectual assets moved and were managed between the two organizations. Needless to say, this caused a lot of hostility. What is even more surprising is that in about a year, the parent organization decided to bring the spin-off back into the parent organization. The spin-off had not delivered on its promises. Now the parent organization had to deal with another set of troubles. The so-called privileged child now had to be integrated with the parent that it had deserted and mistreated. Needless to say, there were rough roads ahead.

The point is that in entering these difficult alliances, organizations should avoid disruption to intellectual assets, which invariably adds difficulties. Most of the time, this occurs when there is lack of clear communication with employees and when an organization does not understand how to manage events to prevent them from escalating into crises. With regard to the former point, I recommend that organizations pay attention to the points discussed in Chapter 2; with regard to the latter point, I note that Chapter 6 provides insights on managing intellectual assets during times of crisis.

- **Licensing agreements**: the movement of intellectual assets is not an issue here.
- **Marketing and distribution agreements**: the movement of intellectual assets is not an issue here.
- **Production and development agreements**: the movement of intellectual assets might be an issue here if the business partner that is being engaged is not seen as a 'good fit' business partner in the eyes of the employees that are involved with the joint production and development.
- **Spin-offs**: as noted in the example above, the movement of intellectual assets is a major issue in spin-offs because of the separation of entities and the chance that one entity will be favoured over the other.
- **Joint ventures**: in joint ventures, as in spin-offs, there may be issues with the movement of intellectual assets as a result of the formation of a new organization and the stress it may put on the resources of the parent organization.
- **Mergers and acquisitions**: this is where the movement of intellectual assets becomes a critical issue, and needs to be managed carefully using the guidelines for managing intellectual assets during crises.

Hijacking and incapacitation of the alliance

What would happen if Microsoft decided to triple the prices of its software products and closed down the maintenance functions for a few products? How would your organization deal with this? Not a pleasant possibility to consider, is it? Why? Well, to all intents and purposes, Microsoft is a giant, and more importantly, the products it develops have made their way into all aspects of the work of business organizations. From the software I am using to write this book, to the project planning tools used by your software engineers, to the spreadsheet programs used by your accountants, we use Microsoft products. Now comes the million-dollar question: do you think Microsoft has the potential to hijack your business?

The answer will depend on the business you are in, but at the bare minimum, Microsoft does have the ability to cause you some pain should it choose to. Similarly, businesses have relationships with some external entities that are so critical that they in fact trust the external parties 100 per cent to act in their business interests – or, to put it more correctly, not to act with guile and hijack the relationship. For example, in the case of outsourcing relationships, certain firms use the same vendors for multiple projects. The good news with this strategy is that the vendor being engaged understands the realities of the business, knows the internal and external environments, and does not have a steep learning curve for every new assignment. The bad news is that the contracting organization becomes vulnerable and cannot switch to a new vendor with ease. Since the organization has engaged with one vendor over a substantial duration of time, it has given up the opportunity to engage with other vendors.

Another security concern arises when the relationship with a business partner is terminated abruptly. This normally occurs when the business partner goes out of business or gets into trouble that limits its ability to function. There have been several cases in which organizations that relied on IT providers, especially application service providers (ASPs), got rude awakenings when these providers declared bankruptcy. In many cases, these firms gave their business partners 24 to 48 hours to move their data and find other partners. Situations such as these put great strains on organizations: intellectual assets may need to be secured and mobilized to new locations, and finding those new locations within a small timeframe might be difficult or impossible.

As we all know, when we are desperate we lack negotiating power. I know of an organization that once had to find a new home for its website and data applications within 24 hours. As soon as word got out that the firm's previous IT provider had gone bankrupt and the firm had little time to act, several of the new providers under consideration increased their fees and asked for guarantees in their contract that were not traditional. The firm had to make quick decisions and had little room to say no.

Hijacking and incapacitation of alliances happens when an organization has not considered the long-term implications of forging alliances. Moreover, the organization has failed to appreciate the fact that alliances need to be managed like portfolios to reduce risks and spread opportunities. In addition, organizations need to have contingency plans in place to address incapacitation of alliances. Here is how things play out in the various alliances:

- **Licensing agreements**: seldom do licensing agreements affect organizations in a significant enough manner to allow hijacking of the alliance or cause serious disruptions if the alliance is terminated – the exception, of course, being in rare cases like Microsoft.

- **Marketing and distribution agreements**: because of the number of choices that an organization has in business partners to engage with in these alliances, the chances of security breaches occurring as a result of hijacking or incapacitation are rare.
- **Production and development agreements**: these alliances are the most susceptible to hijacking by business partners. Also, incapacitation of business partners in production and development agreements will have dire consequences on the organization. This is because the organization has a limited choice in business partners, as business partners are chosen for their unique knowledge. Moreover, the cost of switching business partners is high.
- **Spin-offs**: hijacking and incapacitation are not issues here because of the nature of the alliance.
- **Joint ventures**: hijacking and incapacitation are not issues here because of the nature of the alliance.
- **Mergers and acquisitions**: hijacking and incapacitation are not issues here because of the nature of the alliance.

Preventive measures

In the previous section I detailed five of the major ways that security breaches affecting intellectual assets arise in the context of alliances with external entities. In addition to these breaches, a business partner may suffer any of the other breaches that I discuss in the book: everything from the inability to secure employees' knowledge, to lack of care in handling technology gadgets and failure to secure the organization's physical perimeters, to breaches that may arise during crises. Hence, when discussing security issues with business partners, it is important to bear these liabilities in mind as well.

The good news is that the preventive measures that need to be undertaken by business partners are the same preventive measures discussed in other chapters of this book. For example, conducting background checks on employees is a practice that should be embraced by the business partners an organization engages with. This practice will reduce the incidence of employees exploiting alliances to act with guile. Similarly, as we shall discuss in a later chapter, business partners need to have sound practices for securing assets during times of crisis, just as you would have in your own organization. Hence, in addition to the mechanisms that I will list below, you must check business partners for the protecting mechanisms I describe in other chapters of the book. You must hold your business partners to the same standards to which you hold your own organization. The following mechanisms need to be considered carefully to prevent security breaches and compromises to intellectual assets during alliances.

Build alliances based on trust

As simple as my advice may sound, most organizations fail to heed it. Most organizations are short-sighted in how they view alliances, and argue about issues such as costs. Short-sighted and cost-centric alliances will fail; there is little doubt about this. Alliances that are sustainable over time are rooted in deep trust between the organizations. Trust takes two major forms. First, there is trust that the business partner is well-intentioned, noble and credible. Second, there is trust in the ability of the business to deliver on its promised capabilities. The first kind of trust should be considered a basic requirement, while the second form of trust is specific to the intellectual assets being exchanged or developed in the alliance.

For example, I might trust General Electric to be a responsible organization that is well-intentioned and has high credibility. However, I might not trust GE's capability in the insurance market, whereas I might have full faith in its abilities in the consumer product arena. In order to build an alliance based on trust, an organization must conduct due diligence in selecting a business partner. The cheapest business partner might not always be the best option. Evaluating the credibility and integrity of the business partner is very important. Questions that need to be asked include:

- How did the business partner fare in other alliances?
- Did the business partner act with integrity in past alliances?
- How did the business partner respond in times of crisis? Did the business partner take measures to ensure minimal disruption to its clients?
- How does the business partner negotiate, and is it looking to build a lasting relationship or get a quick win?
- What resources will the business partner dedicate to ensuring that the alliance is managed with care?

It is essential that an organization conducts a thorough background check on its business partner. As part of the evaluation process for choosing business partners, it is necessary that peculiarities of the business partner be uncovered.

Monitoring behaviour and performance

It is absolutely essential that an organization has protocols to monitor the behaviour and performance of a business partner. Behaviour is normally monitored by inspecting the facilities of the business partner. For example, some organizations will send inspectors to the factory floors of their manufacturers to check on the behaviour of the employees, the presence of security measures, and how security measures are followed. Monitoring behaviour may seem to be a sign of mistrust of a business partner. This may be the case if the monitoring behaviour is not discussed upfront, especially if it is conducted in a covert manner. One of my business school professors put it well: 'Respect but suspect.' During the contract negotiations, the organization should make it known that routine inspections are standard business practice, and that this is how the organization conducts business with all of its business partners.

Performance is monitored by tracking progress based on agreed upon milestones. For example, in marketing and distribution agreements, service level agreements (SLAs) articulate what is expected in terms of performance. An organization must routinely get data to ensure that the performance of its business partners is on track. If the organization finds that a partner's performance is not up to par, immediate action should be taken to address the issue. This may include having discussions with the business partner to identify problem areas, or redeploying resources to problem areas. It is important to note that you do not want issues to escalate. If the alliance is rooted in trust, then it is easier to address the issues of performance upfront, as both parties will be willing to cooperate to resolve the issues.

Two things need to be noted when monitoring behaviour and performance. The first is not to overdo it. Overdoing inspections will affect the quality of the relationship and will interfere with the quality of work being conducted. In one case, I know of a project manager who became a pest by constantly asking for information from her counterpart at the business partner. The business partner got so frustrated with this that it decided to terminate its relationship with the organization. The second item to bear in mind is that you need to routinely inspect the well-being of your business partner. Items that need to be checked include the financial well-being of the organization, any new clients that the organization has taken on, new strategic directions, entrance into new markets, and changes to the portfolio of products and services. These details can affect the relationship you have with the business partner. For instance, if the business partner decides to entertain business from your competitors, you might have to reconsider your working relationship, and also re-examine the processes in place to secure your intellectual assets.

Incentives

Just as employees need incentives to follow security procedures and protect intellectual assets, business partners likewise need incentives. Business partners commonly ignore security practices, as they feel that such practices incur additional costs that take away from their bottom line. This might be true. For example, consider the difference between Wal-Mart and Toyota. Wal-Mart squeezes its suppliers into providing the lowest-cost products. If you do not constantly reduce the price of your products, and if you cannot meet Wal-Mart's stringent production requirements, chances are high that you will not be a supplier for the organization. Now, contrast this with Toyota. Toyota, probably one of the most innovative car manufacturers, has an extraordinary relationship with its suppliers. Toyota's suppliers conduct innovation within their own domains (such as building car parts) and then provide Toyota with these intellectual assets, which can then be used in the assembly of automobiles. Should a supplier find itself in a crisis – for example, if a fire causes damage to a factory – other Toyota suppliers will step up to cover the production of the supplier, and will even share some of their profits with the affected supplier. Do you see how different these alliances are? Why would a supplier for Wal-Mart work in the best interests of Wal-Mart? The answer is that they wouldn't! Wal-Mart's suppliers are looking to make their numbers, and know that Wal-Mart will switch to a new business partner if it has the chance. On the other hand, Toyota has built loyalty with its suppliers. These suppliers work in the best interests of Toyota, and even build intellectual assets (innovations) for the company. They know that if Toyota succeeds, so will they. They know that Toyota genuinely cares about their growth and development and will not dump them for a low-cost provider.

It is important that alliances have incentives to encourage good behaviour on the part of business partners. Most alliances do have incentives; however, these incentives are usually designed to encourage good performance on deliverables such as quick delivery times, low error rates and so on. These kinds of incentives help forestall sub-par performance, as well as acting with guile; however, they do not address the issues of intellectual asset development and protection.

Consider the following case. A retail firm that I know of conducts annual inspections of its suppliers' facilities. These suppliers' facilities are rated for their upkeep, attention to detail (such as how the machinery is maintained, and how waste is treated), and even security (such as whether it is possible to take material out of the facility, and how the access controls work). The rankings of suppliers are published annually and made available to all of the suppliers. What is even more interesting is that the company publishes what it deems to be best practices at each of the supplier organizations! The logic behind this is that all suppliers will try to improve their ranking on the list, and more importantly, the suppliers will want to copy the best practices found in peer organizations. Three years since the inception of this programme, the organization has found that security practices in all its suppliers have improved so dramatically that it is now considered a baseline standard, rather than an exception, to have good security practices.

Business partners can be provided with incentives such as increased business and longer contract time periods based on how well they protect intellectual assets. Likewise, business partners should feel severe pain when intellectual assets are compromised. Contracts should stipulate that compromising intellectual assets will lead to severe penalties, or even the termination of the contract. Incentives should be geared toward building loyalty and allegiance to the company and ensuring that the business partner's actions are conducted in the best interests of the organization.

Balancing risks[3]

One of the clear issues that an organization should manage is avoiding becoming a victim of one of its own alliances. This happens when a business partner exerts undue influence on an organization so as to limit the organization's choices and force its actions. Organizations need to be mindful about managing and developing relationships with business partners so as to secure their advantages and limit their exposures. For example, if you have one client giving you 70 per cent of your business, chances are that you will bend over backwards to save the account. Losing this account would bring your business to a quick end. Similarly, if one of your suppliers controls 70 per cent of your inventory, rest assured that it is going to be in the driver's seat when it comes to negotiations.

One way to avoid these unfortunate situations is to take a lesson from the financial investors. Just as you would not want all your money invested in one instrument or one particular stock, so should you not invest all your resources in one business relationship. The ideal organization will interact with multiple business partners. The goal is not to have these suppliers compete with each other, but to help these suppliers collaborate with each other. Think about the example of Toyota. Toyota's goal is not to have its suppliers compete for its business, as in the case of Wal-Mart, but to spread the work around and build collaboration among suppliers. The important lesson to note is that you spread your risks by engaging with multiple business partners. This may raise issues in coordinating the alliances and ensuring that partners do not compete, but this overhead is worth it, especially if the impact of one business partner hijacking a relationship could severely impact the viability of the organization.

Going back to the dimensions of coordination and control, an organization must be clear about how much control it wants over a business partner. If the business partner has a major role to play in the organization's plans, then a high degree of control is likely. The organization must be able to exert some level of control on the business partner. Organizations should look at the various types of alliance as a phase/process model. An organization might consider beginning with a licensing agreement with a business partner. Depending on how the relationship progresses, the alliance may increase in sophistication to a marketing and distribution, or production and development, agreement. If the organization realizes that its dependence on the partner is increasing, it may consider a joint venture. Depending on how valuable the external source is and the organization's dependence on it, a merger or acquisition may be an option further down the road. Starting with a simple alliance and moving towards more complex ones provides an organization with a way to test the elasticity of the relationship and build up integration and coordination capabilities.

You must also consider the worst-case conditions. What happens if you must terminate your relationship with the business partner? What will be the impacts on your organization? Will you be able to continue operations in a normal mode? Who would you turn to for meeting your needs? When crafting a business relationship or an alliance, it is very important to think of an exit strategy upfront. Never engage with external entities until you know how your business will function should the relationship end abruptly. The presence of backup knowledge resources, personnel on hand with expertise and a network of other business partners that you can rely on, are all important ingredients in an exit strategy.

Closing thoughts

Engaging with business partners is never an easy feat; however, this is a business necessity. Ideally, a business would be able to control all aspects of its operations, but this is not reality. The age of specialization and distributed knowledge and expertise makes it a must to collaborate with external entities. Organizations that are able to collaborate and develop a collaborative capability will outperform their competitors.

Collaboration calls for the exchange of intellectual assets with external entities. As I have outlined in this chapter, there are many ways for organizations to collaborate. The important point to remember is that an organization should pay due attention to how intellectual assets work in these arrangements. Organizations need to pay attention to the five ways intellectual asset breaches can occur in these relationships. In addition, organizations should also apply the guidelines and discussion contained in the other chapters of the book. Business partners should have security mechanisms that account for people, technology and other aspects of operations. Indeed, an organization should even apply the guidelines in this chapter to measure how well a potential business partner takes care of its other business partners. In this way, the organization will get a sense of what to expect should it enter into an alliance.

5

Guarding the fortress

Physical security has lost its glamour in recent times. Technology security in all its forms – from data security, to information security, to network security – has received most of the spotlight and will continue to garner centre-stage attention. Most organizations do not take adequate care to secure their physical perimeters, and this oversight may come back to haunt those organizations.

For example, consider the lost and stolen goods from retailers that have made their way onto online auctions. Panties stolen from a Boston-area Victoria Secret's store appeared for sale on the popular electronic marketplace eBay (Scalet, 2005). Paul Jones, CSO of Limited Brands, the parent company of Victoria's Secret, had established a team to monitor online auctions. A member of Jones's team, Joe Hajdu, posed as a small store owner and was successful in purchasing 65 pairs of panties from an online seller on eBay. On inspection, the goods were found to be marked with a return address in Andover, Massachusetts, at a location close to the site of the theft. Convinced that the panties were the ones that had been stolen, the team decided to entrap the thieves. A regional loss manager tagged hundreds of pairs of dog-embroidered panties with ultraviolet ink. The store code was tagged on each price tag. Not coincidentally, that night, 180 pairs of panties were stolen from a store in Marlboro, Massachusetts. The thief contacted Hajdu with information about the new merchandise and asked if he had any interest in making a purchase. In collaboration with the Andover Police Department, the team successfully apprehended the thieves. Jennifer Stevanovich, a mother of three, was caught unloading the stolen merchandise as she was trying to mail it at the post office. Upon raiding Stevanovich's house, the police found other stolen merchandise worth $28,000, consisting of apparel from stores such as Express, Gap and Abercrombie & Fitch, among others. Are your products being stolen and auctioned off? Poor physical security can come back to haunt you.

Consider another reason one should pay attention to securing the fortress: the easiest physical penetrations to orchestrate are in cases in which an organization shares its physical space with a large number of neighbours. Most organizations have co-located physical settings: that is, they are in close proximity to other organizations. For example, many organizations rent floor space in high-rise complexes. They may share office spaces in industrial parks or may even be tenants in large shopping malls. Though these organizations are surrounded by a large number of neighbours, their security plans do not reflect this reality. Moreover, many of these organizations assume that their landlords are responsible for ensuring the physical security of their premises. For example, the landlords normally charge each tenant a small fee to pay for security services (that is, toy cops who monitor the gates and buzz people in) and basic closed circuit television (CCTV) systems, as well as for janitorial services and other communal services. But the landlords only have to do the bare minimum. It is up to each organization to realize the business value of what is housed in its own premises and plan appropriate security measures.

It is also important for organizations to study the interdependency issues that arise from having neighbours. For example, if you are located in a building that houses consulates and embassies, chances are high – especially if the embassies belong to certain countries – that your organization faces severe risks. Moreover, what happens if there is a bank or a bioengineering lab on the ground floor of your building? The security plans that the bank has in place may affect your operations. Risks from experiments conducted at the bioengineering facility could affect the well-being of your employees. Seldom do organizations discuss security protocols and practices with their neighbours. It is even more troubling that these organizations do not share with each other information about potential risks and adverse events. If an organization notices suspicious individuals patrolling the area, chances are it will try to deal with this as an isolated and local incident. Such information may never make its way to other tenants in the building.

Not convinced yet? Well, here is one more reason to be concerned. Think about your mailrooms: how secure are they? Not too long ago, there were fears that anthrax was being sent through the mail. Does your organization have ways of screening what comes onto the office floor? In 2001, 22 infections and five deaths were attributed to anthrax exposure.

Two postal workers died from inhalation of anthrax in 2001, and another seven survived exposure. The Brentwood postal facility in Washington, DC required a $130 million decontamination and renovation before finally reopening in December 2003. A facility in Trenton, NJ underwent an $80 million clean-up. Have you trained your employees about what can (and cannot) be sent via the mail?

Physical security issues are critical if we are to take a holistic view of securing intellectual assets. In recent times, we have seen organizations get very lazy about how they manage their physical security programmes. In this chapter, I shall discuss items that need to be considered when protecting the physical fortress of the organization (see the boxes). The first item of business is to discuss how the nature of the physical fortress has changed in recent times and what implications this has in terms of security programmes.

Causes of security breaches

- Intruders invading the premises.
- Foreign objects entering the premises.
- Offsite facilities.
- Eavesdropping by accident or on purpose.
- Assets taken out of the premises.
- Employee assaults.
- Neighbours as fences or vulnerabilities.

Preventive measures

- Designing the fortress.
- Securing entry and exit points.
- Attending to your guests.
- Inspections.
- Working with friends.
- Security on the go.

Defining the fortress

Not too long ago an organization could feel comfortable if it just protected its office premises. Many organizations had one or two office buildings, and these were the premises that needed to be protected. This was followed by the age of globalization and global organizations, which resulted in organizations with multiple physical locations spread across the globe. This required organizations to be more creative about how they protected their fortresses. In many cases, it was not possible for an organization to 'own' all of its global spaces; rather, the organization used facilities or space rented from local property management partners. The age of globalization was followed by tremendous advancements in information and communication technologies, leading to the concept of virtual work. This put further strains on organizations to protect not only their global offices, but also assets that were used in transit and at the homes of employees, etc. As noted in Chapter 3, an organization must have adequate measures to avoid technology hiccups. We shall not revisit those issues here, but you need to be mindful that they play an important role in protecting the fortress.

These changes in the nature of physical premises point to several interesting trends. First, organizations have more physical space to protect than ever before. Second, the number of access points into an organization has increased drastically because of the spread of organizations. If an organization is located in only one place, there is conceivably only one access point. On the other hand, if the organization is spread out, then there are multiple holes for entry. As I shall discuss, one of the issues of having multiple access points is that an organization is only as strong as its weakest link.

In many global organizations, security policies are written only in English, which is a problem. Employees in locations such as Cairo, Egypt or Beijing, China will neither understand these policies nor have a way to implement them. Hence, those wanting to get access to an organization could try entering from these vulnerable points.

Third, there is a move towards renting space rather than owning space. Owning office premises is an expensive proposition, and hence most organizations today rent space. For instance, an organization might rent eight floors in a high-rise building. The critical issue here is the interdependency of security policies. As noted at the beginning of this chapter, if your neighbours do not have adequate security programmes, a compromise at their end could come back to haunt you.

The final point is that physical security breaches are still easy to orchestrate and are often undertaken, many times without a hitch. These efforts are easy to pull off, as there are few eyes watching for these efforts when compared with the eyes watching for technology break-ins.

To summarize, while the nature of organizations' physical space has undergone change in recent times, this does not diminish the need to protect the fortress. If anything else, the need to protect the fortress has become ever more relevant.

Security breaches

The security breaches that occur in the context of physical security penetrations are by far the most interesting and creative. This is where traditional ingenuity and the old methods of simply attacking human holes come in. While technology greatly helps in the planning and even the execution of these efforts, these efforts are largely human. Skilful and tactical humans are needed to pull them off. Most organizations have fallen victim to such efforts, whether they want to admit it or not.

Intruders invading the premises

One of the most common ways for a security breach to occur is for an intruder to physically enter your premises. Once the intruder is in, it is as easy as taking things and walking out with them. Within the circles that I roam, there are several interesting stories about how intruders have taken advantage of organizations. Here is one story. Two people posing as reporters entered the premises of a large firm to interview the VP of Research and the CEO. During the day they spent at the company they were able to elicit a large amount of information about the firm and relay this information to competing organizations. The firm did not realize it had been had until two years after the incident, as the executives interviewed were too busy with daily matters to follow through and get feedback on how the interviews were being used for a story.

Here is another case, which happens to be a personal one. I have used well over 30 disguises to enter organizations. All of these attempts occurred in cases where the organization in question had asked me to penetrate its perimeters, and in over 90 per cent of these cases, the security units at the organization had been warned that someone would be attempting a break-in.

Here is the easiest way to enter office premises. Have a fake badge made that resembles the layout of the IDs used by the employees, and then dress up like an average employee, whether this means wearing a suit, or going business casual and wearing slacks and a shirt. Then place the badge on your belt with the back of the ID facing out. Get a friend to do the same, and then pretend to be deep in discussion as you walk by the front door of your organization. Chances are high that the security guard will not disturb your conversation. (To be extra sure, wave to the guard and ask him how his day is going.) Another way to enter a building is to do what I described in the opening chapter of the book. Organizations are careless about how they scrutinize the people that enter their premises.

Once an intruder makes his or her way into your organization, getting access to material is quite easy. For example, in one case after I entered an organization, I looked for the telltale empty desk of a person on vacation. Desks of people who are on vacation are easy to spot: there is normally dust on the screen; the papers also have a layer of dust as they have not been moved in a while; and if there is a cup of coffee, you can smell how stale it is. After seating myself at the desk, I proceeded to call the operator. On the operator's phone, the name of the employee on vacation came up. I then was able to get all kinds of information and connect to all sorts of information sources. Before anyone realized what was happening, I was busy briefing the CEO about 10 things the company was working on that were considered confidential.

It is better to keep intruders outside an organization rather than try to track them once they have made their way into it. Here is another example to illustrate this point. A company based in Toronto, Canada posted a job opening for an administrative assistant for its research division. A competitor based in France decided to use this as an opportunity to get an in at the organization. The competitor had an employee based in its Toronto office apply for the job. The applicant doctored material on her CV and made sure that the application would be attractive to the recruiting manager. As the competitor expected, the candidate was called in for an interview and was eventually hired. This employee spent one year relaying information back to the competitor, and when the year was up, she turned in her resignation. By the time the organization realized this breach had occurred it had already committed and/or invested $10 million in efforts that were not going to pay off as expected, as the competitor had the upper hand. Moreover, the organization could never find enough evidence to prosecute the imposter.

Foreign objects entering the premises

How did the anthrax scare hit your organization? Did your mailroom manager get nervous? Were there meetings about how to avoid the fate of the US postal workers? Remember that the perpetrators of these acts have not been caught or even identified. The anthrax scare pointed out flaws in how mail is handled in most organizations. Organizations lack appropriate processes to screen incoming mail and ensure that it is safe for transmittal. However, physical mail is not the only thing organizations need to worry about. Think about other foreign objects that could be nuisances. What about mobile phones or pen-sized cameras? You do not need to be James Bond to use these devices to record sensitive material and take the material out of the organization.

In one organization, a visitor placed a recording device in one of the meeting rooms. This device (I omit the details here as I do not want to encourage others to try it) costs about $200 and is readily available in most electronic gadget stores. The device was used to transmit voice conversations that occurred in that room. Needless to say, a lot of sensitive information made its way out of the organization. Other kinds of foreign objects that can cause security havoc include weapons. As will be discussed in the section on employee assaults, weapons can cause grave harm to employees if they are brought onto organization premises.

Organizations need to have processes in place to limit the entry of foreign objects that might harm the intellectual assets of the organization. Here is one more example to illustrate this point. During a technology company's negotiations with a vendor, an administrative assistant brought a digital recorder into the room. The intent of bringing this device into the room was innocent: to help take good notes and draft the minutes of the meeting. All parties in the room knew that the conversation was being recorded. During the meeting, participants would state, 'Do not record this in the minutes, as this is off the record,' and then would proceed to make some very sensitive statements. These statements included remarks against competitors, other executives, past projects and so on. The assistant lost the digital recorder three hours after the meeting. Guess what? The last time I checked, no one had recovered it! If the recorder were to get in the wrong hands, the company would open itself to several lawsuits. Foreign objects can pose grave risks to the intellectual assets of an organization, especially when the objects are not handled with the utmost care.

Offsite facilities

One of my favourite parts of travelling and giving talks to companies is the exotic locations where these meetings take place. Board-level meetings, corporate retreats and brainstorming discussions occur in places that are supposed to stimulate the mind and allow for free thinking. This normally translates into holding meetings at nice resorts, near good golf courses or facilities for water sports. This is all fine and good, and I encourage you to continue with this practice. However, I ask one question: how secure are these locations for discussing sensitive material relating to your company? The answer? Not too secure!

Here are some nice stories to get you worked up a bit. Enter a hotel, any decent hotel where you would think business meetings take place. Now go to the board where the schedule of events is listed. Do you see anything there of interest? Most organizations are stupid enough to list their names and the types of meetings that are taking place, and the best part is that they even give you the room locations. Here is one of my favourites: 'Board Meeting – Strategic Mapping – Company XYZ – Room 101'. Could you give out any more hints? Now, here is where things get a bit crazier. One executive was hurried in preparing his talk during a retreat. He forgot to print out copies of his presentation for his peers and thus rushed to the hotel's business centre. Frustrated at the speed of the computers at the business centre, he hit the print button multiple times. The problem is that he picked up only the first copy from the printer and hurried to get it photocopied; he left behind five more copies of his 'Strategic Efforts and Key Initiatives' presentation.

Here is another story. How many of you use microphones during meetings? In one case, an executive was speaking – screaming might be a more accurate description – into the microphone during his meeting, and no one seemed to be bothered that the entire talk could be heard a few rooms away. It did not help, either, that the talk was an evaluation of why the company had lost tenders on several key projects.

A lot of security breaches happen on offsite facilities. These facilities are easy targets, as there is little security. Consider the following: chambermaids at one hotel were caught taking digital photos of business papers. The executives who were the targets of these assaults were frequent visitors to the hotel and often bragged about the work they did. The chambermaids found a way to use the information to their advantage and increase their weekly earnings. In addition, offsite facilities are open and accessible to the general public. Anyone can enter a hotel and roam around. The chances that you will be stopped or harassed are minimal, especially if you look busy and fit the image of a tourist or a business executive. Finally, most organizations cannot exert control over the security programmes at hotels during offsite visits. There are some exceptions to this, such as for a visiting prime minister or president, but for most of us, our control does not stretch that far. Hence, most organizations do not bother to get involved with offsite security management, thus leaving themselves vulnerable to lurkers and snoopers.

Eavesdropping by accident or on purpose

How do office rumours get started? One way is people hearing things they are not supposed to hear. They hear pieces of information and then let their imaginations run wild, thereby creating a rumour. Then they engage their closest friends to help pass the message along. In the arena of intellectual asset protection, there have been numerous cases of people hearing about sensitive matters because of poor choices in the security around these conversations. Here are some examples.

A company was considering a strategic realignment effort. Some of the global divisions of the organization were not performing as well as expected, and some tough decisions needed to be made. During one meeting, a group of executives was discussing the fate of the European divisions. Two employees eavesdropped on the meeting and got snippets of information. One of these snippets was the statement that the London office would be closed down. These employees decided to share this information with their friends, and soon there was all-round panic. There was only one problem: the two genius employees had got only half of the message. A decision had been made to close the London office, but this was being done not to get the company out of England, but to move the offices to Liverpool or Manchester. The firm had clients close to these cities and could lower its operating costs by relocating. However, by the time the organization could clean up the rumour, a lot of damage had already been done.

In your organization, how are secure conversations carried out? Do you have secure locations? Do you know when and where to have such conversations? Simply closing your office door is not enough. As the adage goes, the walls have ears. What about those office windows? Do you have a few peeping neighbours? Having secure places to conduct conversations is very important. Here is one other case to get you thinking. A law firm had offices in a high-rise building in a major metropolitan area. During one of its cases, the law firm representing the adverse party decided to engage in some creative strategies: it hired a consulting firm to gather competitive information on its legal adversary. In order to accomplish this goal, the consulting firm rented an office in the vicinity that had a good view of the first law firm's conference room. Through use of some creative surveillance equipment (such as binoculars) and some talented individuals (such as lip readers) the consulting firm was able to extract a lot of good information.

Assets taken out of the premises

In several cases of information leaks I have investigated, it was found that employees had taken material off corporate premises. Most of the time, the leaks did not happen on company premises, but when the asset was outside. For instance, as we discussed in the chapter on technology, an employee might take a laptop containing sensitive company information outside the company, only for the laptop to get lost or stolen. In other cases, disk drives, most commonly USB drives, get lost by employees. These are non-trivial issues. For the most part, paying attention to the guidelines provided in the technology chapter will help address these issues. However, there is one other form of asset leak that needs to be considered; this form of leak occurs when two employees engage in sensitive work outside organizational premises.

Consider the following case: two executives decided to be productive and make the best use of their morning commute into work. These executives lived in the suburbs of Chicago and took the same train into the city. The commute on the train was about an hour long, a good amount of time to be productive and try to get some work done. The executives decided to use the hour to work on company matters and thus avoid or reduce the need to meet at the office, which, they hoped, meant they might be able to leave work early. The only problem was that the matters the executives discussed on the train were sensitive, and a junior employee working at a competing organization regularly travelled on the same train, in the same carriage as the executives. This junior employee was made privy to all of the executives' conversations, and relayed information to his superiors. To the surprise of the executives, their company lost its tenders on four consecutive projects.

Upon discovering how information was being leaked, I advised the executives to engage in a slight act of deception. They discussed false information for a whole week and allowed the junior employee to relay this information back to his superiors. The competing firm used this false information in formulating its bid for the next project, and as expected, did not win this project. Soon the competing firm realized that we were on to them, and we can hope that they learnt a lesson about not eavesdropping.

The point remains, however, that the eavesdropping by the junior employee would not have been punishable by law. Some might consider the employee's actions to be slightly unethical, but when you leave yourself this wide open, you deserve to be penalized and taken advantage of. Most organizations do a poor job of tracking how intellectual assets leave the organization and what employees do with intellectual assets outside the premises.

Employee assaults

In recent times we have seen a lot of crazy things happen in workplaces. One of the scariest and craziest things we have seen is employees who go on the rampage. There have been numerous incidents like this in recent times, especially in the United States. Employees enter their work premises and go on shooting rampages, hurting their co-workers. What is even worse is that even schoolchildren have taken up these practices. There have been several incidents of children going to school with weapons and attacking their classmates and teachers. This is a serious issue. From the perspective of protecting intellectual assets and securing the premises of the organization, these acts represent one of the gravest forms of insecurity. If your employees, the core intellectual assets of your organization, cannot be safe within your organization's premises, there are serious holes in your security programmes.

Employees do not work well when they are scared and intimidated, and hence it is important to have a friendly and safe work environment. Not all employee assaults result in physical altercations. Some of the most dangerous assaults can be emotional and psychological. At one manufacturing plant in the Midwest, female employees were constantly harassed with overt sexual gestures and mistreated on the job by their male counterparts. Even more troubling, this issue was not dealt with by the management for over two years, when a select group of female workers went to the local newspaper with their story. Needless to say, the company faced a slew of lawsuits and fines, and more importantly had to spend a great deal of effort cleaning up its image.

Neighbours as fences or vulnerabilities

As noted earlier, most organizations do not have the luxury of a secluded place that they own, and thus worry only about their own security. Instead, most organizations rent office space. They rent space in buildings, industrial parks, warehouses and so on. This translates into having neighbours. Neighbours, as we all know, can be a blessing or a curse. Good neighbours are hard to find. An ideal neighbour will be one that we can talk to, share common experiences with, and count on for help. I have been quite fortunate these last few years to have excellent neighbours. I am most aware of how valuable they are to me when I am travelling (in an average year, I get on over 100 flights). When I am away, my neighbours ensure that my mail is not left outside, so that people will not detect that there is no one home. They watch my car and move it, should there be any need to do so.

For example, in Chicago the city occasionally restricted parking on one side of the street for street cleaning and required that all cars be moved. There was only a 24-hour notice to move the cars. Hence, if I was away, my neighbours gladly moved my car. Moreover, in times of distress, good neighbours can be great help. For instance, at times when my phone did not work or I needed help, my good neighbours always offered help. Now, just imagine if I did not have a good neighbour: my life would be quite miserable. I would always be stressed out, would never have time to get away, and would just not have a good person to count on to secure my little fortress. Similar dynamics occur with organizations.

Consider the following case: a group of tenants in a building felt the brunt of a disaster when one tenant experienced an employee rampage in its office. Even though the rampage was restricted to one organization, employees working in other organizations on other floors of the building were affected. In another case, an embassy started drawing unwanted attention from a group of protesters who did not agree with the policies of the embassy's country. For about a month, the rest of the tenants sharing the same building as the embassy experienced the protesters' frustration. Employees of the other tenants had to see the protesters as they entered and left the building, and several of them were harassed by the protesters. At one point, a protester managed to get into the building and threw a rock through the windows of the embassy offices.

Unfortunately, situations like these are not rare. Securing the premises of one organization requires that due attention be paid to the security procedures of neighbours, and that care be taken to understand the threats faced by neighbours. The impact of cascading failures can be quite severe. Here is another example. In one building, a tenant had a fire in its office premises. The staff were not trained to respond to this event: the three people nearest to the fire did not know where the fire extinguishers were. Soon the flames grew in strength, and by the time the fire department arrived, the damage was quite severe. The fire was contained to two rooms but affected the floors below and above. The floor below was rented by a different tenant, and the room that was damaged for this tenant was where it stored its computer servers. Needless to say, the disruption to this tenant was as severe as it was for the organization that had the fire.

Preventive measures

The above-mentioned security breaches are only the most common ones, and are not meant to represent an exhaustive list. It would take a lot of time to cover an exhaustive list. The good news is that if you can address the above issues, then many of the other breaches become less of a risk, as you have significantly limited their chances of occurrence.

Designing the fortress

When considering the design of your office premises, do not forget the security dimension. A well-designed office space will be inviting, calming, stimulating and also secure! Most organizations focus on the first three attributes, leaving security as an afterthought. Here are some important points to consider.

Segment your office floors based on access to intellectual assets and different kinds of personnel. For example, it might be wise to have your R&D group on a different floor – and maybe in a different building – from your public relations department. Why? The R&D department will be working on sensitive material, and you do not want visitors with whom the PR department interacts snooping around. Similarly, the HR department, which manages relationships with the external world, should be on a different floor from product design and engineering.

In addition to segmenting office spaces, you should control access to the office spaces. For example, by using ID badges, you can limit who is in a certain space. Not all employees need to roam around the R&D facility. Some organizations limit access to floors by ID badges. ID badges are swiped on the lift for access to the designated floors. Other organizations take security a step further: they restrict who can access lifts by ID badges. An ID badge is required to call the lift. ID badges can be colour-coded for easy inspection and can also be programmed to limit access. For instance, a visitor's ID badge should be a different colour from an employee's badge.

In addition, sensitive areas, such as locations where computer servers and employee data are stored, need to be monitored 24 hours a day, 7 days a week, 365 days a year. These rooms should be fitted with video cameras to record personnel that come in and out of these facilities. Some organizations rightfully take an added step of precaution: access to these rooms is provided only if you are accompanied by one other person. Thus, there are normally two people who need to be there: one person who has work to perform, and another who is there to monitor. Not surprisingly, the other person is normally a member of security personnel.

In designing an office, one of the most important design considerations is the meeting rooms. Best practices dictate that meeting rooms be, at the minimum, soundproofed. In this way, no one outside a meeting room can eavesdrop. It is also advisable to distinguish meeting rooms with a higher level of security. For example, in one organization, there are meeting rooms specifically designated for sensitive conversations. In these meeting rooms, there are no windows, no electronic equipment is permitted, and there is a person outside monitoring traffic around the meeting, among other sorts of precautions. There should be meeting rooms for welcoming visitors (I discuss this in a later section) and meeting rooms for recreational and other social purposes. For example, it's nice to have the lunchroom or cafeteria in a room that has a nice view and that gets excellent sunlight (this cheers people up). Employees should be instructed, however, about what conversations can happen here, and more importantly, what conversations should not take place here.

The final design considerations are the entry and exit points. Entry and exit from the building should be limited. It is best to have one entry point for personnel and a separate one for goods. The entry point for personnel should be used by all employees, and this is where inspection of IDs and other checks should take place. Similarly, there should only be one entry point for goods (such as mail, packages and equipment). Having multiple entry points makes the job of security a nightmare, as there are just too many places for a breach to occur. All entry and exit stations should have CCTVs to monitor the traffic flow.

Securing entry and exit points

An organization must have procedures in place to track the items that come in and out of the organization. For instance, one way a security breach might occur, as discussed above, is through sabotage to physical mail. Organizations need to ensure that their mailrooms have security procedures in place. The mailroom is one entry point from the external world. At the basic level, a process for deciding what mail to allow in and what to do with questionable items needs to be in place and ingrained in the minds of the mailroom employees (Duffy, 2004). Organizations with good mailroom security policies clearly outline the following:

- What items can be mailed (such as official correspondence) and what items cannot (such as sensitive material like business plans, food, personal letters).
- Who has the authority to mail what kind of artefact (80 per cent of employees should not be allowed to mail items out of the organization) and what kind of mail can be received at office premises. (For example, using your office address to receive your spouse's birthday gift that you ordered online is not appropriate.)
- Who has access to the mailroom. The mailroom should be a highly secure area, and only employees who have business being in the mailroom should be allowed there; ideally, there will be a small window to provide access to the external world (such as other employees and mail/courier service personnel), similar to the access provided when you withdraw money over a bank counter.
- Protocols for handling the mail. It should be clear to all employees how packages and envelopes should be addressed. For instance, correspondence should have the name of the sender, the receiver, and a valid address. There should be guidelines on destroying mail, such as how envelopes should be shredded after use. Protocols should also cover details such as how to handle ambiguous items: for example, whether an employee should be called to see whether he/she is expecting something, and whether the mailroom has the right to open mail to check for contents.

Some organizations have far more detailed practices for handling mail, but at the bare minimum the above issues need to be addressed. The nice thing about working through a mailroom security policy is that it will get you to think about managing the other items that enter and leave your physical perimeters. For example, the ideal organization will have a policy that addresses the kinds of artefacts that employees can bring onto premises and the kinds of materials that can be taken off premises. We covered the technological dimensions of this in a previous chapter, but monitoring physical artefacts is also important. For instance, if you enter a highly secure government building, your bags are searched. Bags are searched for recording devices, harmful devices like guns, and anything else that might be suspicious. Moreover, in these installations, movement of electronic equipment (such as laptop computers and disk drives) is not permitted. All material stays within the confines of the organization, except under very rare circumstances.

Access controls are also important. Every thing, human or non-human, that enters or leaves the premises needs to be tagged and monitored. Some might consider this to be overly drastic, but I think otherwise. Employees that enter an organization should have access badges, which they should be required to use to swipe in and out of their work spaces. Under no circumstances – not even if an employee enters the premises with a spouse or a parent – should an exception be made. In one organization, there is a sign at every door that reads, 'All employees must swipe in and out. Failure to do so will result in immediate termination of employment – no exceptions.' This is a very powerful statement, and it reminds employees not to allow others in behind them. This organization learnt the value of security through an unfortunate incident. The organization was a facility that provided women with birth control options, and needless to say, there were some opponents to the organization's mission. One day, an intruder made his way into the premises and went on a rampage, destroying equipment and causing havoc. The intruder was allowed in by a senior manager who did not check for ID and allowed the intruder to tailgate the manager onto the premises.

Access controls should also be placed on sensitive equipment and documents. Today, through developments in radio-frequency identification (RFID) tags, it is possible to track physical artefacts. It is beyond the scope of this book to go into the details of implementing this technology, but trust me when I say that your IT department has already been thinking about this issue. The important thing to remember is that RFID tags can be used to track assets as they enter your organization. For example, you can place them on ID badges to track the movement of employees, or on labels to track the movement of documents. Tracking things as they come into and leave your organization is extremely important, as this is the first line of defence against security breaches. You want to ensure that you know exactly who is on your premises, just as you want to know exactly where on your premises a particular person or artefact is located.

Attending to your guests

Guests come in and out of organizations all the time; while most guests are invited, some just might be crashing the party! An adequate security policy will treat invited guests with respect and warmth, while throwing out gatecrashers and deterring them from trying to come back. An organization must have a policy to address how it screens visitors and manages their visits. Here are some guidelines to follow.

All guests should be at office premises for official business only. Under no circumstances should visitors be allowed into the organization past the reception area without an escort. Some organizations follow a policy whereby an employee is required to get permission from supervisors (managers) to bring a guest on premises. This permission should be given in the form of written authorization that clearly outlines the purpose of the guest visit, what areas of the company the guest will be taken to, and who will be the escort for the guest. These requests should be handed to the security office, which should keep a log of this information and use it during the visit to ensure that the visit is handled with care.

Guests should be asked to provide two forms of identification. At least one form of identification should be government issued, so that the chances of fraud are minimal. The IDs of guests should then be held by the security officer, while a visitor badge is assigned. Visitor badges should have the appropriate access controls (such as RFID tags, unique identifiers, and colour coding that distinguishes them from the badges of regular employees). Only upon completion of the visit, when the visitor badge is returned and the escort signs the visitor out, should the visitor's ID be returned. In case the visitor misbehaves, at least you retain some information on him or her. Moreover, holding a person's ID acts as a clear indication that security is taken seriously and sends a message to visitors not to try anything.

Organizations should severely limit the kinds of items that a visitor can bring onto its premises. In my opinion, no form of electronic devices should be allowed. Objects like phones, pagers and laptops should not be allowed on the premises. A visitor should be aware of these guidelines, and it is the responsibility of the escort to ensure that the visitor knows of them. To be courteous, it is always good to have a few phones and workstations available should the visitor need to check voicemail or e-mail.

Needless to say, these should not be connected to the proprietary infrastructure of the organization.

Prior to a visitor's arrival, personnel in the areas that will be visited should be notified that there will be a visitor on the premises. This notification should serve as a notice to put away confidential matters, to be aware about not conducting sensitive conversations around the visitor, and also to just be alert about how matters are conducted. Some organizations go a step further and place signs that state 'Visitor on premises', so anyone that even casually walks by the area is made aware that a guest is present.

Ideally, an organization will have a separate set of meeting facilities for meeting with visitors. One financial organization that I consulted for had an entire collection of empty offices reserved just for their meetings with visitors. In these offices there was never any sensitive material around, nor could the visitor get a sense of any of the other operations of the organization, as these were not visible. If you plan on doing this, then the above point about notifying staff about the arrival of visitors becomes somewhat irrelevant, as you now have premises that are exclusively used for interacting with visitors.

These policies taken together will help you avoid having uninvited, trespassing guests or guests who go astray on premises, and will ensure that you can account for who is on your premises.

Inspections

One of the most difficult tasks in protecting intellectual assets is building a process for inspections. People do not like being questioned or having their items inspected. Believe me, I understand this, having to pass often through the usual security screening at airports. But this is a normal part of our operations. The cost of not doing these searches is just too high. We tolerate this annoyance as we know that there is a larger good that comes out of this nuisance: our safety and security, we hope, are protected. Organizations face a similar challenge. Organizations that opt not to have inspections are just placing too much faith in all their employees to be good. While I would like to hope this is a reality, my experiences tell me to 'respect but suspect'. Thus, I advocate that organizations should have processes for conducting inspections. That being said, there is a right way and a wrong way to do something.

First, one thing that really annoys people is preferential treatment. This takes multiple forms. For example, an executive's luggage is not checked while an engineer's bag may be heavily scrutinized, or there is a gender or age bias in how searches are done. Any sort of preferential treatment raises people's blood pressure, so the first thing to do is to establish a consistent and uniform policy. You should have a policy that states that all employees' bags will be searched, and if things do not look right, they will be put through further searches. Be clear about this. Do not allow ambiguity to set in.

Second, the other thing to be mindful of is not allowing inspections to be so cumbersome and time-consuming that they prevent people from attaining their task objectives. This translates to being mindful of the traffic that is entering and leaving your premises. During rush hours in the mornings and evenings, have extra staff to help ease the traffic. Similarly, during these times, have your most pleasant and best-trained staff working. This is not the time to train a new person! I remember an experience where I was queuing to enter a large high-rise commercial building. The building had a process whereby all bags and employees went through a security check. There was only one problem: the security guard who was attending to this matter was being trained at 8 am. That was not a wise thing to do! The building was disrupting its employees' schedules and adding to their aggravations.

The third issue that you need to be mindful of is that any inspection that follows a set process is breakable. As long as I know your security process, I can find a way to break it. Hence, there is always a need for randomness. Random inspections need to be conducted, and simply making employees aware that these inspections will occur is a major deterrence that prevents security breaches. Remember, all of the assets, intellectual and physical, that reside within the organization belong to the organization, so you should have no issues getting access to them. As discussed in the chapter on technology, you can routinely scan e-mail messages or check phone records. Most organizations have access to this data by the very fact that they provide these resources to employees for official use. Similarly, physical inspections of property should not be a problem from a legal standpoint. However, when these do occur, the staff conducting these inspections should be on their best behaviour. Employees will be annoyed, and to some degree, they have the right to be: it is a disruption to their work. However, if these inspections are done in a courteous manner and employees are reminded that they are being done in the best interests of the organization and that people are chosen randomly for inspections, this may calm their tempers a bit, especially if they think you are singling them out.

Organizations need to be mindful about their policies on inspection. Quite a few organizations go to extremes. Their most common trajectory is starting out with no inspection policy and then, when a breach (or, in some cases, breaches) occurs, swinging to the other extreme of all sorts of inspections and scrutiny. This is a reactive stance (we discuss this issue in greater length in the chapter on crises), but for now it is important to note that reactive gestures are seldom welcomed by employees, nor are they respected. It is best if the inspection policy is one that is thoughtful, and implemented during a time of normalcy rather than after a breach.

Working with friends

Securing physical spaces, especially when you are in close proximity with neighbours, is not an easy feat. You need to go and talk to your neighbours about their security policies. Unless your neighbours are really nice, chances are you will get only a little bit of good information. Cooperating on security efforts is not easy to achieve. Your neighbours will not want to divulge too much about their plans or, in the event that they do not have plans, they will not want you to be aware of that. So how do you get around this?

If you are renting space in a building or another co-located entity (such as a research park), the first thing to do is check with the security team of the owners or managers of the space. If the people who are leasing or managing the space do not have such a team in place, then run fast and choose another property. If you cannot run, then twist the arms of the owners to get a security team in place. You should work with (or more accurately, through) this team to ensure that all your neighbours have their security programmes in order. One way might be to call a meeting of the directors or managers of security programmes at each of your neighbours. During this meeting, you should be able to start a dialogue. Pay particular attention during the dialogue to the issues discussed in this chapter and the chapter on crises. You will want to make sure that your neighbours are not allowing friends to roam freely in the building. Agreements need to be arrived at for questions such as, what happens if a person is found wandering? Who will take responsibility? Who are the points of contact at the other organizations? Ensuring that your neighbours are following good practices to secure their physical space is important.

In addition, you need to make sure that your neighbours have plans in place for dealing with crises. We discuss the protection of intellectual assets in times of crisis in the next chapter. Pay close attention to those details, and ensure that you know how your neighbours have planned for crises. A common best practice is to get the various tenants to share their crisis management plans with each other. In this way, all are made aware of how to address situations as they arise. As a simple example, if your neighbour has a fire and plans to evacuate employees from the area as a result of a potential biohazard, you should know whether the biohazard might endanger your employees as well.

Finally, the best policy is to choose your neighbours wisely. Depending on the kind of business you are in, there are certain neighbours that you just do not want to have. For example, it is quite risky to have your offices in buildings that house consulates. You also want to stay away from a bioengineering lab, unless you are also a bioengineering facility. Similarly, you do not want to be near local government offices, where there is a lot of traffic and the possibility of nuisance is high. Conduct environmental assessments of your localities. Do your homework to identify previous security breaches that have occurred. Conduct background checks on your neighbours. This can be done by using the power of Google. Search the news releases of these organizations, and see whether any of them have been victims of recent attacks or are drawing the wrong kind of attention.

Security on the go

A good security programme for intellectual assets will have plans in place to protect assets when they are outside the traditional physical confines, such as of those of the office. As noted in the previous section, breaches of intellectual assets can happen quite easily during offsite meetings. These breaches must not take place, and unless an organization can secure these locations it will not do the organization any good to have meetings offsite.

To protect intellectual assets with security on the go, the first thing to do is to ensure that the security team knows the purpose of the offsite meeting. If the meeting is a simple team-building exercise you probably do not need a lot of security. However, if it is a meeting of your board, you had better have the security programme in place. Communication with your security team is vital.

Once the need for security has been established, the next step is to choose the locations of these meetings wisely. Obviously, you will want to go to a place that is enticing and nice. You do not have to sacrifice on this point, but be smart about it. If you do choose to go to a resort, ensure that the resort has a security team in place. Have your security team talk to the site's security team. Make sure the site has contingency plans in place, check whether you can keep the names of the attendees confidential, and see whether you can pay for extra personnel to help your guests when they arrive. Basically, plan the programme with mindfulness about security.

The next step is to ensure that you communicate with the meeting attendees. Just as you should track what comes in and out of your physical premises, track what is going to be taken to the meeting, and ensure that it is either destroyed at the meeting or taken back to the office. As much as possible, tell your attendees to carry the bare minimum and only essentials. Also provide people with instructions about connecting to technology resources (see the discussion in the previous chapter). For example, set up a printer for attendees rather than having to go to the business centre. Set up a secure network for them to connect to the internet.

After this, make sure your attendees keep their business quiet. For instance, do not hand out folders labelled with the name of your organization or the purpose of the meeting. These get left on tables and can attract the wrong attention. Do not post the locations and purposes of your meetings around the hotel. Attendees should be given a phone number they can call or a room number they can visit to get this information, should they forget it. Then, clearly inform your attendees about what are safe spaces for holding sensitive conversations (for example, a golf course can be ideal as long as you do not have people next to you) and what are not (such as the bar). Ensure that employees do not leave sensitive materials in their rooms. If needed, have a place where they can store sensitive materials during the day. This might be the same location where you provide them with technology support and where your point of contact is located.

Make sure there is no one wandering around near your conference rooms. Ensure that all material that enters a conference room is legitimate. Do not allow anyone not known to you in these rooms. If you hold meetings in certain countries, it might be good to check for electronic bugs and recording devices. If possible, do not allow food to be brought into the meeting rooms; require people leave the meeting rooms to eat, and secure the rooms during this time. Bringing food in provides ample opportunity for unwanted snoopers to enter.

Finally, have a mechanism by which employees can report suspicious behaviour. If items get lost during the meetings, have a point of contact employees can report this to. You must be able to attend to these issues in a quick and agile manner. Following these guidelines ensures that your meeting will be productive and pleasant, while also ensuring that security will be maintained.

Closing thoughts

This chapter has provided guidelines on how to protect the physical space of the organization. It is very important that an organization pays the same amount of attention to physical security as it does to other forms of security, such as IT security. Failure to secure the physical fortress can be quite costly. As noted earlier, one of the beauties of physical penetration is that you can leave without a trace. This is quite difficult to pull off in other environments. Hence, if you do not know who is coming in and out of your organization, no amount of technology security is going to save your intellectual assets. The final warning should come from this: most of the time, it takes only an average person to penetrate physical security, while technology penetration requires a higher degree of sophistication. What does this tell us? There are many more people for you to worry about who can just walk right through your doors, smile, take something, say 'Thank you,' and leave, than there are hackers and crackers to disrupt your information systems.

6

From abnormalities to crises

Organizations are vulnerable to a wide assortment of crises. These crises can be natural (such as floods, hurricanes and earthquakes) or outcomes of human actions (such as terrorism, wars, hostage taking and kidnappings). In recent times we have seen a whole slew of crises. It is astonishing that as societies have advanced, the incidence of crises has increased rather than decreased. It is also interesting to note that organizations are no more apt at preventing, curtailing, or responding to crises in comparison with historical times. For instance, today we have more incidents of terrorism, cybercrime and other forms of criminal activity. Moreover, naturally occurring incidents, such as floods and droughts, have also not become any less severe or frequent. There is an ongoing debate that industrialized societies have damaged the environment to the point where we are now witnessing negative consequences such as global warming. Needless to say, crises are not going to go away any time soon.

Organizations today have to demonstrate agility and resilience in how they face crises. Agility is the ability to mobilize resources in a proactive manner to address changing conditions in the environment. The mobilizing of resources should occur in an effective and efficient manner, with minimal overhead and disruption to ongoing operations. Resilience is the ability of an organization to repair itself and restore impacted areas after crises. It is essential that an organization be able to repair itself and restore disrupted functions in a feasible manner: that is, with minimal cost, effort and suspension of activities. Organizations that fail to demonstrate these characteristics will be continuous victims of crises, and will not be in a position to compete in the environment.

In the context of intellectual asset security, it is important to note that crises are an important factor that an organization needs to prepare for. It is not sufficient to prepare for issues of intellectual asset security just in the context of employee work practices, business alliances, or other conditions that occur during normal operations. Securing intellectual assets during times of crisis is very important. Consider the case of events such as during times of war (like the recent incursion into Iraq by the United States) and natural disasters (such as Hurricane Katrina in the United States). What transpired soon after these incidents was absolute chaos. Citizens were frustrated, there was widespread looting and theft, property was destroyed, and havoc was unleashed. Now, just think about the case of the organization that never prepared a security plan that could be mobilized. Do you want to be the CEO of this organization? Probably not! Why?

First off, there was ample warning of both these impending events. In the case of Katrina, weather reports dating back several days to weeks prior to the hurricane were signalling the upcoming weather patterns; in the case of Iraq, anyone who was at all tuned into world politics could have predicted the outcome. Thus, CEOs of organizations cannot claim that these events caught them off guard. Now consider the location of these crises. Katrina's major wrath was unleashed in Louisiana. Was it a surprise to anyone that the levees would break? In the case of Iraq, organizations operating in this geographic area were well aware of the threats they faced. Hence, if these organizations did not have a security plan in place, this should not be excusable and might even be considered gross negligence. Finally, consider the following: if organizations did not have a backup plan for operations and were banking on the assumption that all would be well in their primary area of operation, wasn't that just too much wishful thinking?

It is absolutely essential to have a plan of action to protect intellectual assets during crises. During disasters, organizations are reactive, emotionally charged, and are seldom thoughtful in their actions. This is natural, given the nature of the impact of what they have just witnessed or been affected by. This is why it is important during times of normalcy to think through the issues that might arise during a disaster, plan for them, train for them, and then be prepared to call on routines as needed during the event. An organization that has not planned for a disaster will exponentially complicate and increase the severity of the impact of the disaster, as a result of its incompetence and inability to act in a timely manner.

In this chapter I outline the security dimension of protecting intellectual assets during crises (see the boxes). We shall begin with an exposition on organizational crises. It is important to realize that while crises may come in different shapes and sizes, their underlying features are fairly constant. For example, the process by which a crisis develops is the same for a natural or human-induced incident, and even the same for a small or a large-scale incident. Hence, an appreciation of the nature of organizational crises will create a framework from which you can plan for the security operations. The various forms of intellectual asset security concerns will be outlined next. I conclude by outlining various mechanisms that can be used to help plan for and secure against intellectual asset losses during crises.

Understanding the beast

- Recognizing signals.
- Preparing for the event.
- Responding to the event.
- Learning and bolstering the organization.
- Intellectual asset losses during crises.

Preventive measures

- Contingency plans.
- Scenarios.
- Immediate response capabilities.
- Learning capabilities.
- Virtual monitoring stations.

Understanding the beast

We must understand the nature of crises in order to uncover the security issues that arise during these incidents and to put in place preventive mechanisms. Organizational crises can be defined as rare or unexpected events that cause stress to an organization (Shrivastava et al, 1988; Mitroff, 1988; Pearson and Clair, 1998; Hensgen et al, 2003; Hensgen et al, 2004). 'Rare', 'unexpected' and 'stress' are all subjective terms, and need to be evaluated in the context of the organization and the environment in which it operates. For instance, for a financial trading firm, losing a few million dollars on a given day of operations might be considered normal. However, if the corner pub lost about 20 per cent of the same amount (as a result of fire or vandalism, perhaps), the incident would be considered a major crisis. Hence, what is considered rare in one organization may not be rare for another. Any event needs to be evaluated by the context of the organization and the specificities of the impact before a judgement can be made about whether it constitutes a crisis.

Crises have the element of surprise. By this, I mean that the entity does not expect it. Unexpected events can take one of two forms. One form of the unexpected occurs when an entity is totally blindsided by an event. There has never been any thought put into the possibility of the event, and the event strikes. Imagine, for example, that you go into a bank one day to take care of your financial matters. Suddenly, the bank is getting robbed. To you, this is an unexpected event, as you did not think about or prepare for this. You did not go to a class where you were trained in how to deal with bank robbery situations. For the bank, the robbery is still a crisis, but it has prepared for this kind of event. Bank tellers and managers take classes and learn how to address these situations. The bank witnesses the other type of the unexpected: here, an entity thinks about an event but assumes that the probability of its occurrence is so low that when it does happen, it manages to surprise the entity.

Any event that pulls an organization out of its normal mode of operation and causes it stress may be considered a crisis. Consider the case of an organization that experiences increased interest in one of its products. Let's say the organization was expecting to sell 100,000 units over the life of the product, but the day the product was launched, over 90,000 units were sold! This event will be viewed as a crisis, albeit a good crisis, as the organization can now receive greater revenue from the product. The crisis is that the organization now must figure out how to mobilize its resources to increase production. While crises do not necessarily have negative consequences, all crises do cause some level of stress, as they require organizations to shift and move resources under strict time pressures.

It is important to be in an open frame of mind when thinking about crises. As noted above, crises do not always have bad or negative consequences. Whether an organization can take advantage of changes in the environment as opportunities, or is forced to accept them as negative crises depends heavily on:

- how it has recognized the signals of the impending event;
- how it has trained and prepared for the event;
- how it handles the event when it materializes;
- how it learns from the event;
- how it uses the lessons learnt to improve future operations.

Recognizing signals

Numerous postmortem analyses of crises have come to two universal conclusions. First, all crises have been preceded by warning signs, which, if recognized at the right time may have helped the affected organization avoid the crisis or, at the bare minimum, lessened the impact of the crisis; and second, most organizations do a hopeless job of processing signals from their environment (both internal and external), and as a result, are unable to prevent and manage crises. Consider the case of the 9/11 attacks in the United States. Long before the event there were numerous signs of the impending terrorist attacks (Desouza and Hensgen, 2003a, 2003b). Most of these signals were not processed in time by the various intelligence agencies, and as a result, the activities of the terrorists went unnoticed until it was too late. In financial crises, such as the bankruptcy of Enron, or industrial crises, such as the Bhopal disaster and Exxon Valdez oil spill, the warning signs were present but went unnoticed. The natural question to ask then is, 'Why?'

Warning signs go unnoticed for several reasons.[1] First, most organizations have a poor understanding of the sources of information in their internal and external environments. A source of information can be thought of as any entity, either physical (such as a human or a machine) or logical (such as a team or department), that emits information. Information emitted may be of varying types (for example image, text, sound), forms (structured or unstructured), volumes, and frequencies (Desouza, 2006; Ramprasad and Rai, 1996).

Consider the case of an organization trying to understand threats to its intellectual assets. These threats may come from internal sources (for example, an employee might go on a shooting rampage, injuring or killing co-workers) or external sources (for example, a competitor might release a new product, making the intellectual assets of the organization less valuable). Information about these signals can also come in from multiple channels: we can get information from discussions with employees, news feeds on the internet, newspapers, discussions at conferences and trade shows, and discoveries in academia, among other sources. The challenge to the organization is to understand clearly what information sources it needs to pay attention to. This is no easy feat, as the sheer number of sources that an organization needs to attend to has increased in recent times. Advancements in technology have made it easier for us to collect a greater volume of information with greater granularity, but organizations still must take the first step of identifying the sources of interest. Otherwise, it will get useless information from unnecessary sources. Recall the adage, 'Garbage in, garbage out': if an organization does not receive good information from its sources, it will not fare well in the activities of crisis management.

The second challenge is to ensure that the organization pays due attention to the information emitted from the sources. Today, most organizations are inundated with information. Information overload is common, and this trend is not about to change. Most organizations suffer from attention deficit, and hence cannot focus on important signals, as their capacities for information intake are stretched to their limits. Consider the common case of the executive managing several projects. During the course of a single day, the number of e-mails he or she receives may number in the hundreds. Chances are high that the executive will not get through all the e-mails on any given day. Moreover, in terms of allocating time to information sources, there will be a bias toward reading e-mails from a boss or peers first, and then, if time permits, reading e-mails from those lower in the proverbial food chain (such as employees who report to the executive, or employees who report to a project manager who then reports to the executive). Now consider the nature of signals of impending crises: these normally come from the frontlines of organizations, from employees who are interacting with the critical work processes or customers. If the executive does not pay attention to these signals, chances are high that they will go unnoticed until it is too late. In a recent case of workplace violence involving an employee who went on the rampage and shot his co-workers, it was discovered that there were e-mails to senior executives from the assailant's peers, as well as from the assailant himself, containing warning signals. None of these e-mails received any attention until too late.

The third challenge faced by organizations is to interpret signals in an open and creative manner. Most of the time, organizations process and look at signals in a highly narrow and specific manner, thereby missing the big picture. Some organizations rely too much on history and thus always process signals using the context of history: that is, if a signal led to a certain outcome in the past, the signal will be expected to lead to the same outcome today and in the future. Unless an organization is working in a static and unchanging environment, this kind of thinking is flawed. Dynamic environments, which characterize the contexts in which most businesses operate, undergo changes on a continuous basis. Hence, the information that is emitted from a source needs to be analysed in a dynamic context.

The simplest example can be taken from the world of national security and government intelligence programmes. Today, information emitted from a source needs to be understood and evaluated in a highly localized context of the specific environment and time period. In the past, information was analysed at a higher level and within one environment: the Cold War. This thinking has no room in today's operations, as each culture, country, time, person and so on adds many dynamics to the evaluation of a given piece of information.

Falling prey to the history trap is easy. For example, most organizations that are blindsided by competitive moves often claim that they never saw them coming. What they really mean is that they never thought that the information they were gathering on their competitors was actually signalling X when they had assumed, on the basis of historical records, that the outcome would be Y. Take the case of global terrorism. Preceding the 9/11 attacks, most pundits believed that the primary motive for the takeover of commercial airlines was to capture hostages. 9/11 woke us up to the reality that the terrorists' goal is not taking hostages, but destroying human lives mercilessly. There was a fundamental failure of imagination in the intelligence communities to interpret signals in an open manner. Tom Clancy and other writers had constructed more creative plots in which terrorists used airlines as weapons of mass destruction.

As we can see from the above, the issues involved with processing signals before an impending event are critical. If we manage to understand and analyse signals optimally, we have several options in addressing an impending crisis. We could, if possible, prevent the crisis from occurring. In August 2006, the British security service acted on information in a timely manner to prevent large-scale commercial aviation attacks. The authorities arrested a group of individuals before they could carry out the bombing of commercial aeroplanes using improvised liquid explosives. This is a case in which information was used in the appropriate manner to prevent a large-scale human-made disaster. When it is difficult, if not impossible, to prevent a disaster, we can work to mitigate the effects of the event. Natural climatic events such as hurricanes can have devastating impacts; while not all the impacts, such as loss to property, can be minimized, the loss of life, which is more important, can be avoided, if not reduced, if there is early warning of the incoming crisis and people have ways to evacuate.

Preparing for the event

Crises are meant to inflict shock. Shock can be thought of as any sudden incapacitation of an entity (person, equipment, organization or whatever) as the result of an event. The incapacitation may be for a few minutes, hours or days, or may even be permanent. The longer an entity stays in shock, the longer it will take to respond to a crisis. Consequently, the longer you take to respond to a crisis, the more time the crisis has to take hold and intensify its impact. While in a state of shock, the chance of a rational and well-thought-out response to events is minimal; what occurs instead is a flurry of haphazard reactions. In an interview, one executive related that facing the immediate reality that a condition of crisis has set in is tantamount to a teenager losing his or her first love. At first, the emotional and hormonal commotion is so great that the individual's entire value system is thrown into total confusion, and any attempts to arrive at an appropriate response or course of action will be unsuccessful. Feelings of anger, guilt, denial, betrayal and blame simultaneously affect any attempt to be rational, and any immediate actions in response to the situation are likely to be ill-fated and counter-productive to the interests of any of the parties involved.

Having a contingency plan is one necessary element in preparing for a crisis. Contingency plans can be called upon to prepare an organization for a crisis and to help the organization manoeuvre through the initial period after a crisis. For example, most organizations have plans in place before major launches of information systems. The project team will think through all the possible scenarios that might unfold during the system launch, and plan actions to address each of the negative possibilities. In addition, the team will chart out areas of responsibility for each team member, so that in the case of emergent and novel discoveries, there are designated people responsible for attending to those issues. For example, one person might be in charge of database connectivity, and another person will be in charge of the communications system. The crisis management literature has much advice on how to build such contingency plans, so I shall not cover this topic here. The important thing to note is that most contingency plans are plans about risks. They identify the most high-probability events that will cause the most damage, and then work to put protocols and policies in place to prevent these events. It is important to have a contingency plan, and many organizations do have such plans to address crises. However an important issue remains: most organizations fail to mobilize these plans during crises. It is not sufficient for today's managers to presume that the availability of a crisis plan means that the associated strategy, as a whole, will yield the desired results without careful regard to the parts making up the whole plan. Such posturing is detrimental to the organization.

Organizations need to be more cognizant in preparing for disasters; the first step towards this is to realize the shortcomings of relying exclusively on contingency plans.[2] Most organizations reduce crisis management to having a contingency plan. This plan is usually documented in a large book (or on a CD-ROM), and consists of procedures and protocols which need to be executed should a crisis occur. For many reasons, I consider these to fall under 'management by myths'. Here are the three most important reasons.

First, contingency plans provide overarching guidelines for dealing with foreseeable crises. But most crises that unleash maximum damage are hidden and never accounted for in crisis plans. A core characteristic of a crisis is the element of surprise. For example, airport baggage screeners prior to 9/11 had guidelines for dealing with suspect objects that looked like guns or bombs. But as we all know, the 9/11 terrorists used box cutters to accomplish their mission. Now baggage screeners are instructed to look for box cutters. What are the chances a terrorist will use the same device twice? Close to nil. They could, however, use a basic plastic explosive, which is not easy to detect. Will our baggage screeners be ready? Most likely not, because of the narrow 'in-the-box' thinking that plagues many organizations. This is what we found out. In 2006, the attention in airport security shifted to liquid explosives; this happened only after the plot to blow up UK airliners on their way to the United States was thwarted.

After the discovery of the plot, airlines restricted the carrying on of liquids. This was the only response possible, as they had not planned for this contingency.

A contingency plan is a prime example of in-the-box thinking. I had the opportunity to review the response plans of three Fortune 100 organizations based in the US Midwest. I found it surprising that the three looked 85 per cent alike. None of the plans did enough to account for the peculiarities of the organization concerned (see next point below); moreover, none had been adequately updated. The original plans were designed in the late 1980s; all three had only been slightly modified to reflect changes in the environments of the organizations. This is analogous to having a baggage screener look only for bombs and ignore box cutters or any other sharp devices, or even any liquid explosives that could be used as weapons in our current times.

While the nature of the abnormalities an organization has to contend with may not change over time, the manner of response does change. Consider the example of dealing with the press. Before the internet era, news reports on crises were delayed in reaching audiences. Today, news is delivered in real time. This can be good or bad, depending on how prepared an organization is in dealing with crises. A prepared organization can use the news media efficiently and effectively to mitigate the impact of the crisis and communicate effectively with stakeholders. On the other hand, an unprepared organization can open itself up to legal troubles, bad-mouthing in the marketplace and loss of reputation.

The second problem with existing contingency plans is that they are 'espoused plans'. These plans are written not in times of crisis but in times of normalcy. Hence, they are seldom applicable in the period immediately after a crisis, as they do not account for all the chaos and havoc. In most organizations, there are traditional fire extinguishers located near computing equipment. If a fire were to occur, using a traditional fire extinguisher on a PC would irreparably damage the computer. If a crisis scenario were executed, the organization would learn that it must replace the traditional fire extinguishers (which use a corrosive acid to contain fires) with a more appropriate type of fire extinguisher (such as a gas extinguisher that contains fires by sucking in the fire without causing any corrosive discharge). While having the right equipment in place is important, it is not enough. Many individuals in the organization have never been trained to use such a device; hence, expecting them to use it effectively during times of stress is absurd. One of my clients, a retired aircraft pilot, likened this to asking a pilot to read the aircraft manual while the plane is closing in on an altitude of 5000 feet during an emergency. Espoused plans work nicely on paper; however unless they are actually practised using scenarios, they will not be helpful in times of crisis.

The third problem with contingency plans is they do not do enough to assign roles and responsibilities. Most contingency plans are generic. As they are built mainly by consulting firms that seek to maximize economies of scale, they seldom address the peculiarities of each organization. For instance, there might be a line in the chapter on communications stating, 'Please contact your communication specialist for updates on the crisis.' Now pick 20 employees from your organization and ask them to identify the communication specialist. You will probably end up with 10 different answers. Imagine if during an aircraft emergency the passengers did not know who constituted members of the airline crew. This is not a rare occurrence in times of organizational crises. In 2005, during a fire in an office building in the Chicago Loop, people trapped in the building received communications on how to evacuate the building from an individual who did not possess adequate training and did not have the authority to send out such communications. As a result of this and other mishaps, the fire ended up costing more casualties than necessary, as individuals became trapped in stairwells and had no way to exit.

For the reasons outlined above, I have stressed to organizations that having contingency plans is not sufficient for crisis preparation. These plans might help, but only if we are able to respond adequately to the event during the initial period of the disaster.

Responding to the event

Unless you have prepared well for a crisis, there cannot be any hope or comfort that plans will work out as expected during the event. Most organizations lack capabilities for immediate responses to disasters. This can be described as the time just after a disaster hits and before a contingency plan goes into effect. For example, if your servers were hit by a worm on Friday afternoon at 4:46 (let's assume your company workday normally ends at 4:30 pm), what do you do between 4:46 pm and the time you can move your databases to your disaster centre? Do you have a protocol in place and ready to execute based on this scenario? Do you know whom to contact? What happens if the primary contact is unavailable? Who then has the decision-making authority? In my research and consulting, these questions trouble the most prepared organizations and the most informed of managers. If the crisis and/or information systems team has not practised this scenario in the past, chances are high that chaos and confusion will set in during the time of the crisis. This will reduce the potential impact the contingency plan will have on mitigating the crisis.

It is important for an organization to be able to respond to a crisis. Responses can be characterized as being short or long term. Short-term responses, as discussed above, are the moves that an organization needs to make immediately following a crisis. These responses need to be put into motion quickly, and their efficacy is gauged by how soon they take place to minimize the damage. Long-term moves are more detailed and require some deliberation. These moves are put in place only once the initial phase of the crisis is over and the organization has had time to 'stop the bleeding', so to speak.

For example, if a building is being consumed by a fire, the short-term response would be to rescue the people inside and contain the fire. A long-term response would involve estimating the loss and seeking alternative premises for personnel affected. Note that how well an organization does in executing the short-term moves will have a distinct and direct bearing on the longer-term moves. To continue with our example, if lives are lost as a result of the mishandling of rescue operations, the owners of the building may be so consumed with public relations and legal challenges that they may never have a chance to reconstruct the building or put their long-term responses into play.

An organization must have a way to respond to a crisis. Responses to crises must be thoughtful and careful, not reactive and haphazard. As will be discussed in a later section, one mechanism that has proven to be helpful for organizations in responding to crises is the use of scenario-based planning efforts. Unless employees prepare well for a crisis beforehand, you cannot expect them to perform under conditions of stress. One of the sayings my coach used to use is, 'If you train hard then you will find the game easy, and if you train easy the game will be hard.' Training and preparation is important in orienting people about how to react and attend to crises. The chances that misuse of knowledge will occur during a crisis will be considerably lower if there has been training in high-stress situations.

The unfortunate news is that many organizations do not spend the appropriate time and effort to train and equip their employees. The reason for this is simple: training employees is costly. In today's highly competitive world, pulling out resources from revenue projects is not easy, and thus, training becomes an afterthought. Only after organizations are hit, and hit hard, do they take the time and effort to train their personnel. As an example, I spoke to several bank managers whose branches had been robbed. Only after the robberies occurred did the managers take the training of employees for bank robberies seriously. In one case, it was only after the bank robbery that the manager hired a security firm to help train and bolster the bank's security programmes. Prior to this, the manager had his brother play the role of the security guard, even though he was never trained for the position.

Learning and bolstering the organization

Learning from rare events such as crises is an important organizational activity. Organizations that learn from these events, rather than sweeping them under the rug or blowing them out of proportion, will be better prepared to deal with future incidents than their peers. Learning from crises is a tricky and often cumbersome process. Several challenges for the organization exist in this regard.

First, there is a tendency to hide crises, sweeping them under the rug. I cannot tell you how many times I have been called by organizations to help them with crises, and most, if not all, of those times the event, its impact and other peculiarities were handled in secret and behind closed doors. If it could help itself, the organization did not want to alarm its employees about the crisis. Moreover, it did not want to alarm the external world. Imagine that a company has a breach of security during which an employee successfully embezzles $100,000. Upon discovery of this breach, most organizations would not call the police or report the incident; the reason is that the losses they would incur if this news were to reach the market could be 10 to 100 times more than the initial loss. Instead, the company would find ways to sweep this event under the rug. It might, for example, contact the employee and tell him that if he kept quiet about the incident, the company would not pursue legal action or would enter into some other kind of mutually beneficial agreement.

If, according to an organization, an incident 'never happened,' how is the organization to learn from the event? Even if there is, in such a case, a conscious effort to learn from the incident, the process of learning will be compromised by the need for secrecy. For instance, if lessons are extracted from the incident, their implementation may not be as effective as possible, as most of the organization will lack an understanding of the context in which these lessons were created.

Consider the following. A couple of employees of a manufacturing plant got into a fight after work at a local pub, off company premises. The two employees, along with other co-workers, had gone to the neighbourhood pub for drinks and had got into a heated debate. You might ask why the organization should care about this. Upon investigation, the organization was found liable, as organizational resources had been used to promote the social hour. The organization was considered to have condoned the event, and hence, it was forced to pay for some of the damage to the pub and the medical expenses of one of the employees. This event was then hushed up, as the organization did not want to attract media attention or open up the organization to more scrutiny. As a result, the two employees were urged not to talk about the event, and the organization settled the charges with the pub.

The next day, a senior executive issued a memo stating that no notices about social events could be posted on office premises. This was meant to address future issues and prevent the organization from incurring any further liability. However, the memo sparked a huge negative backlash from the employees, as many of them felt that the organization was not supporting their social engagements and did not care about their well-being. Needless to say, it was difficult for the organization to communicate the lessons learnt from this event as it did not want to bring attention to the event itself.

Hiding incidents lies at one end of the spectrum; blowing the lessons of a crisis out of proportion is at the other end. Let me share an example of this. In one organization, it was discovered that a couple of employees were using the communication infrastructure (telephones, internet and so on) for personal use (such as international phone calls to family members) and entertainment use (such as surfing pornographic websites and visiting chat rooms). Upon discovery of this, the organization's IT department blocked all external communication on the internet (that is, it only allowed access to corporate systems via the intranet) and required employees to receive authorization by managers to place international calls. Now was this an exaggerated response? Sure. Did it help the organization? No. Such reactions to crises limit the ability to learn. When an organization engages in such exaggerated responses it not only blows the crisis out of proportion, but in addition it annoys innocent employees and precludes any chance of influencing those employees' actions in a positive manner. Exaggerated responses take the crisis out of context and have the potential to cripple an organization.

Another issue that hinders learning is that organizations find it difficult to admit that they have made mistakes and must take responsibility for their actions. A common reaction follows most crises: the blame game. Everyone's first reaction to a crisis, after the initial state of shock, is to find someone to blame for the event; most of the time, blame is assigned to someone else. No one wants to admit playing a part in a crisis, and as a result, no one feels that they have anything to learn from the event. The reluctance to admit responsibility also gives rise to the propensity for crises to go unreported.

Assuming that learning from a crisis does occur, the next step is to ensure that the lessons learnt are reflected in the policies and procedures of the organization, so as to better prepare the organization for future incidents. Spending effort on learning from the crisis will pay off only if the lessons learnt are taken seriously enough to change the underlying behaviours of the organization. Consider a personal example. When I first arrived in Chicago in December 1996, I decided to drive a sports car. This was one of those bright ideas that come with being young. I had no experience with manoeuvring a car during a snowstorm, nor did I have a lot of experience driving sports cars. (A simple note for the non-automotive junkie: sports cars are not meant for driving during snow storms!) I ended up skidding off the road, as I did not know that pressing the brakes when you are on a sheet of ice is not the wisest move. After this incident, I did not stop driving in the winter. But I ended up being cautious about what car I drove in the snow, and if I was using a sports car, I had a better feel for the controls and learnt how to manoeuvre in unfavourable road conditions. Organizations more often than not fare poorly in incorporating learning from crises into their future operations.

One issue that plagues most organizations is forgetting incidents and lessons learnt. Soon after a crisis, most organizations are on a heightened state of alert. All attention is focused on the incident and its impact. Fast forward a few weeks or months, and most of the alertness will be replaced by traditional ways of doing business. You would never know that this organization had been hit by a crisis. The next headline will catch everyone's attention, and the learning from the crisis will not have time to be absorbed or to get any traction.

Consider the dynamics of reporting in the global media. One day, the attention of the world can be focused on a war between Israel and Lebanon; the next day attention is diverted to a foiled airline hijacking plot; and the very next day, this news is replaced by arguments among politicians. Similar dynamics occur in organizations. There is not enough attention and time given to a crisis after it has been attended to. As a result there is very little effort spent on incorporating lessons learnt from the event into organizational policies and routines. As a consequence, the organization is no better prepared than when the crisis first struck, and it will likely be the victim of a similar crisis in the near future.

Lack of adequate oversight from external stakeholders also prevents incorporation of learning into an organization's routines. Consider the case of government agencies: soon after a scandal breaks or a crisis occurs, what is the first thing to transpire? A committee or a commission is set up. Committees are normally involved in investigating the issue, coming up with learning points for the organization, and then making recommendations to the policy makers. They are seldom responsible for ensuring that the recommendations are heeded or implemented by the organization. As a result, most investigations are not treated with any seriousness and are just considered a normal nuisance. Similar situations occur in the business world. After a major crisis, the board of directors (or overseers) will usually commission an executive-level team to investigate the issue and make recommendations. But the ball stops there. Seldom is there any investigation into whether any recommendations were actually implemented, and if they were implemented, whether there is any valuable feedback to collect and reevaluate.

Learning and the incorporation of learning are serious tasks in which many organizations fare miserably. Not surprisingly, many organizations unfortunately go through the painful process of facing crises time and time again; some even face the same kind of crisis multiple times. For example, American car manufacturers have lost ground to their Japanese counterparts not once, but twice. Japanese car makers not only took over the market with more fuel-efficient vehicles, but in recent times, they have again taken the lead with new hybrid cars that use alternative fuel.

Intellectual asset losses during crises

Given the nature of organizational crises, we can appreciate the fact that managing crises is no easy feat. However, managing crises is not an impossible assignment. As noted previously, most organizations fare poorly in crisis management not because they do not know how to manage during these times of stress, but because they are unwilling to take the necessary measures to conduct themselves in a responsible manner. In this section, I shall focus my remarks on how such challenges in crisis management affect the security of intellectual assets. I highlight the various mechanisms by which intellectual assets are compromised during crises, then go on to suggest ways to implement preventive mechanisms.

First-order impacts

The most visible effect a crisis can have is the destruction of physical facilities and infrastructures and the loss of human lives. These outcomes are common in the case of natural disasters such as hurricanes and earthquakes, as well as in human disasters such as terrorist attacks. Intellectual asset losses occur in these situations in the form of:

- loss of critical personnel, who have knowledge housed in their minds;
- loss of information systems, both traditional (paper-based) and electronic;
- loss of organizational knowledge artefacts, such as physical processes;
- loss of infrastructure that connects an organization to its internal and external stakeholders.

While all organizations will mourn the loss of human life, the effects that an organization will feel from these loses will vary. One point needs to be made here. I am not talking about the emotional and psychological losses associated with the loss of human life. There is no method to quantify these losses, and while these losses are severe, I shall not discuss them here. In our previous discussions, we addressed the need to protect the knowledge housed in the minds of employees, as they might be victims of unexpected events. If an organization has backups of requisite knowledge and personnel who can take over the roles of lost personnel, the impacts it feels will be lessened. Having backups of knowledge and having employees who can step in and take over are both critical; one without the other is not good enough.

Consider the case of a financial investment firm that has its employees routinely record their knowledge and ideas, dealings with clients, trades made and experiences. Let us even assume that during a disaster, the technology apparatus that stores all this valuable knowledge is secured and allows the data to be used. Would a novice trader be able to get up to speed about making major trades simply by reading through this knowledge? Surely not! The trader would lack the necessary contextual details, the hands-on apprenticeship and so on. The knowledge will not be able to mobilize itself. Similarly, there is limited value in having trained personnel who are ready to step in, but who cannot access requisite knowledge about the ongoing happenings of the business and the intricacies of recent dealings. To continue with our example, imagine that the investment firm had experienced traders who could step in to make the necessary financial calculations and execute million-dollar transactions, but there was no knowledge about the risk preferences of customers, the nature of dealings with current customers or the risk tolerance in given markets. Such details are highly contextual to the given organization, the trader and the customers of the trader. Without these details, it would be impossible for a skilled trader to step in and start contributing to the organization in the short term. Hence, both requisite knowledge about the organizations' business processes and the expertise housed in the minds of personnel are important for executing business. If one of these is missing after a crisis, the chances of recovery are severely diminished.

Information and knowledge residing in technology systems is sometimes damaged or compromised during crises. About a decade ago, it was common for technology crises to result in complete loss of information from technology systems. These incidents are rare today due to the large investments organizations have poured into backing up their technology systems. An important issue needs to be considered here, however. While your organization might be prepared for technology disasters, are your business partners prepared? What about the information system of the small corner shop that you deal with? Protecting your own technology systems is not sufficient to feel comfortable. An organization may be impacted by failures on the part of its business partners and other stakeholders. Interdependencies in a coupled world can have significant impacts. Cascading technology failures, which occur when interlinked systems go through a domino-style failure sequence following disruption to one of the systems in the chain, can be quite severe.

Imagine, for example, that a customer's systems fail, and as a result, the system starts to output incorrect orders to a given retailer. The retailer's system, in turn, will take this data and feed it up to a warehouse, which might feed it to the original manufacturer, which may feed it to its suppliers, which may have to order raw materials from other suppliers. Wrong information from one source goes through the entire network and causes cascading disruptions to a number of organizations. Hence, it is always wise to ensure that your business partners have the appropriate measures in place to protect their technology systems.

In addition to losing information and knowledge that reside in technical systems, we can also lose information and knowledge artefacts in paper-based forms. These losses may be minimal, so long as the organization has made digital copies of papers that are of significance. Once again, prepared organizations will fare much better than their unprepared counterparts in lowering the impacts of these losses. It is neither expensive nor cumbersome today to scan documents and store digital copies. As a result, many organizations are spending a great deal of time and effort to preserve knowledge artefacts that normally are not captured in electronic form. For example, after group discussions and meetings, it is not uncommon for digital photographs of whiteboards to be taken and for these to be stored with the notes from the meetings. In a similar vein, it is possible to digitally record video conferences so that they can be retrieved at a later date. Obviously, these steps are not necessary for every paper or meeting. Failure to be discriminating when it comes to recording and storage will result in wasteful and futile efforts. Organizations must have strategies in place for recognizing which assets need to be captured digitally and stored, and how frequently.

Business processes and procedures may also be lost during a crisis. For example, an organization could lose an entire manufacturing plant or a call centre. The organization would lose the business processes that occur at these facilities. The challenge for an organization is to quickly find other locations where it can carry out the business processes with minimal effort and cost. In today's world of outsourcing and lean manufacturing, the loss of a single business centre can have devastating impacts for an organization. Most organizations do not have any slack resources or additional spaces that they can call upon; this is a consequence of going lean and engaging in 'just-in-time' manufacturing. As a result, the loss of a single centre could result in crippling shutdowns for the organization's entire production system. Moreover, today it is common for organizations to outsource large chunks of their business processes to other organizations. If a business partner is hit by a crisis, does the organization have a backup plan to get the work done and meet the needs of its customers? We have already discussed this issue in the context of business partners, but it is worth repeating here in the context of crises. Unless you have a plan in place to transfer work from one business partner to another in a swift and effective manner, you are flirting with trouble.

You could also end up losing infrastructure during a crisis, most notably communications infrastructure. Communication infrastructures include telecommunications, but may also include roads, seaways and airways.

For instance, after the 9/11 attacks, not only was mobile cellphone communication disrupted, but so was air travel and even ground transportation in the north-east United States. Disruptions to communication infrastructure make it difficult to coordinate response and recovery efforts. Disruptions can affect how we communicate information and knowledge between the organization and its internal and external stakeholders. For instance, if secure communication channels are disrupted, does that mean unsecured communication channels should be used to exchange sensitive material until secure channels can be established again? The prepared organization – that is, one that has worked through these scenarios before an actual crisis occurs – will know exactly what communication channels to use for which kind of knowledge transfer so as to minimize loss of knowledge and disruption to business operations (see the box).

Loss of critical infrastructure

As a simple example of why the need to practise and prepare is essential, consider the case of a prominent investment firm. I was asked to observe the firm's crisis management preparations and scenario exercises. One exercise simulated the loss of an entire office building, in which there were some survivors. The survivors then had to call a central number to report that they were alive and receive further instructions. The first run of the scenario went well, and all survivors dialled in and got through as expected. I then urged the crisis manager to give me a little authority to modify the scenario a bit to make it more realistic. I added the following condition: only one in every 10 phone calls made through a mobile phone would get through, and not all survivors would have a mobile phone available. This condition was added to simulate a more accurate situation. I also told the manager not to inform the participants of this change until the new run of the scenario was under way.

The scenario started just like expected: all of the survivors assumed they would have a phone handy and knew the number to call. Upon the destruction of the building and the identification of the survivors, only half of the survivors were given phones. The rest were told that their phones had been destroyed by heat and rubble from the disaster. They were then instructed to search for other means of communication. Those with the phones were busy trying to reach the designated number, but many could not get through as the lines were dead. Only two people were able to connect to the central number. Needless to say, the addition of my stipulations exposed great holes in the plans of the organization. The organization had not taken care to simulate an accurate scenario, and had never envisaged the true impact of the loss of communication infrastructure.

None of the survivors lacking mobile phones were able to find alternative means for communication in a reasonable amount of time. However, if the organization had informed them about neighbourhood stores, cafés and other places connected to a communications infrastructure (such as payphones, internet cafés, spots that got better reception), they might have been better prepared.

Second-order impacts

Second-order impacts from crises can be as devastating, if not more devastating, than the first blow. During crises, employees are unsure about the future of an organization. This is when they are most likely to leave their current employer and search for new opportunities. Consider the case of a major manufacturing organization whose employees one day learnt of an ongoing government investigation into the behaviour of three of its senior executives. The senior executives were being investigated for charges of corporate fraud, sexual harassment, and offering bribes to their foreign contractors. The investigation was supposed to be conducted behind closed doors and was not meant for public release. However, one of the witnesses cooperating with the government in the case broke her silence out of frustration with the slow pace of the investigation.

Soon the press picked up the story, and it was on every radio station. Employees entering the office that day could learn of the incident either by turning on their local radio station or by scanning their morning papers. This news item was the talk of the morning around the office cubicles and water coolers. The senior executives involved in the investigation were not allowed to release a statement, as their lawyers felt that any statement would have a negative impact. The organization's public relations department worked feverishly on releasing internal and external statements. An external statement was released by about 11 am local time (three hours after the start of normal business operations), and an internal statement was released at about 2 pm.

When the employees received the official statement on the incident, many of them did not believe it. They questioned why it took so long to come up with a statement. Was the organization trying to hide something? Were the executives really guilty? Was this going to be another Enron incident? The stock market was not helping the organization's cause, either: its stock price took a hard hit that day, and various news pundits predicted the impending demise of the organization. Within a few months of this incident, the organization had lost a large proportion of its knowledge workers. Most workers were not ready to risk their futures with the organization, and left for competing organizations.

What is most notable about this case is that after the story broke, the government disclosed that it did not have enough evidence to conduct a full-blown investigation. But the damage had been done. Employees were scared, fearful and distressed, all of which was the result of a crisis. The crisis was in and of itself not what caused the most damage; it was the organization's failure to assure and secure its knowledge workers that led to chaos, confusion, gossip and rumours, all of which resulted in even more anxious and confused knowledge workers.

It is very important for an organization to minimize the impacts of a crisis by having good communication mechanisms. Communication of direct and straightforward information will go a long way in minimizing the impact of a crisis. If the organization in the case above had had a plan to communicate a clear message in the event the story was leaked, it could have responded in a more timely and capable manner. Scrambling for communications at the last minute is undesirable. Most people in crisis situations communicate on the basis of incomplete information and in an emotionally charged manner. In the above case, reporters began interviewing executives and middle managers about the investigation. None of the interviewees had all the information, yet they saw this as their opportunity to get on the morning news and become famous. Many of them found it necessary to say something, and as a consequence, there were contradictory statements coming from various sections of the organization. The result was more disbelief and stress for those in the company.

The other issue that is critical in situations without a clear communication plan is demystification. This was highly problematic in the case above, as there was not enough information being provided to the employees. At 2 pm, the employees were told that there was an ongoing investigation into the activities of three executives, but not much else could be released at the time, as the investigation was ongoing. This is not good enough. By 2 pm, the employees had already heard this information numerous times from other sources; they wanted more from their organization. A more apt communication mechanism would have been for the organization to brief senior personnel about the situation in greater detail. (These individuals should have already been vetted by the organization for their ability to protect sensitive information.) These individuals, who are closer to the employees on the front lines, could then be the people with whom the employees could speak; they could also be the people who helped the organization deliver their message.

It is critical that an organization minimizes the loss of vital intellectual assets during a crisis. These knowledge assets are what the organization will desperately need to get the organization back up and running. Losing knowledge assets during a crisis just exacerbates the impacts of the crisis and slows down the process of recovery and restoration. Moreover, if the organization's stakeholders (such as customers and business partners) see the movement of key knowledge personnel out of the organization, their confidence in the organization will start to fade. This may lead them to pull out their business, making it even more difficult for the organization to return to a state of normalcy.

Third-order impacts

During a crisis resources are moved from their designated areas to areas of impact. For example, law enforcement personnel may be asked to leave their traditionally assigned zones or districts to help out in affected areas. When a factory suddenly receives a larger-than-normal order for products, it may have to call upon workers to put in overtime, move personnel around, and even shut down other operations so that it can focus on meeting the greater demand. The logic behind the transfer of resources from their original positions to impact areas is that these are temporary moves. Resources are relocated to give immediate attention to a crisis and to more quickly return the organization to some level of normalcy. In cases where resources are not quickly mobilized to the places of need, a crisis can escalate.

For example, what unfolded in the hours after US troops originally entered Iraq and captured the city of Baghdad? Looting, destruction of property, and rape. The United States was too busy celebrating its brief victory, and failed to put adequate resources into securing the area.

Similar chaos unfolded in the days after Hurricane Katrina hit Louisiana.

Diverting resources is an important part of responding to a crisis, but this should be done in a measured manner, as it pulls away resources from other areas of an organization. In addition, there is the case of attention diversion during a crisis: the attention of personnel moves from daily details to the crisis. The crisis will be the main thing on everyone's mind, while everything else takes a backseat. Executives will not have the intellectual bandwidth to address daily matters; their schedules will have to be realigned and time reallocated to address activities that surround the crisis.

Combining near-complete attention on a crisis with the mobilization of resources to address the crisis invites knowledge losses to occur in areas that are not getting any attention and that have limited resources. The art of deception is based on the premise that you can deceive someone most easily by having him focus on things that distract him from your true intentions. There is seldom a better time for a crook to conduct unscrupulous tasks than in the hours, days or weeks following a crisis. Knowledge losses that are the outcomes of planned and deliberate acts by humans are best conducted when there are not so many eyes watching. For example, during times of crisis, normal security protocols may be in a state of hiatus. People may get access to sensitive material and may feel the urge to use these assets to their own advantage. Competitors watching an organization go through a crisis may plan surprise moves to catch the organization off guard. For example, it is not uncommon for competitors to go on the offensive when an organization is going through a corporate scandal. Competitors may use this opportunity to showcase how they conduct work, lure away customers of the organization, and just make it difficult for the organization to get back on its feet.

It is very important for an organization to plan how resources will be mobilized during a crisis. The plan must strike a good balance between attending to a crisis and conducting the day-to-day business. Obviously, it may be difficult or even impossible in the case of certain events to conduct day-to-day business, but even in these cases, the organization must have a plan to balance resources. Almost no organization can afford to focus completely on the crisis and ignore other areas of operations; doing so just invites the development of a new crisis.

Another common third-order effect of a crisis is the misuse of intellectual assets. Misuse of assets occurs when people are not in the right frame of mind or do not have the appropriate training to employ knowledge assets. This normally occurs as a result of one of two general conditions. The first is where an employee cannot perform a regular task under times of high stress and chaos. The second is where an employee is given a new task but lacks the requisite knowledge to perform the work. Both of these conditions are highly undesirable.

Intellectual asset misuse is dangerous for several reasons. Often, intellectual asset misuse occurs as a reaction, which, like any reaction that lacks thought, will always be poorly executed. Hence, knowledge misuses can actually exacerbate a crisis. Consider the case of the airline industry following 9/11. Soon after the terrorist attacks, the Transportation Security Administration requested airlines to provide passenger lists and other information on travellers; clearly, these constituted knowledge assets for the airlines. Many of the commercial airlines gave out this information as an obvious reaction to the heightened interest in national security. They never thought this action through. Soon after the story broke that airlines had released passenger information, many commercial airlines (such as Northwest and JetBlue) were hit by lawsuits and backlashes, as the disclosure of passenger information violated agreements with customers about confidentiality and privacy. This action, needless to say, caused a new crisis for the organizations. They not only lost the trust of customers, but also had to rescind earlier statements that they had not shared confidential passenger information.

Second, intellectual asset misuse can be dangerous. Consider the case of medical installations. During times of crisis, medical professionals who do not have all the necessary training may be thrown into situations where they are expected to act. This may be dangerous as, one, they may not be able to perform the medical procedures needed by the patients, and two, they may not be able to cope with the pressures of the situation. There have been cases in which medical professionals did not act with the appropriate care during a crisis and harmed patients rather than saving them, thus creating another crisis: a malpractice lawsuit, or a series of them.

Third, intellectual asset misuse can lead to undesirable longer-term impacts, which may be as severe as the complete demise of the organization. If an organization makes a great misstep during a crisis, that single misstep could compromise the entire organization. For example, in mission-critical centres, such as air traffic control centres and nuclear reactor monitoring stations, a misuse of knowledge can have consequences that are devastating.

One case that was quite troubling for me to witness was a start-up technology company, poised to make a big mark in biotechnology, which ended up closing its doors before it could even make it big. A few weeks before the launch of the company's product, three of its designers got seriously ill. The illness was caused by one employee who had the flu but decided to come to work anyway and ended up infecting his co-workers. With the three critical developers out, the organization faced severe crisis, as there was external pressure to release the product. Instead of doing the right thing and trying to delay the launch of the product, the firm decided to plough through and pass on responsibilities to the junior programmers. The junior programmers ended up making serious errors in the code, which made their way into the first release. These errors were so catastrophic that the four test clients who had agreed to try the new product ended up terminating their trials within two weeks, costing the company its reputation and putting the quality of its product – its primary intellectual asset – in question. The company never recovered from this incident and ended up closing its doors.

Preventative measures

Protecting intellectual assets during crises requires appreciation of the nature of crises and the security risks that intellectual assets face during these times. We have covered these two issues in the preceding sections. I now highlight mechanisms that can be implemented to secure intellectual assets. Several of these mechanisms not only help an organization better secure its intellectual assets but also help improve its capabilities in overall crisis management.

Contingency plans

Even though I am not a big fan of contingency plans, they do serve some important purposes. A contingency plan in and of itself is not sufficient; however, it is a prerequisite for doing other essential items. Each of the items that follow needs to be accounted for as well in any programme designed to protect against security issues during times of crisis.

Most contingency plans are based on simple calculations of risks. They go something like this. First, you enumerate all the possible risks an organization might face. In our context, this might entail making a list of the knowledge security issues that could arise during a crisis. The second step involves assignment of probabilities. Here we ask the question, 'What is the probability that a risk will materialize?' A probability of 1 means that the risk is almost certain to arise, while 0 signifies no probability of occurrence; and in the same vein 0.2 means low probability, and 0.9 signifies high probability of occurrence. Risks that have a low or almost no chance of occurring are given little, if any, attention, while risks that have high probabilities of occurrence are given due attention.

Third, we need to assign impacts or outcomes. Here we ask the question, 'If the risk were to materialize, what would be the outcome?' In the context of security issues, outcomes refer to the damage that might be inflicted on an organization by knowledge losses or misuses. Once the damages are calculated, we must then move to the fourth step, which entails deciding how much risk is tolerable. No firm will be able to protect against all forms of risk; the cost of doing this is just too high. Hence, the organization must decide what risks it will tolerate and address the rest. Tolerable risks are normally those that have the lowest probability of occurrence and that have the lowest impact.

The fifth step is to put in place measures to address the risks. These measures are the security procedures and protocols that we have been talking about in this book. The sixth step is to actually test out the mechanisms and make sure that everyone understands what they are. Here is where most organizations fail. Many will have grand-scale plans to address a crisis, but may never test those plans out (we shall address this issue in the section on scenarios below). The final step is to continuously revise plans on a periodic basis or when conditions in the internal and external environments warrant a revision. Outdated plans are of no use and can cost an organization dearly should a crisis materialize.

In terms of intellectual asset security, contingency plans need to account for several things. First, they need to address how critical assets will be protected. This can take the form of any of the preventive mechanisms we have discussed in the book. Second, they need to address the issue of how assets should be replaced should they become impaired or damaged. This is quite critical. An organization must think about the backup resources and reserves that can be called upon in times of crisis. Here is where organizations can learn from a special type of organization. Think of nuclear reactor operations centres and aircraft cockpits: these both represent mission critical operations (MCOs). MCOs are places where people conduct operations that are absolutely vital for an organization to realize its mission.[3] In the case of an aeroplane, activities conducted in the cockpit are central to the pilots' mission. Similarly, the control tower of an airport is an MCO that is responsible for the operation of runways, aircraft gates and hangars. MCOs are interesting to examine, as they do not witness disasters on a routine basis, yet are some of the most complex organizations. The way they conduct business and run operations allows them to prevent events from becoming catastrophic crises.

MCOs have several interesting practices in place, one being flexible knowledge architecture. MCOs take great effort to maintain flexibility in their operations. By flexibility, I mean that these organizations can organize, reorganize, dismantle and reassemble their assets in minimal time with minimal disruption to overall operations. This ability is very valuable in managing crises, as resources can be diverted to areas of concern immediately, which often allows MCOs to nip the crisis in the bud.

There are two contributing factors in creating a flexible architecture: first, having knowledge redundancies, and second, a mentality of constant disruption. Knowledge redundancies can be seen in the way members of MCOs are trained. Each member has not only an intimate knowledge of his or her job, but also working knowledge of colleagues' work. This is essential for mobilizing knowledge quickly and filling knowledge gaps during a crisis. A mentality of constant disruption puts everyone on their toes; disruption to normal business is not considered an exception but is expected. Hence, feelings of complacency and permanence are not present. Employees routinely switch and rotate jobs with their colleagues, which helps them appreciate the work their colleagues are involved in and promotes a greater understanding of how the overall system works.

Most organizations have compromised their capability to be flexible through the fad of downsizing (or rightsizing). Organizations place emphasis on being lean at the cost of being flexible. I am quite concerned about this, as lean organizations are good only for operating in known contexts. When dealing with a crisis, which most organizations have to do at some point, leanness is not desirable, as it lowers the number of resources available. We can use the analogy of a buffer. The greater the buffer (assuming that the buffer is ideally planned and executed), the greater the slack one has in dealing with a crisis. For example, if a grocery store has additional stock of a product, it can easily handle small surges in product demand. However, if there is no buffer, then small surges in demand may disrupt grocery operations and cost the organization in terms of sales and reputation.

Buffers in knowledge skills and assets should not be considered wasted or unwanted resources. There are smart ways for organizations to build these capabilities. An ideal way is to train employees in multiple functions and to solidify job rotation programmes. Employees should be encouraged to learn things outside their primary functions and get an appreciation for other job responsibilities. In addition, using simulations, which we discuss next, employees can be trained to apply their broad sets of skills to evade and manage crises and learn how to work in environments where disruptions are a normal part of business.

The third thing an organization needs to do is constantly test and retest its contingency plans. The organization must use scenarios to test its reflexes and stress points.

Scenarios[4]

Organizations must do more to imagine disasters and work through them with scenarios. Working through scenarios adds to the viability of an organization's contingency plans by putting the espoused plans to the test. Working with scenarios is critical for putting the plans into action and seeing how they hold up during times of duress and stress. Scenarios bring a sense of realism to the possible threats, dangers and abnormalities an organization might face. Scenarios can be handled in multiple ways: they can be physical or live demonstrations; they can be simulated using computer technologies; and they can also be enacted. Regardless of how a scenario is executed it must meet two goals.

First, scenarios should help reduce the shock of the crisis. Shock is the stage immediately following the impact of the crisis. A shock can put the affected entity in a state of unconsciousness (or semi-consciousness, depending on the nature of the impact). It is during the stage of unconsciousness or semi-consciousness that organizations make errors in responding to a crisis. Moreover, the longer the organization is paralysed after the impact – that is, the longer it takes to regain full consciousness – the greater the chances of the crisis escalating.

Second, scenarios should help individuals and organizations calibrate effective and efficient actions after the state of shock. After the initial shock wears off, organizations (and individuals) often conduct haphazard actions that exacerbate the situation. Reactionary actions are never wise, unless you have had ample time and opportunity to run through the plausible consequences. Running through scenarios provides us with room to test such actions and see their consequences.

The aeronautical industry does a resoundingly good job with scenarios. During the training of pilots, scenarios play several important roles. The first is to simulate the environment prior to the real experience. Before taking command of a real aircraft, trainees must learn the ins and outs of flying and the governing laws of physics in simulators. Simulators provide trainees with room to make errors and learn from them. Even though the consequences of errors are simulated, they help in getting the point across. A pilot must gain a good sense for the various components of the flight instrument panel, and learn how to determine the performance of the aircraft, monitor the flight plan and the travel routes, deal with changes in environmental conditions (such as turbulence), communicate with other stakeholders (the other members of the cabin crew, passengers, ground airport staff and so on), and most importantly complete the mission.

The second role scenarios play is to simulate crisis conditions. Simulators help pilots learn how to maintain control of a flight when things go awry: for example, how to fly when an engine is on fire, how to land an aircraft in times of emergency, how to communicate with ground staff during times of internal crises such as hijackings or passengers falling ill. This training is critical in building a good pilot. Imagine the following situation on a plane: the right wing engine blows out. The pilot does not immediately detect the area of damage. Guesses are made about why the aircraft is not performing normally, but because of a wrong diagnosis, an incorrect resolution is applied. The situation deteriorates. After a period of delay, the damaged area is discovered. Then the pilot and his co-pilots begin to scan through 900-plus pages of technical documentation on how to deal with the situation. During this time there are conflicts about who has responsibility over what. Communication with the cabin crew and passengers is haphazard. This situation would almost certainly lead to disaster. However, this seldom happens. Pilots have been trained to work through these scenarios. They have pre-programmed responses to many situations, which helps them save lives and mitigate the impact of crises.

Scenario planning has been used by businesses to deal with strategic issues, such as product pricing, marketing campaigns and human resource incentive packages. However, their use in crisis management and the management of technology disasters is weak at best. Apart from a select few organizations, no one pays much attention to using scenarios in the context of crisis management. Many complain that scenarios are too expensive to run, that the drills disrupt work practices, and that scenarios can instil unneeded fear in employees. At the end of the day, however, scenarios are your best bet at preparing your people to deal with a crisis.

Regardless of their nature and scope, scenarios must be realistic. They must give the sense of reality to the item of interest. Moreover, they must also welcome the questioning of assumptions and contexts. There is no such thing as a bad scenario; even the most improbable scenario will help an organization learn something. Errors made during a scenario exercise should not be shunned; they should be considered avenues for learning. Shunning errors is a sure way to waste a good scenario exercise. In the context of crisis management, this is especially true. If employees do not follow the outlined protocols in a contingency plan, we need to know why. It may be because of an incomplete contingency plan, a misinterpretation of the plan, or a flaw in the design of organizational processes.

A good scenario for simulating disasters must have five components. I list these in no particular order of significance. First, the scenario must address roles and responsibilities. Who is responsible for what? Who is the backup for a given task or activity? Questions such as these must be worked out. The last thing you want during a crisis is internal conflict. There is enough to contend with without making the situation worse with in-fighting and finger pointing. Having backups for each role and responsibility is critical, as chances are high that when a crisis hits, all your primary personnel may not be available.

Second, the scenario must address communication protocols. How will the organization communicate, and with whom? Who is responsible for communicating? There is nothing worse than haphazard communication during a crisis. Communications should be planned and delivered by the appropriate personnel. Communications normally take two forms, internal and external. Who is responsible for communicating to the internal members of the organization? What communication protocols will be used: e-mail, voice mail, a toll-free number or a website? How can individuals retrieve such communication? Managing external communications is equally important. The organization should have one front and face for the press and external stakeholders. Rumours, leaks, probes and investigations all result from poor communication with external parties, such as issuing multiple versions of a report or conflicting stories.

Third, a crisis scenario should address the issue of protection. How do we protect the assets affected by the disaster and mitigate further loss? If there is a fire in the building, how can we prevent the fire from spreading and make sure all personnel are secure? It is always wise to run through multiple scenarios and have two or three backups for a protection protocol, lest one should fail.

Fourth, the scenario should involve damage assessment. Knowing the casualties of a crisis is important. After the 9/11 attack, the death toll for the World Trade Center changed from original estimates in the neighbourhood of 10,000 to under 3,000 at the latest count. This was obviously poor damage assessment. Now consider the case of the Pentagon: death toll figures from that attack did not change much, and the reporting was fairly accurate. Obviously, the Pentagon had means for adequately detecting the loss of personnel. Timely damage assessment is critical for reducing the impact of the initial shock and also for calibrating immediate actions.

The fifth essential component of a crisis scenario is having the organization conduct operations without all of its resources. This is analogous to having an aircraft pilot land in the desert or with only one operational engine. Unless an organization has conducted an exercise in operating without all resources, the chances it will survive during a crisis are low. Running without all cylinders is a sure way to test the vulnerabilities of the organization and learn how to manage in times of stress.

Immediate response capabilities[5]

During the autumn of 2002 a series of sniper attacks around Washington, DC led to a local law enforcement crisis which drew national attention and interest. There were questions not only about whether the perpetrator would be caught, but also about how the situation was being handled by the authorities. Once it was established that the shootings were likely to be the work of a single person rather than multiple parties, law enforcement efforts focused on identifying and locating the sniper. A telephone 'hot-line' was established to obtain information from the public. On at least two occasions, the sniper phoned the hot-line and attempted to get past an operator to speak to operations command personnel. The operator, ill-equipped to handle such a request, thwarted both attempts. It is likely the operator was never trained for the situation in which he or she was asked to function. Whether the sniper was intending to turn himself in or would have provided information that might have expedited his capture is unknown. What is known is that a system intended to enhance information flow during a crisis situation failed because of a single fault that was built into it: placing an agent of limited capacity in the crucial role of gatekeeper to an entire operation. The sniper and his accomplice were later captured due in great part to the diligence of a concerned truck driver.

While there are numerous examples of unfolding events that were driven to crisis by the actions of initial responding agents, few illustrate this concept as dramatically as the nuclear disaster at Chernobyl. Several events were taking place simultaneously at reactor four of the Ukrainian atomic energy plant on 26 April 1986. The plant was undergoing annual maintenance and testing. At the same time, the city of Kiev requested to be taken offline, which required engineers to make adjustments to the reactor's capacity. These adjustments were made manually rather than mechanically, and individuals, all skilled, who were working outside of project planning made the decisions about when and how the adjustments would be made. In doing so, and because of a preoccupation with schedules, these engineers breached their own safety protocol that allowed automated systems to kick in. This effectively negated any manual attempts for correction or override that were being attempted elsewhere within the facility. In the early morning hours of 26 April, the roof of the reactor facility was lifted as a result of the ensuing explosions, which were caused by activities by a team of respected experts working under conditions of broken communication.

In analysing this case and many others like it, we find similar reasons that communication engagements went bad. The organizations commonly failed to put enough value and attention on their ability to communicate during crisis situations, or they did not completely understand the nature and value of communication in the period immediately after a crisis developed. Having a contingency plan that addresses recovery following a crisis is inadequate if there are no provisions addressing the crucial first response: that is, what circumstances must be communicated internally and externally, as well as how they are to be communicated, during the initial stages of a crisis and up until the full extent of the contingency plan effectively kicks in.

Proponents of emergency planning and contingency programmes acknowledge that crisis is always inevitable, and so they are constantly revising and redesigning plans to meet the changing parameters associated with new crisis schemes. Organizations generally assume that crises with serious consequences have a low probability of occurrence:

that is, neither the crisis nor the magnitude of its impact are ever realistically anticipated. Compare this with the actual occurrence of disasters with high consequences and high probability, which suggests negligence, as was likely to have been the case in the Bhopal disaster and NASA's *Challenger* tragedy. In many of these cases, there were opportunities during the initial stages of the impending crisis for responding agents – if they had been able to view conditions through the wider lens of organizational interests – to make critical decisions to minimize, if not avert, the crisis before it reached a critical stage. If no decisions or the wrong decisions are made, conditions become exacerbated at best, and at worst are likely to contribute to the problems at hand.

The conditions leading to wrong decisions or a failure to make decisions reside in existing emergency and contingency plans and/or in the execution of those plans. Current planning focuses on the 'big picture' and on creating a cohesive sequence of steps from initial execution to completion. These steps focus on minimizing the loss of life and property as well as establishing a timeframe for organizing the resources for response, establishing a location for response operations, and identifying the existing impact. Such plans are usually meticulous in detail and are expected, when executed, to produce similarly meticulous results for the organization.

When the Exxon Valdez oil tanker ruptured, there was a plan which, if executed within two hours, could have dramatically reduced the effects of the subsequent oil spill. However, initial responding agents decided not to implement the plan because their assessment grossly underestimated the initial crisis situation and its impact. On 11 September 2001, the World Trade Center buildings were struck within 15 minutes of each other by hijacked commercial airliners. An hour after the first incident, the Pentagon experienced a similar attack. No military planes were scrambled despite the President's message during the intervening time that the country had experienced an 'apparent terrorist attack'. During this time, the Executive office may have assumed that the military was taking reasonable preemptive precautions in defence of the nation, while in fact, instead of dispatching fighters, the military was most likely waiting for Executive direction or orders related to engaging civilian airliners. This sequence of events becomes more frustrating when one considers that the North American Aerospace Defense Command (NORAD) had trained for and simulated aircraft hijackings in which commercial planes might be used as missiles to target buildings. Their exercises included specific details about

From abnormalities to crises ■ 163

buildings that might come under attack, and included one scenario that suggested the Pentagon would be a target.

A critical function of an immediate response is to stop the bleeding from the crisis and to take a quick assessment of the status. The ability for an organization to communicate during this time period is critical.

Social networks exist in organizations, and it is essential they be represented in some manner other than a hierarchical chart that merely *implies* perceived communications. Generally, a formal organization chart is used to represent the implied communication structure that is meant to work for an organization and the defined paths through which information and communication is meant to move. There is a distinction between the perceived and actual communication lines that exist within the organization. Figure 6.1 shows the communication routes in a small organization. Rounded nodes represent individuals and lines indicate regular communication between two individuals. Note that the CEO of this organization is 'connected' fairly well to the lines of communication within the organization and is placed in the centre of the organization. There is a tighter group of communication paths at the top of the network than at the bottom. This would be important if these were two different work groups.

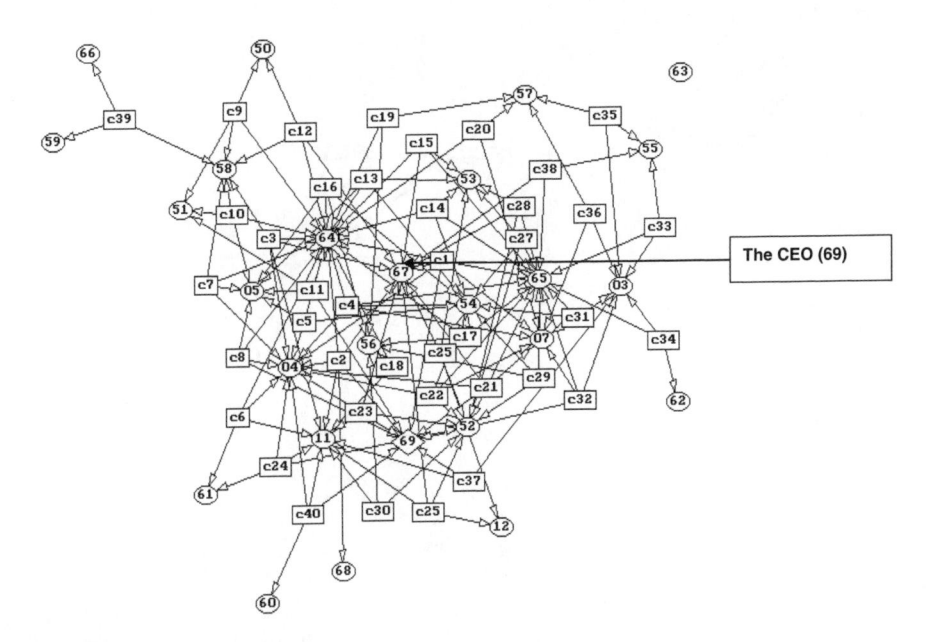

Figure 6.1 Organizational lines of communication

164 ■ Managing knowledge security

Figure 6.1 also indicates that there are individuals who serve as conduits to the CEO. That is, not all individuals report directly to the CEO; rather, they report to personnel in specific departments, such as marketing, sales and manufacturing, and those personnel in turn report to the CEO. The network represented above is a fairly well-connected group with no cutpoints (points at which if a connected individual was severed from the network, others would be cut off from all communications). Similarly, there are few bridges: that is, lines which, if removed, would cause the network to 'split'. Communication would continue between or among remaining individuals on either side of the split, but not to the organization as a whole.

Now consider what happens to the lines of communication at the impact of a crisis. The first change we notice is a dramatic decrease in the channels of communication because some groups or individuals are not directly involved with the unfolding crisis situation. Since some lines of communication are now severed, people who might be of assistance are unaware of what is happening. It would be particularly troubling if a crisis were developing in or around clique 7 in Figure 6.2, which represents what might remain of an organization's communications during the onset

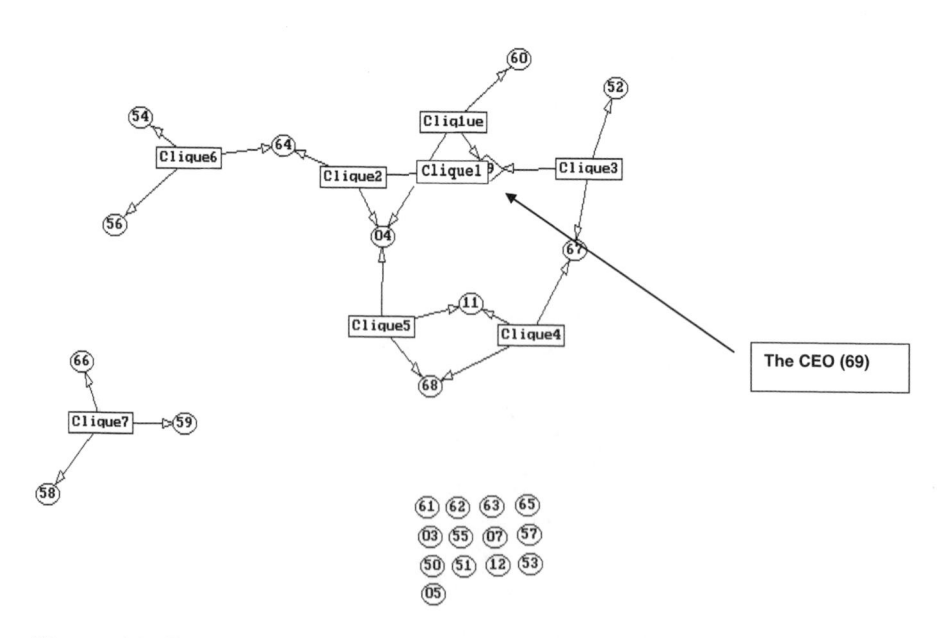

Figure 6.2 Communications lines during the onset of crisis

of a crisis. While there might be exchange of information, or perhaps speculation, about some problem with clique 7 via the remaining channels, the lines of communication to clique 7 no longer exist.

Although Figure 6.2 indicates the CEO (69) may be made aware of what is transpiring, there are many more isolated individuals who are effectively cut out of the communication loop. This indicates that although there is a fairly tight network overall, the structure for actually working as a team, for building towards a united organizational response, is not as strong. The chances for immediate recovery are determined as the crisis unfolds; it is at this point that a programme design must be implemented to avert further calamity before full implementation of the company's contingency plan.

Companies do not typically prepare employees for communication despite the fact that this very topic is often bantered about when 'improvement' meetings are held. Often, the only real thought on such preparation or training is done in retrospect, either after a crisis or following the discovery of some problem that might have been avoided if the proper steps had been taken initially. Alternatively, communication is considered in advance, but is thought of as a static event, which is unfortunate. Crisis examples provide evidence that there is at least one problem few contingency plans are equipped to handle, namely, the initial crisis–agent response impact syndrome. If this syndrome takes hold, decisions made in the beginning phases of an unfolding crisis will not only be in error, but will also be ultimately detrimental to the interests and stability of the organization (see the box).

Communication agreements

1. Use a social network application to define the organizational communication structure(s).
2. Determine hidden communication resources (individuals, cliques).
3. Determine threats to communications.
4. Identify communication strengths.
5. Review current contingency planning and align to identified communication network(s).
6. Develop a curriculum and implementation plan.

7. Provide training.
8. Evaluate training and based on the results, determine an operations schedule for full implementation.
9. Evaluate implementation.
10. Be available for follow up.

Learning capabilities

We discussed some of the unique features of MCOs earlier in this chapter. Another interesting feature of MCOs is that they are never satisfied with their successes; rather, they dwell on their failures. They examine failures systematically and thoroughly to come up with improvements to their processes and systems. Compare this behaviour with that of private sector organizations, where even small gains and successes are routinely exaggerated and disseminated all over the news media. When crises do strike, MCOs manage them and, more importantly, seldom forget them. MCOs take great care in conducting postmortems after a crisis. Postmortems are used to study how and why the overall system failed, what were the root causes of the failure, and how to fix them.

In my experience, private sector organizations after a crisis are quick to claim that they have reached a sense of 'normalcy' in business functionality. This forces them to divert attention, both internal and external (for example, media attention), from the crisis and what exactly transpired. One might say that postmortem analysis in private sector organizations gets swept under the rug, and everyone hopes the situation does not repeat itself. Writing postmortem reports should be ingrained in the organizational fabric. Postmortems should also be written upon completion of projects. These should be similar to after action reports conducted by defence agencies to debrief personnel about lessons learnt.

While writing postmortems is important, it is even more important to get personnel to use past lessons to improve the success of future operations. Organizations should implement incentives, as well as strict penalties, to encourage project managers, directors, managers and so on to review prior engagement reports before embarking on new projects. This minimizes the chances of repeating past failures.

Virtual monitoring stations[6]

Three types of information processing are critical in the management of signals. An organization must be able to generate decisions from informational signals, to move decisions and information across a variety of channels, and to learn from its past. A well-managed symbiotic information centre – a virtual crisis centre – is needed to bring these dimensions together and accomplish these three goals. The word virtual emphasizes its remoteness from the physical organization, since there are a number of security concerns about an onsite presence. Use of a different ISP to host the virtual crisis centre could provide the simplest solution. Virtuality also demands that all the tools and technologies for monitoring such signals be accessible via virtual means, such as the internet, PDAs, wireless devices or telephone communications. Once it appeared on 9/11 that Washington, DC was under attack, the US President and his immediate staff were moved to a remote control centre equipped with technology to monitor the developing situation. We suggest that similar (but less resource-intensive) arrangements be developed for organizations concerned with crisis evasion.

Unless an organization has a virtual crisis centre in place it will be very difficult, if not impossible, to monitor information signals in an effective and efficient manner. The need for a virtual crisis centre is even more apparent now, given our current economic and political conditions. Management of information is critical to the success of organizational efforts. Information today comes in multiple forms and formats and at a nearly continuous rate; failure to synthesize information in a timely manner will prevent us from building a real-time enterprise. Having a real-time enterprise is an imperative if we must compete in today's uncertain and fiercely competitive marketplace.

The first step to building a virtual crisis centre is to make an inventory of all sources of information with which the organization should be concerned. Information signals need to be gathered from relevant sources both within and around the organization. A number of automated tools exist for this task. Such devices include scanners, automated transaction processing systems, and identification devices such as RFIDs. Existing systems are becoming increasingly sophisticated and can now handle greater volumes of data at higher levels of detail than was previously possible. Recent advances in distributed artificial intelligence have led to the proliferation of intelligent agents, which act as representations of humans in electronic environments. Such devices are common in environments such as business-to-business transaction systems, negotiation software, supply chain management systems, search engines and web monitoring tools. Agents generate data when transacting business or on behalf of their owners, and are valuable existing sources that can be monitored.

The second step is to aggregate like-source information (that is, to build classes) and establish links or relationships between classes of sources. Those familiar with object-oriented design techniques will be aware of this approach. For example, in traditional batch processing systems of organizations, programs aggregate and process similar transactions together; single entries are available for multiple applications. At this stage it is important to ensure cohesiveness and proper coupling in systems. Each subsystem must be cohesive: that is, it must have one goal. The subsystem's level of cohesiveness is reflected in its ability to manage the class of data that is involved.

Links among subsystems must be coupled in a manner that facilitates a smooth flow of information while preventing extensive dependence on the other subsystems. This appears to be where most signals get lost during a developing crisis. While many organizations use a class of systems intended for enterprise resources (ERP), the architecture is not truly enterprise-oriented but rather represents a hodgepodge of inherited systems, sometimes recently installed with older equipment or from other organizations they have merged with or acquired. Rather than trying to integrate these systems in an effective manner, many organizations have tied them together loosely without any global concept in mind. This leads to poor information movement across departments and groups in the organization.

The virtual crisis centre should provide a seamless map of information movements across sectors of the organization. Integration of existing information processing systems is an important undertaking. We must strive to achieve the seamless flow of information through the disparate and heterogeneous systems of an organization. This can be accomplished by building pipelines or connectors. Translators also play a critical role. Translators are programs or devices that enable two disparate systems to communicate with each other. A translator either serves as a lowest common denominator in the sense of speaking a common language, or interfaces between the schemas of two distinct languages. We are not revisiting the general discussion of data integration cost-benefits from 15 years ago; we are calling for a judicious choice of crisis-relevant data connections between those systems not yet appropriately connected. Making sense of information from different information systems will become easier in the near future with the diffusion of markup languages such as XML, which do more to describe the data contained within information packets or objects.

The next step is to have adequate tools and technologies in place that allow for cohesive sense-making. Two elements are essential for accomplishing this. First, a repertoire of past signals and their effects should be catalogued so that an organization can gain cyclical information from historic feedback. Unless an organization can learn from the past, its chances for future success in evading crises are restricted. This requires a data or information warehouse which allows for interoperable and temporal databases. There is a need to be able to link to artificial intelligence sources, such as neural networks that will continuously learn new patterns and signal an impending crisis. Prototypes of such designs might study daily loads and traffic patterns, and signal when a server is expected to fail.

The second element of sense-making is having adequate decision support and planning tools to establish a repertoire of 'what if' scenarios. This practice facilitates the decision-making process by augmenting human processing, which has limitations. One of the key elements of decision support systems is their ability to aid in problem visualization or 'spatial' representation. Such approaches foster problem structuring by connecting the various components of interest, presenting the information in a meaningful manner and calculating costs of decisions. While information systems can aid in suggesting directed information or insights and deducing patterns, they cannot generate completely actionable meaning. The human aspects of tacit knowledge and experience with the problem domain are employed at this stage. We can have expert systems that automate reasoning and suggest actions at a rudimentary level, but human intelligence is still needed for more complex tasks.

The last step – the creation of the virtual centre itself – involves presentation and representation of the information. This is accomplished on the internet. The goal here is to design a website with all the necessary bells and whistles to make information presentable, much like the layout of a car's dashboard. The use of Active Server Pages (ASP) and other database export languages should make this relatively easy. The goal should be to make all necessary information cleanly presentable.

Lastly, you need to ensure the integrity and protection of the centre. While much of the centre can be made available to members of the organization, only a dedicated group of individuals should have the ability to modify the core architecture. Each person in the organization should be allowed to personalize his or her view of the system to reflect specific needs and tasks, but authorization determines who will have access, and at what level of security.

Establishing remote service in contingency planning and emergency preparedness comes with some expense. But this expense is justified given our current political and economic climate. Each of the Fortune 200 Companies (F2C) will need to have its own virtual crisis centre. The sheer volume of signals generated and dissipated by these organizations, coupled with their global reach and round-the-clock operation, demands specialized attention. It would be futile for two F2C organizations, in attempts to save cost, to consider sharing such a resource. If the same crisis were to affect both organizations, a single centre would be unable to sustain them.

Virtual crisis centres will become a necessity as we face even more uncertain economic and political times. After 9/11, affected organizations that were not able to restore services within a couple of days did not survive the crisis. The losses of information and knowledge experienced in those few hours represented irreplaceable damage. Organizations need to be capable of establishing their online presence within minutes, not hours and days, after disruption of their services. Remote crisis centres will enable them to do at least that and most likely more. The clear benefit of such centres stems from an initiative which reflects preparedness and determination to mitigate and possibly evade some of the consequences related to crisis.

To the naïve, virtual crisis centres may seem to be a luxury item, but those who are willing to gamble on the probability of a crisis not striking are playing with fire. The experienced and knowledgeable among us will consider the idea of a virtual crisis centre seriously. To propose a closing analogy, ask yourself whether you would be able to drive your car without an adequate dashboard. You might be able to. However, the risks of your car not operating effectively and efficiently are high, as you will not have information on the functioning of critical components. Similarly, you might be able to run an organization without appropriate attention to signals and information, but you must be able to predict the future in order to avoid a catastrophe resulting from poor information management and negligence.

Closing thoughts

Protecting intellectual assets during times of crisis is absolutely critical. As this chapter has outlined, the severity of losses from damage to intellectual assets can be quite critical; it is important that an organization does not enhance the impact of a crisis by loss of intellectual assets. Organizations that do not consider worst-case conditions during times of normalcy, and prepare for them, will fail to secure their intellectual assets during times of crisis. This will almost surely lead to one outcome: the inability to recover from the crisis and the demise of the organization.

7

Securing your intellectual assets

Are you convinced of the need to protect secure intellectual assets? Obviously, I hope so. In this final chapter, I want to conclude by sharing some guidelines on how to go about building a security programme. In the previous chapters, I explored the technical and operational solutions needed to help secure intellectual assets. As you can probably imagine, these solutions need to be put into a comprehensive framework, which should guide the strategy behind intellectual asset management. This chapter will provide the strategic framework.

In order to articulate a strategic framework, I shall provide you with some best practices that I have gleaned from my work with several organizations. My hope is that you will see the wisdom behind these practices, but do not rush to immediately apply these to your own organization. Instead, you should consider these practices, examine the realities of your organization and the environment in which it operates, and then make informed decisions on how to tailor these practices to help your security programmes.

The seven strategic considerations

In order to build a viable security programme for intellectual assets the following seven considerations need to be carefully thought through. These considerations should not be dealt with through operational lenses or even tactical frames; rather, they need to be considered as strategic matters (see Figure 7.1).

Building the security team

The individuals who make up your security team are your most important assets in the defence against intellectual asset breaches and sabotages. The ideal team will have several desirable characteristics. First, each individual will display the utmost integrity and allegiance to the organization. Security professionals are called upon to conduct difficult assignments. These assignments may require them to access sensitive material (such as logs of an employee's computer usage, or background information on potential employees) and will normally involve some

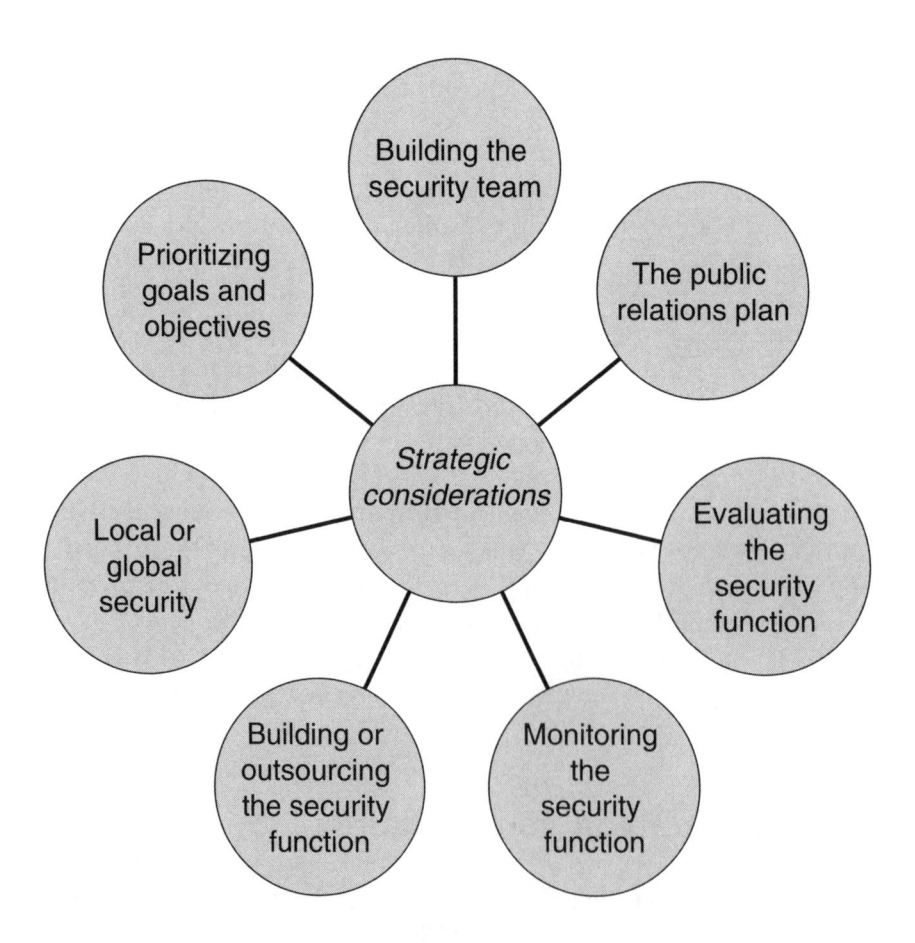

Figure 7.1 The seven strategic considerations

ethical questions (for example, in covert security operations, the extent to which an individual should be monitored, and the methods used to monitor the individual). In these situations, it is absolutely essential to use individuals who work with the highest level of integrity. In the same vein, you should use individuals who display unfettered allegiance to the organization. No one should be able to compromise the security personnel of the organization. If your security personnel can be compromised, you might as well leave the doors of your office open and give all intruders open access to your intellectual assets.

Second, the security team will be comprised of individuals with a wide assortment of skills and capabilities. Having only techno-geeks on your team is not sufficient, even if 90 per cent of the threats in your organization arise from technology-centred attacks. You will need a communication specialist to write up reports, build presentations and communicate with your external stakeholders. You will also need a project manager who can direct the efforts of your staff. Employing a person with a background in psychology will also pay off. This individual will be able to help you profile the minds of intruders and predict their next moves. Having a good researcher/information analyst on staff is also advisable. This individual will help you analyse information from public sources, integrate and interpret it, and come up with actionable recommendations. Finally, you will need personnel with deep experience in the industry in which your organization operates. Security operations differ markedly depending on the industry. The protective services given to movie stars or pop idols differ from those given to the CEO of a company. No two security teams will have the same look and feel. However, the set of skills I have listed here is the most desirable.

Third, the ideal security team will be comprised of individuals with a variety of experiences. Experience most often translates to their previous work experiences. It is good to build a team of people who are not going to engage in groupthink because of their similar backgrounds. Work experience is only one dimension of diversity. Other dimensions include age, gender and cultural background. Novices, with their curious natures, may be able to challenge invalid assumptions held by experts. Similarly, differences in gender and cultural background will result in creative discussions and more holistic analysis of problems. Having cultural diversity on the team is an absolute must. Let me share my own rule here: whenever I have hired people for my own organization, I have applied the following screening criterion. If an individual does not speak two or more languages fluently, with some experience in a third language, he or she does not have the requisite appreciation for the cultural complexities that one faces when engaging in global business dealings!

Fourth, the security team must be a cohesive unit. That said, it is important that the culture of the security team be unifying, binding, open and warm. The tasks that the security team need to engage in will, at times, be difficult. You do not want to have team culture disrupting things further. Hence, spend the required time to help your team bond. Send the team on retreats and give the members time and space to get their act together. You cannot expect this unit to perform right away at a high level, as it is going to take the unit time to figure itself out. The best strategy is to engage the group in some intellectual exercises: for instance, have the team work through various simulations of intellectual asset breaches. Have the team members voice their arguments, engage in constructive debates, and get to know the skills and capabilities of each person.

One thing I have found is there is no single academic degree or certification that can establish credibility for security personnel. For example, universities do not hand out degrees such as a PhD in Breaking In or a MSc degree in Counterintelligence! Nor will a Microsoft or Oracle certification in IT security do the trick. The place where the pedal hits the metal or the rubber hits the road is how an individual performs when faced with a problem. Here is where the intellectual exercises will pan out. Each individual must feel comfortable in his or her role, and must also know what skills other team members possess and be able to trust their capabilities.

Fifth and finally, pay your security personnel well. I am not talking about giving them stock bonuses or luxurious cars. I am, however, talking about paying them at a level at which you pay your other core knowledge workers. As noted earlier, if you want your security personnel to build an allegiance to your organization and protect your assets, you must provide them with the necessary remuneration. If you are miserly in paying them, you are asking for trouble, as they most likely will not perform as you wish. After all, why should they?

The public relations plan

The security programme of any organization is often a point of contention. Employees do not like the headaches of passing through detectors and having their behaviour monitored. The external world (that is the press) is waiting for the security group to mess things up, at which point it will jump on the juicy story to report. It is thus very important that a security group has an adequate public relations (PR) plan. The PR plan must account for the two faces of the public: the internal employees of the organization and the external stakeholders, which include business partners, government, academia and the press, among others.

First and foremost, it is important to designate points of contact (POCs). If the external world wants to inquire about the security programme, there should be one, and only one, person it needs to access. Similarly, for internal matters there need be one person only. Most organizations will employ one person to serve as the POC for both internal and external communications. Why is having one person important? You control the message. You can get one unified message out to your audience. It should be made explicit that if any other security personnel talk to the external world about the security programme, this is grounds for immediate termination. There should be absolutely no leaks and no stories in the press that have the following: 'an unnamed senior source that has knowledge of the security programme'.

Second, have in place an ombudsperson so that security personnel have a person to go to for bringing issues to the attention of management. Having such a person acts as deterrence against individuals leaking information. Ideally, the ombudsperson should be appointed by the board of directors or examiners of the organization, and should report directly to the board. The ombudsperson should be external to the organization and should not be under the control of any of the C-level officers of the organization.

Third, ensure that your unit has a process for ensuring that responses to the external world are thoughtful and complete. For example, if an incident were to happen at 8.30 am, it would not be wise to give a response to the press at 8.45 am. Anything that might be said, except for acknowledgement of the incident, will be incomplete. A PR plan will have a process by which information can be gathered, verified, analysed and then prepared for external consumption. It is important to note that not all information should be made available. If the incident calls for information to be withheld, this must be done with care. For example, it is common practice to hold back information if an official investigation by law enforcement personnel is planned. Similarly, it is reasonable to protect the source of information that foils a possible threat. Protection of sources is only one aspect of the problem; sometimes it is also important not to disclose the methods by which an incident occurred, or the way in which an incident might have been prevented. These considerations also need to be accounted for before making statements.

Fourth, the concerns of internal employees need to be handled with care. On one hand, you want to inform your employees about the safeguards that protect them and the organization's intellectual assets. On the other hand, you must preserve the element of surprise and the clandestine nature of security operations. If your security plan is disclosed, most skilled individuals will be able to find a way to compromise it. Hence, it is best if the security team discusses upfront what information will be shared and what will not. For example, it is common practice to inform employees that correspondence such as phone conversations, e-mail exchanges and text messages is subject to monitoring. In addition, most employees will understand the need for random searches of physical spaces. However, it is when the security team starts to disclose the 'how' of such searches that things get problematic. How are e-mails scanned, and how does the security team determine which space to search? These are tradecraft and process issues that should be held in strict confidence. Under no circumstances should sensitive operations be divulged to all employees.

Fifth and finally, the security team must work hard to maintain and preserve the trust others place in it. A good PR plan can be a great contributor to this goal. The security department can build good rapport with an organization's internal employees by sharing some statistics of their work on a regular basis (such as the number of attacks prevented, and the number of training classes provided to employees). However, if the security operation remains a complete black box, then difficulty will arise. The chief security officer (CSO) of one organization writes an e-mail every month to inform the organization about happenings in the security division and general news about security programmes in other organizations in the industry (for example, if one of its competitors has hired a new CSO).

Evaluating the security function

How do you know whether the dollars, rupees or pounds that you are throwing into security are paying off? What is the return on investment? Is the security department overly paranoid and building defences that are over the top? These are difficult questions to answer for one obvious reason: security programmes are normally called into question only after a breach has occurred. Once a breach occurs, people realize that the security programme had gaps and holes that could be exploited. Hence, following the logic through, the money spent did not achieve its intended objective. So what is a CSO supposed to do?

Building security metrics is not an unattainable goal; it just takes a little bit of creativity. For one thing, collect the obvious measures. These include the number of attacks that were attempted but failed. In the case of technology attacks – for example, attacks on servers – capturing this information is fairly straightforward. Similarly, it is easy to collect data on how many 'bad apples' are kept out of the organization as a result of good background checks. Continuing, you can collect data on the number of breaches that occur in firms similar to yours and then compare your organization's numbers against this number. This is not easy to do, but it is possible. You can scan newspapers, trade publications and even the newswires for reports on breaches in other organizations and use this data for benchmarking purposes. Just remember, though, that not every breach is reported. So if you have no breaches while others have breaches being reported, you are doing a bit better than the other firms. These measures are the bare minimum and should not be considered sufficient.

Data should also be collected on security interventions. For example, one organization built a rewards programme to encourage employees to report suspicious behaviour. When this programme started, there was a lot of noise in the system. A lot of false alarms were being reported. The security department then conducted a series of training classes to give employees more direction about identifying threats. The annual statement prepared by the CSO included data on:

- the amount of information coming in before the rewards programme;
- the number of information nuggets coming in after the rewards programme;
- the number of sources doing the reporting;
- the number of threats thwarted using the information;
- the change in the quality of information after the training was held.

All of this data made a very powerful statement to the board of directors and showed that money being spent was actually paying off. For example, the board could see that the $50,000 spent on training paid off, as the quality of information rose by 30 per cent. The rise in quality of information increased the efficiency and the effectiveness of the security group. In a similar vein, you can be creative in how you gather data on security interventions. The important thing to remember is to measure the state of affairs before you apply any interventions. This will give you a baseline against which to measure the contributions of the interventions.

External experts should be brought in to test the resiliency of your security programmes. However, be aware of this: when you bring in a group of experts to penetrate your systems, 99 per cent of the time, your systems will be penetrated. The reason is simple: experts are on top of their game and know how to take a system down. Now does this mean that you need to panic? Probably not! The average Joe who wants to attack your system will not have the skills to pull off such an operation. So what do you do if your systems are penetrated by the expert consultants? One thing is to identify the places that were broken into. Seek input on how to bolster these areas. Then do a reality check: are the measures for bolstering these areas reasonable given the profile of the average Joe? If the answer is no, think carefully before investing in these measures. Remember, if someone really wants to come after your organization there is almost nothing you can do to stop him or her. You will never be able to protect against everything. In terms of strategy, you must use your funds in a manner that lets you get the highest payoffs for your security programmes.

Finally, remember that any evaluation is only as good as how it is perceived by the evaluators. Here is where I think CSOs and security directors need to do some work. It is a must to understand which measures get the attention of senior executives. Let us examine the case of an R&D organization, for which an important indicator is the number of successful new product introductions into the market. A CSO in this organization must be able to link security interventions to reductions in the number of unauthorized leaks of new product developments, reductions in the number of surprises once the product reaches the market and so on. A good security function must be able to help the other functions of the organization reach their goals and objectives. The CSO must be able to track this contribution and use this to evaluate the contribution of the security function to the overall management of intellectual assets. A straightforward way of doing this might be as simple as showing how security programmes help in the creation, storage, transfer, application, protection and destruction of intellectual assets across the various organizational units.

Monitoring the security function

Who monitors the monitor? This is a difficult issue to contend with. Security units have the potential to go bad, and if they do go bad, they can go really bad! In one organization, a security unit started looking into the personal details of workers for whom it had no authorization to do so. In another case, a rogue security guard began tampering with employee information. In yet another organization, one member of the security unit abused his power to harass a female employee. These situations give security personnel a bad name. Employees are thus very sceptical of the powers vested in the security function. A good system to monitor the security function will help alleviate employee concerns and will also act as a good check and balance. Here are things to consider.

First, have a board of overseers for the security function. This board should comprise at least five people. Three out of the five should be from outside the organization. These may include directors, trusted advisers or external experts. The other two members should be senior officers of the organization. The board should be responsible for monitoring the security function. The monitoring may include giving authorization for sensitive activities and asking for reasons before allowing activities to be undertaken. For example, the board has the right to ask why a background check needs to be run. The board will also report to the employees and serve as their eyes and ears.

Second, ensure that there are checks and balances in place. While the board will handle rare and unusual requests, there must be processes in place for regular activities. For instance, if a background check is to be conducted, at the very least authorization must come from the human resources manager who is considering hiring the applicant. If an employee's computer usage is to be heavily scrutinized, there must be just cause for doing so, which may involve getting a request from the employee's manager. Having clear-cut processes will help reduce the anxiety felt by employees.

Third, as part of the PR programme, make it clear to employees that the security department reports to the board, that the security department's actions are being monitored, and that there are processes for ensuring that no security action is conducted without appropriate authorization. The board should also have a point of contact with whom employees can communicate should they want clarification or other information.

Building or outsourcing the security function

Do you want to outsource the management of security operations or do you want to build this capability in-house? This is a non-trivial decision. The decision to make or buy is one that needs to be considered with care. If your firm has a history of running its own security operations, it might be best to continue with that, unless the current operations are failing. Transferring security to outsiders will simply be too costly. Moreover, your current personnel have knowledge about firm operations that will be quite valuable and irreplaceable.

If your firm does not have a security function for its intellectual assets, or if the current function is not performing up to par, you might consider outsourcing. My previous book with Kogan Page, *The Outsourcing Handbook* (Power et al, 2006), was on the topic of outsourcing. In this book, the process of outsourcing is described from the first step of strategically assessing organizational readiness for outsourcing to the subsequent steps of choosing what to outsource, selecting a vendor, negotiating a contract, starting and managing the outsourcing relationship, and terminating the relationship. I strongly recommend this book if you are considering outsourcing your security function.

Outsourcing security requires you to work with a business partner. To this end, I would strongly urge you to pay attention to the issues raised in Chapter 4, 'When friends become liabilities'. You must have the appropriate agreement in place with your security vendor, which assumes that you have thought through the issues of coordination and control. Pay close attention to the alliance and ensure that you work with the security vendor to resolve issues in the early days of the alliance. During the early days, it is quite possible that things will not go as planned. This is acceptable. The important thing to do is to ensure that you identify problem areas and work on these to get them resolved. Allowing issues to fester will result in reduced trust, poor communication and lack of effectiveness.

Do not allow the security vendor to hijack the relationship. As my co-authors and I note in *The Outsourcing Handbook*, always have an exit strategy. An exit strategy should detail under what conditions you will terminate your relationship with the security vendor. Moreover, the strategy should outline how you will cope with the security issues in the short and long term after the relationship is severed. It is absolutely essential to craft an exit strategy before you begin a relationship with a vendor. Thinking through the issues that might arise during the termination of the alliance will help you craft a better contract with the security vendor, and also devise an appropriate working relationship.

The final thing to pay attention to is the incentives provided to the security vendor. Just as you should provide employees with incentives to uphold security procedures and secure intellectual assets, so should you provide security vendors with incentives. Incentives should entice the security vendor to be on its best behaviour, work with alertness, and secure the intellectual assets of the organization. Incentives should be provided for behaviour that goes above and beyond what is called for in the contract.

The important thing to remember is not to simply compare the cost benefits. The decision whether to build or outsource should be made based on the strategic benefits. Cost benefits change depending on the time horizon. Moreover, it is easy to find contractors who can do the job for less, but the important questions to ask are whether they have the right capabilities and whether they are trustworthy.

One of the functions that you cannot outsource is the process of vetting security personnel. The process of ensuring that the security vendor has the requisite integrity and that the security personnel pass their background checks needs to be conducted by the organization. One thing should be noted here. If you decide to outsource security, the evaluation and the monitoring of the security function needs to be conducted internally. The same rules apply in terms of creating a board to evaluate and monitor the function. In addition, when outsourcing the security function, ensure that you control the PR process. Your organization needs to be responsible for PR, both internal and external, when discussing security matters.

Local or global security

Given that most organizations are global in nature and are spread across multiple locations, a common question is, what is the appropriate governance mechanism for security programmes? Should the organization follow a unified approach across all its locations? Should each location be able to customize its security programme to meet the peculiarities of its local environment? The answer is: it depends!

For a company like McDonald's that operates a franchisee model, where all locations follow similar processes and practices, albeit with small variations, a unified security approach is possible. This is because there will be economies of scale. Securing McDonald's trade secrets should take a uniform approach. Similar issues arise for a company that produces a single product or service. However, there is a slight caveat that needs to be addressed. If a McDonald's is located in a troubled neighbourhood, such as a locality with a high crime rate, it makes sense to take extra precautions to secure the premises. Hence, while uniform practices will work across the organization, there will need to be some level of customization depending on the locale.

Now consider the case of security governance for an organization that produces multiple products across multiple locations. In this case, having a unified set of security practices will be difficult. Securing an R&D lab will be quite different from securing a call centre. Moreover, securing an R&D lab in Israel will be different from securing a call centre in Mumbai or Chennai, India. Security programmes will vary according to the product or service, and also by location. Here each unit (either geographical or product/service) should be allowed to build up its own security programmes to address its unique needs. The role of the overall organization is to provide a general framework within which these local programmes can be constructed. For example, the organization, through its CSO or security director, will establish metrics to gather data on the performance of security measures, share best practices, and integrate protocols across units. Each local security director will report to the CSO who will then ensure that at an overall level, the organization has adequate security coverage to protect its intellectual assets.

In addition to local or global security programmes, we must consider the issue of centralization or decentralization. In highly centralized security programmes, the resources and decision making are controlled by a select few individuals (or even one individual). These normally occur in organizations that take a unified approach to security. In decentralized programmes, the decision making is distributed and spread out across the organization. Not surprisingly, organizations that take a local approach to security take this approach.

The challenge that needs to be considered by organizations is how to coordinate the security programme, yet make sure that it is flexible and agile. On the one hand, centralized programmes have the advantage of coordination and structure, yet they are seldom agile as decision making is slow. On the other hand, decentralized programmes can quickly react and adapt to local conditions; however they face challenges in terms of coordination. Ideally, an organization will choose a structure that permits adequate coordination while retaining flexibility and agility. To this end, it is important for the organization to model and test out multiple organizational design structures. Thinking through multiple forms of a command-and-control structure, to use the analogy from the military, will help in the generation of the ideal structure based on the realities of the organization.

Most organizations should have at least the following:

- a centralized decision-making and oversight authority;
- local security managers who address peculiarities around specific products, services and locations;
- the ability to deploy a quick-response unit, akin to a special-forces unit, should a crisis arise;
- an integrative mechanism to connect the various members of the security unit.

Prioritizing goals and objectives

No security budget will be adequate. Nor will you ever find an organization devoting ample resources to security. I hope this book moves executives to provide greater resources to their security programmes, but I do not think an organization will ever provide sufficient resources. The reason for this, which I understand, is that there are other competing demands for these resources. Given that you will not be able to secure all the intellectual assets of the organization, you must prioritize where to spend your energies.

Consider the case of securing employees of the organization. Not all employees are equal. This may not sound like a politically correct statement, but it does represent reality. There are certain classes of employees that are more expendable than others. I am not talking about this from the perspective of human or social welfare, but from the simple perspective of economic cost. Why do we pay certain employees more than others? Why do some employees get away with things while others are held accountable for even the most minor errors? Simply put, organizations do not value all employees equally, at least not when it comes to attention, resource distribution and so on.

As noted in Chapter 1, if an employee possesses knowledge and capabilities that are rare, non-imitable, non-substitutable, and are of value to the organization, then the organization needs to pay attention to him or her and ensure that there are adequate mechanisms in place to protect the person's knowledge. In most organizations the challenge is to clearly identify these employees. Sometimes the most visible employees are not the ones that rank high on the metric of intellectual assets. There are many employees who keep their heads low, work on their projects, and do not make too much noise; they are too engrossed in their work. These employees remain hidden in the organizational space and need to be identified.

The most highly valued employees need to be protected first; then you can move on to the rest. It is important, however, to note that at times you may not be protecting the most highly valued assets as much as you are protecting against the most severe risks. For instance, for a financial trading firm that deals with the trading of financial instruments, protecting against employee sloppiness is of the greatest importance. Ensuring that employees do not jeopardize the integrity of the firm by applying intellectual assets incorrectly will be the first priority. The entire operations of a financial firm can be brought to a screeching halt if it is discovered that trades are suspect and possibly illegal. Hence, it is important to put into place measures that minimize or remove this risk.

In a similar way to employees, intellectual assets of other forms need to be prioritized and secured. The loss of some assets, though painful, can be tolerated, while there are other assets that need to be secured at all costs; failure to do so will result in extinction of the business. Upon conducting an audit of intellectual assets, an obvious conclusion you will come to is that you cannot protect against everything. This is only natural and should not be seen as a point of despair.

This book has put forth a number of preventive mechanisms that can be utilized to minimize the risks to intellectual assets. We need to distinguish between short-term and long-term measures, and first-order and second-order (or *n*-order) measures. It is not uncommon to see organizations react to security breaches very hastily and put in place what are at best weak mechanisms to protect work. For example, the instant a company discovers a data breach the company often prohibits all employees from taking work home. This is a classic example of a reactive measure, which is counter-productive. By barring all employees from taking work home you have slowed down the productive capacity of your organization. Worse yet, you have aggravated and irritated your employees and made their work very difficult.

The opposite of a short-term fix is to engage in a thoughtful exercise to put in place mechanisms that are of interest to the organization in the long term. For example, a long-term fix might be to require all employees to receive basic training on knowledge security and ensure that they are educated about the issue. The difference between a first-order and a second- or *n*-order measure is also critical. First-order mechanisms can be thought of as foundational mechanisms; without them other fixes would not be effective. For example, without having a good process to check associates within the organization, any training to inform employees about the sensitive nature of their work will have minimal impact. If you allow rogue employees to penetrate your organization, what are the chances that they will actually listen to the training material? A second-order fix builds upon the first-order fix. For example, once you have desired employees within your premises, you need to put in place access controls and communication protocols to ensure that intellectual assets are used appropriately. These mechanisms would be meaningless if you failed to screen for bad apples before they enter the organization, as such employees would likely devise ways to break these protocols anyway.

The ideal organization will fortify itself by choosing the right combination of preventive mechanisms to implement. The preventive mechanisms will be implemented in the right structure (that is, making sure you have first-order measures in place). An organization's priorities in terms of intellectual assets, threats it faces, and preventive mechanisms, need to be evaluated and updated on a regular basis. Conditions in the environment (such as the termination of an alliance with a business partner, or the outbreak of war) may call for changes, or there might be internal changes to the organization (such as the opening up of a new division).

Closing thoughts

I now conclude this book. Security programmes for the protection of intellectual assets are still in a stage of infancy. Organizations need to invest more in their security programmes if they are to truly secure their intellectual assets. Intellectual assets are the life-blood of an organization, and if these vital assets are not secured, the viability of the organization will be called into question. It is very important that an organization should not overdo security. Security for intellectual assets is important and vital; there is no doubting this statement. However, security should be an enabler to the development and management of intellectual assets. Security measures that cripple a business will serve no purpose. The security programme should be viewed as an asset and not as a painful thorn by the employees of the organization and the external entities that interact with it.

This has been the most difficult book so far for me to write, as there was too much to tell and too much excitement behind each of the vignettes I presented for me to stay focused. Even with this difficulty, I have never had a better time putting together a text as I did with this one. I hope you enjoyed reading the book. While I have had to omit some details of each of the cases presented to protect the innocent, I hope they have driven home their points. My goal is not to scare you, but to raise your awareness of the issues. While the current picture of security is grim, it does not have to be this way. This book contains actionable pieces of knowledge that you can incorporate. As with all implementations of knowledge, learning must follow.

I want to learn from your experiences. I welcome comments and suggestions (kev.desouza@gmail.com), and look forward to hearing from you. Thanks for persevering through the book. Good luck on securing your intellectual assets!

Notes

Preface

1 My first book, *Managing Knowledge with Artificial Intelligence: An introduction with guidelines for non-specialists* (Westport, Conn: Quorum Books, 2002) grew out of my work in the area of technical analysis of information for competitive intelligence assignments.
2 My work in the area of knowledge management can be found in *Engaged Knowledge Management: Engagement with new realities*, co-authored with Yukika Awazu (Desouza and Awazu, 2005a). In addition, there are several hundred articles where you will find my thoughts on the topic of knowledge management and organizational innovation.
3 See Desouza and Vanapalli (2005); Desouza and Awazu (2004a).
4 Details of our work can be found in my book, *Managing Information in Complex Organizations: Semiotics and signals, complexity and chaos* (Desouza, 2005a).

1 The basics

1 Excerpts from this section have been drawn from Desouza and Awazu (2004a).
2 Excerpts from this section have been drawn from Desouza and Awazu (2005b).
3 My graduate assistant, Caroline Dombrowski, gathered the evidence for and documented this case study.
4 Excerpts from this section have been drawn from Desouza and Awazu (2004b).

2 The human stain

1 This section draws heavily on Desouza and Awazu (2005c).

4 When friends become liabilities

1 This section draws heavily on my previous work with Yukika Awazu. See Desouza and Awazu (2005a) and Desouza, Awazu and Jasimuddin (2005).
2 Excerpts from this section draw on Desouza and Awazu (2006).
3 The topic of how to manage risks in alliances can be further explored in Power *et al* (2006), of which I am a co-author.

6 From abnormalities to crises

1 See Desouza and Hensgen (2003c) for more detailed coverage on barriers to optimal information processing.
2 Excerpts of this section have appeared in Desouza (2004).
3 A good source of reading on the topic of MCOs is Weick and Sutcliffe (2001). In this book, the authors refer to MCOs as high reliability organizations (HROs). See also Desouza (2005b).
4 This section draws heavily on Desouza (2004).
5 This section is based on my work with Tobin Hensgen (Hensgen *et al*, 2006).
6 This section is based on my work with Tobin Hensgen (Desouza and Hensgen 2003c, 2006).

References

Berinato, S (2005) How to get rid of old computers, *CSO Magazine*, December

Business Week (1975) The office of the future, *Business Week*, 2387, 30 June, pp 48–70

Datz, T (2006) Loss prevention, *CSO Magazine*, January

Davenport, T H (2005) *Thinking for a Living: How to get better performance and results from knowledge workers*, Harvard Business School Press, Boston, Mass

Desouza, K C (2002) *Managing Knowledge with Artificial Intelligence: An introduction with guidelines for non-specialists* Quorum Books, Westport, Conn

Desouza, K C (2004) Simulating disaster scenarios: a missing link in crisis management, *Disaster Recovery Journal*, 17(3), pp 56–59

Desouza, K C (2005a) *Managing Information in Complex Organizations: Semiotics and signals, complexity and chaos*, M E Sharpe, Armonk, NY

Desouza, K C (2005b) Vital dimensions of mission critical organizations: how MCOs use KM to survive a crisis, *KM Review*, 8(3), pp 28–31

Desouza, K C (2006) *Knowledge Management Maturity Model: Theoretical development and preliminary empirical testing*, dissertation, May, Liautaud Graduate School of Business, University of Illinois at Chicago, Ill

Desouza, K C and Awazu, Y (2004a) Securing knowledge assets: how safe is your knowledge? *J@pan.Inc*, 58, August, pp 22–25

Desouza, K C and Awazu, Y (2004b) Don't get caught sleeping: why physical security still matters, *J@pan.Inc*, 61, November, pp 20–23

Desouza, K C and Awazu, Y (2005a) *Engaged Knowledge Management: Engagement with new realities*, Palgrave Macmillan, Basingstoke, UK

Desouza, K C and Awazu, Y (2005b) Segment and destroy: the missing capabilities of knowledge management, *Journal of Business Strategy*, **26**(4), pp 46–52

Desouza, K C and Awazu, Y (2005c) Harp on your organizational mission, *Today's Manager*, April–May, pp 10–12

Desouza, K C and Awazu, Y (2006) Managing knowledge in spin-offs, *IET Engineering Management Magazine*, October/November, pp 16–18

Desouza, K C, Awazu, Y and Jasimuddin, S (2005) Utilizing external sources of knowledge, *KM Review*, **8**(1), pp 16–19

Desouza, K C and Hensgen, T (2003a) On 'information' in organizations: an emergent information theory and semiotic framework, *Emergence*, **4**(3), pp 95–114

Desouza, K C and Hensgen, T (2003b). Semiotics of 9/11, *IT Professional*, **5**(2), pp 61–64

Desouza, K C and Hensgen, T (2003c) *Managing Information in Complex Organizations: Semiotics and signals, complexity and chaos*, M E Sharpe, Armonk, NY

Desouza, K C and Hensgen, T (2006) Virtual crisis centers, *Disaster Prevention and Management*, **15**(5), pp 778–82

Desouza, K C and Vanapalli, G K (2005) Securing knowledge in organizations: lessons from the defense and intelligence sectors, *International Journal of Information Management*, **25**(1), pp 85–98

Duffy, D (2004) Handle with care, *CSO Magazine*, July

Fitzgerald, M (2003) Big savings big risk, *CSO Magazine*, November

Galin, D (2003) *Software Quality Assurance: From theory to implementation*, Addison-Wesley, Reading, Mass

Gray, T (2005) FTC, CartManager settle on data release, Internetnews.com, 10 March

Greenemeier, L (2006) No more excuses, *InformationWeek*, 29 May

Greenemeier, L, Malykhina, E, McDougall, P, Ricadela, A and McGee, M K (2006) The high cost of data loss, *InformationWeek*, 20 March

Hensgen, T, Desouza, K C and Durland, M (2006) Initial crisis agent-response impact syndrome (ICARIS), *Journal of Contingencies and Crisis Management*, **14**(4), pp 190–98

Hensgen, T, Desouza, K C and Evaristo, J R (2004) Ad-hoc crisis management and crisis evasion, *International Journal of Technology Policy and Management*, **4**(3), pp 257–74.

Hensgen, T, Desouza, K C and Kraft, G D (2003) Games, signal detection, and processing in the context of crisis management, *Journal of Contingencies and Crisis Management*, **11**(2), pp 67–77

Kotha, S and Nolan, R (2005) *Boeing 787: the dreamliner*, Harvard Business School Cases 9–305–101.

Marlin, S (2005) Former bank employees are charged in data heist, *InformationWeek*, 23 May

McMillan, R (2006) Unisys subcontractor arrested in VA computer theft, IDG News Service, 15 September

Messmer, E (2006) Coda to the VA data-loss incident, NetworkWorld.com, 31 May

Mitroff, I A (1988) Cutting through the confusion, *Sloan Management Review*, **15**, pp 15–20

Nonaka, I and Takeuchi, H (1995) *The Knowledge-Creating Company: How Japanese companies create the dynamics of innovation*, Oxford University Press, New York

Pearson, C M and Clair, J A (1998) Reframing crisis management, *Academy of Management Review*, **23**(1), pp 59–76

Pelton, R Y (2003) *The World's Most Dangerous Places*, 5th edn, Harper Collins, New York

Power, M J, Desouza, K C and Bonifazi, C (2006) *The Outsourcing Handbook: How to implement a successful outsourcing process*, Kogan Page, London

Ramaprasad, A and Rai, A (1996) Envisioning management of information, *Omega*, **24**(2), pp 179–93

Scalet, S D (2005) Auction blocks, *CSO Magazine*, August

Shrivastava, P, Mitroff, I, Miller, D and Miglani, M (1988) Understanding industrial crises, *Journal of Management Studies*, **25**(2), pp 283–303

Thomas, D, Ranganathan, C and Desouza, K C (2005) Race to dot-com and back: lessons on e-business spin-offs and re-integration, *Information Systems Management*, **22**(3), pp 23–30

Weick, K E and Sutcliffe, K M (2001) *Managing the Unexpected: Assuring high performance in an age of complexity*, Jossey-Bass, San Francisco, Calif

References

Abdulla-Raheem, Khalil 92
ABN Amro 3
advertising 16
Alexia 83
alliances *see* business alliances
Amazon 80
Ameritrade 3
Apple 27
Arthur Andersen 76
assets
   financial 6
   intellectual 3–9
   inventory of 72–73
   physical 6
   security of xiii
   see also intellectual assets

Bank of America 3, 4
Bhopal disaster 133, 162
Boeing 83–84
   Dreamliner jet 83–84
breaches *see* security breaches
business alliances xiii, 9, 23–24, 75–103
   balancing risks 101–03
   collaborative capability 103

exit strategy 103
incentives 100–01
intellectual assets and 84
interdependence 76–77
monitoring 99–100
outsourcing 77
security breaches 88–97
   acting with guile 90–92
   highjacking and incapacitation of alliance 95–97
   leaks from partners 92–93
   movement of intellectual assets 93–95
   preventive measures 97–103
   sub-par performance 88–90
trust 98–99
types 76, 79–87
   control 79–80, 82, 84, 87
   co-ordination 79–80, 82, 84, 85, 87
   joint ventures 86–87, 90, 91, 93, 95, 97
   licensing agreements 81–82, 89, 91, 93, 95, 96–97

marketing and distribution agreements 82–83, 89, 91, 93, 95, 97
mergers and acquisitions 87, 90, 92, 93, 95, 97
production and development agreements 83–84, 88, 89–90, 91, 93, 95, 97
spin-offs 4–86, 90, 91, 93, 95, 97
business relationship 79, 102

call centres 14–15, 78
CartManager International 3–4
Central Intelligence (DCI) 65–66
Chernobyl 161
Choice Point 4
Churchill, Winston ix
Coca-Cola 7
Commerce Bancorp 4
communication 150–51
  agreements 165–66
  organizational lines 163–65
  scenario planning 159–60
  see also public relations (PR) plan
competitive advantage 3
competitive intelligence x, 15–20
  insider information 17
  open/public sources 16–17
computer networks 4
  attacks on 4, 10
Confucius xiv
contingency plans 136, 137, 138–39, 154–57
corporate espionage xi
counterfeit operations 90–91
crisis management xii, xiii, 5–6, 24, 97–98, 111, 129–71
  business processes 147–48

communications 148–49, 159–60, 163–65
damage assessment 160
flexible knowledge architecture 156
immediate response capabilities 160–65
learning from crises 141–45, 166
loss of intellectual assets 130, 145–54
mission critical operations (MCOs) 156, 166
misuse of intellectual assets 153–54
preparations 136–39
  contingency plans 136, 137, 138–39, 154–57
  scenarios 136–37, 157–60
  surprise element 137–38
policies and procedures 143
preventive measures 154–70
responding to the crisis 139–41
risk management 155
scenario planning 157–60
sense-making 169
terrorism 135, 162–63
training for employees 140–41
types of crises 129
understanding crises 132–54
use of resources 151–53
virtual monitoring stations 167–70
warning signs 133–36

Deutch John M 65–66
DHL 82
due diligence 89
Dunn, Patricia 19

Index

eavesdropping   17–18, 113–14
e-mail   58, 64, 69–70
emergency planning   161–62
  see also crisis management, scenario planning
employees   23, 27–53
  allegiance of   46–48
  assaults by   115, 134
  background/security checks   40–42, 97
  behaviour   44
  check-ups   42–44
  competition for   34–35, 45
    case example   35
    recruiting researchers   25
  communication with   151, 178
  counter-intelligence   45–46
  crises and   140–41, 149–51
  educating   50–53
  entrapment   36–37
  ID badges   117–18
  incentive schemes   48–50, 179
  information leaks   29–29, 31
  intellectual assets   28
  interviews with rivals   32
  malicious intent   37–39, 67
  obsolescence   33, 49
  preventive measures   39–53
  public conversations   23
  risk management   50–51
  rogue   4–5, 37–39, 67
    case example   38, 39
  screening   43
  security breaches   30–39
  sloppiness   30–32, 61
  theft   39
  training   140–41
  travel arrangements   60–63
  use of technology assets   73
  valuing   46–48, 185–8

virtual work   108
Enron   27, 76, 133, 150
evaluation   179
Exxon Valdez   133, 162

FedEx   80, 82
Fiorina, Carly   19
Ford, Henry   xi
Ford Motor Company   3

Gates, Bill   27
General Electric   27
Geometric Software Solutions Ltd   5
globalization   108
Google   34–35

Hewlett Packard   19
Hurricane Katrina   6, 130

Industrial Espionage Act (1996)   5
information leaks   28–29, 31, 92–93
  data breaches   57
information systems   xiii
information and communication technologies (ICTs)   10, 23
  see also technology
intellectual assets   6–9, 59, 187
  agreements on use   73
  compromising   3–6
  employees   28
  identifying   12–15
    competitive intelligence   15–20
  labelling   52
  loss during crises   145–54
  misuse during crises   153–54
  movement of   93–95
  obsolence   33, 49
  securing   130, 173–88
  transporting   67–69

types   51–52
see also knowledge management
internet, the   55–56
Iraq   130

Jobs, Steve   27
joint ventures   86–87
   guile of business partners   91
   highjacking/incapacitation   97
   leaks   23
   movement of intellectual assets   95
   sub-par performance   90
Jones, Paul   105

knowledge leaks   4, 23
knowledge management   xii, 9–25
   outsourcing   77
   resources   13–14
   sharing   11
knowledge workers   14–15

Lay, Ken   27
Leo Burnett   82
licensing agreements   23–24, 81–82
   guile of business partners   91
   highjacking/incapacitation   96–97
   leaks   92
   movement of intellectual assets   95
   sub–par performance   89
Limited Brands   105
Los Alamos National Laboratory   57–58

mailroom security   119–20
marketing and distribution agreements   82–83
   guile of business partners   91

highjacking/incapacitation   97
leaks   93
movement of intellectual assets   95
sub-par performance   89
Marriot Corp   3
McDonald's   183
meetings
   offsite   17
mergers and acquisitions   87, 93
   guile of business partners   92
   highjacking/incapacitation   97
   leaks   93
   movement of intellectual assets   95
   sub-par performance   90
Microsoft   27, 34–35, 76, 81, 95
mission critical operations (MCOs)   156, 166
Mitsubishi Heavy Industries   83
Mortgage Group   3

NASA   162
non-disclosure laws (US)   5
non-disclosure agreement (NDA)   xi
North American Aerospace Defense Command (NORAD)

offsite meetings   xiii, 112–13, 125–27
outsourcing   xiii, 18, 77
   agreements   9–10
   exit strategy   182
   incentives   182–83
   relationships   90
   security function   182–83

physical security   xiii, 20–22, 24, 59, 105–27

attitudes to   21–22
breaches   107–17
design issues   117–18
eavesdropping   113–14
entry and exit points   119–21
guests   121–22
inspections   122–24
neighbours   106, 116–17, 124–25, 125
offsite facilities   112–13, 125–27
policies   108
preventive measures   117–27
security breaches   109–17
   assaults by employees   115
   assets taken out of premises   114–15
   carelessness   110
   eavesdropping   113–14
   foreign objects   111
   intruders   109–10
   neighbours   116–17
   offsite facilities   112–13
   preventive measures   117–27
   visitors   121
PNC Financial Services Group   4
production and development agreements   83–84, 88
   guile of business partners   91
   highjacking/incapacitation   97
   leaks   23
   movement of intellectual assets   95
   sub-par performance   89–90
project management   12
public relations (PR) plan   176–78
   communications   177
   employees   178
   ombudsperson   177
   points of contact (POCs)   177
   trust   178

radio–frequency identification (RFID) tags   120–21, 167
reverse engineering   8
risk management   155

scenario planning   157–60
secure conversations   113–14
security breaches   xiv, 4
   business alliances   88–97
      preventive measures   97–103
   employees   30–39
      preventive measures   39–53
   physical   105–17
      preventive measures   117–27
   technology   59–67
      preventive measures   67–74
security guards   20–22
security management   20–22
security programme   173–88
   centralization/decentralization   184–85
   evaluation   178–80
   local/global   183–85
   monitoring   180–81
   public relations (PR) plan   176–78
   outsourcing   182
   prioritizing goals/objectives   185–87
   resiliency   180
   security team   174–76
security team   174–76
   characteristics   174–75
   cohesiveness   176
   experience   175–76
   pay   176
   skills and capabilities   175
Skilling, Jeffrey   27
spin-offs   84–86
   guile of business partners   91
   highjacking/incapacitation   97

leaks   23
movement of intellectual assets   94, 95
sub-par performance   90
strategic alliances   5, 23–24, 80
surveillance   19
  e-mail   19
  physical   19
  pretexting   19

technology   55–74
  applications   66–67, 72–74
  conferencing   59
  dependence on   57
  disposal of   65, 71–72
  e-mail   58, 64, 69–70
  gadgets   56
    mobile   63–64
  inventory of assets   72–73
  security breaches   59–67
    employees' travelling   60–63, 67–69
  preventive measures   67–74
  software development   77–78
  storage and duplication   64–66
    security of   70–72
  virtual work   108
  wiping data   72
Time Warner   3
Toyota   100, 102

Unisys Corporation   92
UPS   80, 82, 83

Verma, Shekkar   5
Veteran's Administration (VA)   60–61
virtual crisis centre   167–70
Vougut   83

Wachovia   4
Wal-Mart   100, 102
Welch, Jack   27

Visit Kogan Page online

Comprehensive information on Kogan Page titles

Features include:

- complete catalogue listings, including book reviews and descriptions
- sample chapters
- monthly promotions
- information on NEW titles and BEST-SELLING titles
- a secure shopping basket facility for online ordering

Sign up to receive regular e-mail updates on Kogan Page books at www.kogan-page.co.uk/signup.aspx and visit our website:

www.kogan-page.co.uk

ALSO AVAILABLE FROM KOGAN PAGE

"Provides information imperative to your understanding of the application of Risk Management."
Sophie Williams, Operations Manager & Deputy Chief Executive, the Institute of Risk Management

ISBN 13: 978 0 7494 4949 0
ISBN 10: 0 7494 4949 7
Hardback   2007

Sign up to receive regular e-mail updates on Kogan Page books at www.kogan-page.co.uk/signup.aspx and visit our website:

Order now at www.kogan-page.co.uk

ALSO AVAILABLE FROM KOGAN PAGE

"A guide for managers and executives responsible for compliance and IT management. Explores new legislation including ISO/IEC 27001, the single global standard for information security best practice."
Risk UK

International IT Governance

An Executive Guide to ISO 17799 / ISO 27001

Alan Calder & Steve Watkins

ISBN 13: 978 0 7494 4748 9
ISBN 10: 0 7494 4748 6
Paperback   2006

Sign up to receive regular e-mail updates on Kogan Page books at www.kogan-page.co.uk/signup.aspx and visit our website:

Order now at www.kogan-page.co.uk

ALSO AVAILABLE FROM KOGAN PAGE

"A practical guide for managers in developing and implementing appropriate strategies for online risk management."
Management Services

ISBN 13: 978 0 7494 4642 0
ISBN 10: 0 7494 4642 0
Hardback   2006

Sign up to receive regular e-mail updates on Kogan Page books at www.kogan-page.co.uk/signup.aspx and visit our website:

Order now at www.kogan-page.co.uk